ON Q : JACK AND BEATIE de LEON AND THE Q THEATRE

by Kenneth Barrow

THE Q THEATRE was the foremost of London's 'little theatres' where new plays were tried-out prior to West End presentation. Hundreds of aspiring playwrights, among them such ultimately distinguished writers as Sir Terence Rattigan and William Douglas Home, saw their first plays presented there.

Vivien Leigh, Sir Dirk Bogarde, Joan Collins, Sir Anthony Quayle and Margaret Lockwood were among the legion of actors who trod the boards for the first time at Q. Fledgling directors included Peter Brook, Tony Richardson and William Gaskill. Film directors John Schlesinger and Bryan Forbes acted there as did two James Bonds - Sean Connery and Roger Moore; not to mention the likes of Dame Peggy Ashcroft, Sir Richard Attenborough, Dame Flora Robson, Sir Michael Hordern, Dame Gwen Ffrangcon-Davies, Sir John Clements, Dame Lillian Braithwaite, Sir Donald Wolfit, Dame May Whitty, Sir Godfrey Tearle, Dame Irene Vanbrugh, Sir Felix Aylmer and the legendary Mrs Patrick Campbell.

The story of Q is inextricably bound up with that of a charismatic theatrical partnership, Jack and Beatie de Leon. From London's East End she yearned to be an actress and settled for being one of the most shrewd and astute of theatre managers, eventually becoming a brilliant teacher of actors inspiring, among many others, Anna Calder-Marshall and Windsor Davies. He from a Central American background, trained to be a solicitor, but was introduced to a life in the theatre by marriage to become a talented playwright, director and impresario. The story of their haphazard career is illustrated with many memories, observations and anecdotes from their own writings, together with tributes from some of the thousands who shared with them the fascinating adventure that was Q.

ON Q

ON Q

Jack and Beatie de Leon
and the Q Theatre

KENNETH BARROW

FOREWORD BY DIRK BOGARDE

THE DE LEON MEMORIAL FUND
In Association with
HERITAGE PUBLICATIONS
Hounslow Leisure Services

First published 1992
© Kenneth Barrow 1992
ISBN 0 9519089 01

Published by

THE DE LEON MEMORIAL FUND
King's Lodge
Kew Green
Richmond, Surrey
TW9 3AA.

Printed by

Darwin Press Limited, Gordon Works
Inwood Road, Hounslow, Middlesex, TW3 1XR

CONTENTS

AUTHOR'S NOTE

WHEN JACK DE LEON died in 1956 he left behind him a three-quarters completed manuscript entitled *The Q and I*. These memoirs, dictated to Margaret Shepherd his secretary, traced the story of the Q Theatre from its beginnings in 1924. A three-quarters written story is, sadly, not a book. The manuscript was shut away in a cupboard with boxes of theatre programmes, account books and assorted other memorabilia from the theatre which died with its founder.

Jack's widow, Beatie, plunged into a teaching career which ended only when she was forced into premature retirement at the age of eighty-three. With time suddenly on her hands she took out the old manuscript, dusted it off and decided to write her own version of events with Jack's work as a guide and source of illustration. At Sir Dirk Bogarde's suggestion, with her daughter Jean she began taping memories of the past, summoning friends, colleagues and relatives to the microphone to add their recollections. When it came to the writing, although the early memories of her East London childhood flowed easily, the day-to-day running of the theatre over thirty years seemed impossible to document without resorting to a series of lists of this, that and the other.

If there was one thing Beatie learned during her years of running the Q Theatre as a well-oiled machine, it was that if she found herself incapable of performing an important task then she would call in the professionals. In the case of her proposed history of that theatre she chose to do the same. Enquiries were made, contacts contacted and the project finally landed on my doorstep.

I read Jack's manuscript with its marvellous insights into a period of theatre history which has frequently served as the background to my deliberations, here with a perspective I knew little or nothing of. I pondered Beatie's attempt which, at that stage, I was being invited to 'ghost'. The problems seemed insurmountable, the chief of them being the difficulty in charting the story of a theatre which presented plays for one week only without a permanent company of actors. Could it ever be anything *more* that a series of lists? I had pressing professional commitments which served as a reason and, listing a few (albeit some of them rather lame) excuses, I committed the unforgivable sin of *turning Beatie down* ...

As I was to discover, "No" is an answer Beatie seldom accepts. In the months that followed she worked diligently to come up with the proof that the lamer of my excuses had no foundation in reality.

One winter's day blithely unaware of all this diligent research, I was at home with little more than a bit of thumb-twiddling to occupy my time and imagination, when the telephone rang. Someone else answered it and reported that there was a mad woman on the phone for me. Indeed it seemed to be true. Obviously confused at not having summoned me personally to the instrument she was yelling instructions in a voice I had never heard about lunch at Kew, to the accompaniment of a shrill, piercing whistle. Later I would learn that at such moments Beatie would tune her deaf-aid to the 'attack' mode. Thus I turned up at Kew Green for the first time and Beatie set about telling me exactly how wrong I had been in turning the project down. Within a matter of days I had changed my mind and set about the task of changing Beatie's.

In my previous books I had adopted the role of story-teller, using the memories and opinions of my subjects drawn from personal interviews, letters, jottings or journals included in italics throughout the narrative. Writing a book in the first person on Beatie's behalf with italicised extracts from Jack's manuscript was one option, but one I preferred not to pursue. By that method there was no conceivable way of including the full participation of one of the more colourful and fascinating characters in the story of Q: Beatie herself. I proposed a straightforward joint biography of Jack and Beatie with the Q Theatre as a background.

I had to pass an audition to prove my point with a few sample chapters. But it was with her blessing that eventually I began to research and write what Beatie would, enigmatically, continue to refer to as her memoirs. Despite differences in our temperament and the occasional collision of her stubborn will with my own the work continued because, at the end of the day, we respected one another. As almost anyone who ever worked with her would attest, she could be infuriating, but it was impossible not to feel an overwhelming affection for her.

Although I had frequently warned her that this was not the kind of book which would have immediate appeal for publishers in today's market she was neverthe-less deeply disappointed when rejection slip followed rejection slip. She continued, however, to be gamely optimistic, planning the champagne and smoked salmon victory celebration when eventually the book was placed and the party we would have on publication. Her death in February 1991 means that she won't be with us in person at that party. But she will certainly be there. Eyes light up the moment she's mentioned and all the old stories and some new ones will be told, as they are here in the book that fulfilled the last dream of her life.

Of the many people whose help must be gratefully acknowledged, first and foremost I would like to thank Jean Mason, Jack and Beatie's only child who, apart from her many vivid recollections and observations, was also the provider of generous hospitality throughout the life of this project. Mention must here be made of her stalwart husband Jim who, uncomplainingly, endured many a lunch and high tea when the sole subject under discussion was a world which his life had unwittingly touched upon. How he, more than anyone else, must have lived for the day the book was finally finished.

I am extremely grateful to Delia de Leon who, with her brother Jack, was the original licensee of the Q, also to her sister Evey Carley and to her brother Stanley and his wife Evey de Leon; and of the succeeding de Leon generation, to Pat

Gribbin, Marilyn Maclean and Gloria Halman. Of the same generation of Beatie's family I am extremely grateful to Anthony Lewison, Nora Burke-Scott, Vera Derer, the late Joan Hillman, Marion Lever, Peggy and Nick Nicholls and a whole band of Lewisohn men: John, Robert, Philip, Teddy, Neville and Bruce.

On behalf of Beatie and myself, I would like to thank Sir Dirk Bogarde for distinguishing the book with his excellent and perceptive foreword.

Grateful acknowledgement must also be made of the following for the various ways in which they helped bring the project to fruition: Joss Ackland, Terence Alexander, the late Dame Peggy Ashcroft, Sir Richard and Lady Attenborough (Sheila Sim), Maxine Audley, Alan Barker, Michael Bennett, Lady Bethune, Jim Biddulph, Lady Black, Bernard Braden, Lyndon Brook, Peter Brook, Anna Calder-Marshall, Phyllis Calvert, Joan Chapple, Helen Cherry, Jackie Collins, Sean Connery, Peter Copley, Constance Cox, Cynthia Cruickshank, Eileen Cruickshank, Hugh Cruttwell, Peter Cushing, Windsor Davies, Robert Eddison, Brian Forbes, Alan Garnham, Mary Gaskell, Sir John Gielgud, Joan Hickson, Sir Michael Hordern, Freddie Joachim, Henry Joachim, Joan Kemp-Welch, Sarah Lawson, Margery Leslie, Bernard Levin, Gillian Liverton, the late Margaret Lockwood, Barbara Lott, Elspeth March, the late Lord and Lady Miles, Sir Ronald Millar, Bruce Montgomery, Mark Moore, Roger Moore, Christopher Morahan, Barry Morse, Barbara Nash, Michael Northen, Joseph O'Conor, Daphne Odin-Pearse, David Owen-Bell, Richard Pasco, Geoffrey Passmore, Richard Pearson, Angela Peters, Ellen Pollock, the late Sir Anthony Quayle, Margaret Rawlings, the late Dennis Roberts, Gloria Sampson, Joan Sanderson, Sir Peter Saunders, John Schlesinger, Joy Shelton, Donald Sinden, Shaun Sutton, Gordon Warnecke, Joan White, John Wiles and John Witty.

Especially warm thanks must go to Euphan Scott and Margaret Shepherd who not only shared with me their memories of Q but laboured long and hard on various aspects of the manuscript, and to Flora McInnes for her clerical assistance.

Though one would never congratulate the staff of the British Library's Newspaper Collection at Colindale for their courtesy or celerity, where would we be without such a resource? I used it exhaustively in researching the chronology of Q, and the careers of Victor Lewisohn and Aminta de Leon.

Grateful thanks must go to the management and staff of Print-a-Sec, 23-25 Praed Street, London, for their patient and painstaking photocopying work throughout the whole process of this book.

Even a decade ago it was quite a simple and straightforward process by which one would seek permission to quote from copyright material in such a book as this. However, the subsequent upheaval in the publishing world, when houses formed and reformed in different alliances, has made this now an extremely complicated process. For example, the Random Century Group which now owns the rights to the Bodley Head lists can trace no record of *Stars In My Hair*, the late Reginald Denham's autobiography which was published by Bodley Head in 1958. Fortunately, when I was researching the official biography of Dame Flora Robson I met Mr Denham in New York. On that occasion he gave me his personal authorisation to quote from this book. I feel sure he would have similarly authorised the quote about the Q Theatre. Emlyn Williams wrote me a letter some years ago in which he said, "Feel free to quote anything of mine" for my book about Clemence Dane. I am certain he would have extended a similar courtesy for the fragment quoted from *Emlyn* (Bodley Head, 1973).

Every effort has been made to trace the owners of the other copyright material used in the text. I am grateful to Victor Gollancz Ltd for permission to quote from *How To Grow Old Disgracefully* by Hermione Gingold, and for graciously waiving any fee. Similar permission has been sought from Macdonalds to quote from Henry Kendall's autobiography, *I Remember Romano's*, and from Longmans for a quote from *A Pride of Terrys* by Marguerite Steen, but has not thus far been received. Letters pertaining to permission to quote from the Collins publication *The Unsinkable Hermione Baddeley*, being that lady's autobiography, and the W.H.Allen publication *Past Imperfect* by Joan Collins, have been returned marked 'Gone Away'. Alternate addresses will be sought.

I am particularly grateful to Times Newspapers Ltd for permission to quote from numerous reviews which appeared in The Times, and for the writings of James Agate originally published in The Sunday Times; also to the Richmond & Twickenham Times for reviews which appeared in that newspaper and in the Brentford & Chiswick Times. Both organisations graciously waived any charges, and for this too I am extremely grateful.

I would like to dedicate my work on this book to the memory of Allan Walsh, a remarkable character actor and a valued friend. He died too young.

KENNETH BARROW
Maida Vale
London
April 1992

THE DE LEON MEMORIAL FUND:

I feel deeply grateful that the beloved memory of my dear and devoted parents, whose care for me equalled their care for drama, especially that drama which extends and deepens human understanding as well as the drama which refreshes and delights, is to be kept alive by the book ON Q. My gratitude extends to the many people who have generously contributed with writings, with money and with support.

The De Leon Memorial Fund acknowledges a debt of gratitude to Donald Sinden, its patron, and to Sir Richard and Lady Attenborough, Phyllis Calvert and Anna Calder-Marshall its trustees. Also to the following whose generous contributions made publication of the book possible:

Joan Longland
Edie Lukyn
Flora Macinnes
Rachel Mackay
Marilyn Maclean
Elspeth March
Ann-Margaret & A.E. Martin
James Mason
Alan McMahon
Bruce Montgomery
Mark Moore
Barbara & Eric Nash
Anthony & Pat Nicholls
Peggy, Nick & Tricia Nicholls
Daphne Odin-Pearse
Doreen Ollett
Terence O'Neill
Joy Osborn
David Owen-Bell
Ken & Patricia Oxman
Richard Pasco
Jean Pearson
Richard Pearson
Dr Malcolm Pines
Primrose & Derek Powell
Margaret Rawlings

John Reeves
Richmond Adult & Community College
Richmond Drama School
Richmond Parish Lands Charity
Hon. Philip Samuel
Joan Sanderson
Sir Peter Saunders
Jean Scott Rogers
Sue Sheffer
Paul Shelley
Margaret Shepherd
Gail Smith
Sheila A. Smith
Lesley Street
Shaun Sutton
Theatre Despatch (Philip Ormond)
Theatreprint
Gilliam Thorpe (Orange Tree Theatre)
Joan Tiffin
Victoria & Albert Museum
Ted & Midge Warner
Edna & Willard Weiss
Joan White
John Witcomb
Margot Woodstock
Lord Wyatt of Weeford

I would like to express personal thanks to Euphan Scott who typed both my mother's original sixty-page memoirs and the final manuscript; to Margaret Shepherd who did research as well as handling correspondence; to Bruce Montgomery who acted as Fund Secretary; to Michael Northen who drew up ground plans of the Q Theatre which were useful in the process of writing the book; to John Bardsley who made sparkling new photographic prints from a set of battered originals; to cousin Anthony Lewison through whom we finally met Kenneth Barrow; to all the family, especially my godmother Delia; to friends; to the many people who worked at Q, and its patrons, for their continued support and encouragement; to students and colleagues at Richmond Adult and Community College; to Margaret Fenn, Theatre Museum, for allowing the book's Press launch to take place there; to Mr Reginald Willson and Theatre Print for a free advertisement; to Nikki Biddle, John Good Programmes, for a free advertisement in the Richmond Theatre Programme; to the Society for Theatre Research for a free advertisement in Theatre Notebook; to Andrea Cameron, Local Studies Librarian, Hounslow Leisure Services, who told my mother shortly before she died that, as Q was a pioneer theatre in Hounslow, the book would be published, and for her diligent work in bringing this about; to Brenda Matthews of Hounslow Library for laying out the manuscript into the Pagemaker desktop publishing programme; to Nigel Elmer and staff at Wordperfect Typesetters for their assistance in this and for producing copy for the printers; to Tony Forster and staff at Darwin Press for their help and advice and for printing the book; to Kenneth Barrow for his extensive and patient research work, and more work writing and remaking, and for devising the cover; to my parents for what they gave us all in their example of love and endurance and dedication to the good; to my husband, Jim, for his patient good humour; and finally to Sir Dirk Bogarde whose devoted encouragement to both my mother and myself inspired the book in the first place and whose lovely and amusing foreword brought us such happiness.

To you all, I shall always be grateful.

JEAN DE LEON MASON
King's Lodge
April 1992

Foreword
by
DIRK BOGARDE

THIS is not a book simply about a quite astonishing theatre, it is also the story of a remarkable partnership and an intense and quite unshakeable love affair. The partnership was between Jack and Beatie de Leon: the theatre was theirs, and so was the love affair.

There was never a team like them and, alas! there will never be one again. We who were, even for a short time, a part of it all were the blessèd indeed. There was no nonsense about this intense pair. The only thing that mattered to them, apart, I imagine, from each other, was getting 'the curtain up' no matter what. And this they succeeded in doing brilliantly in the face, sometimes, of very daunting odds. But it went up, and it stayed up, in spite of fire, disasters, lost actors, a war and anything else which fate chucked their way. Even with the untimely death of Jack, the show still went on. That was the rule; it was what he wanted and what Beatie insisted on. The play was the thing.

The theatre had been all manner of things before Jack and Beatie got hold of it. They made it, in an amazingly short time, into one of the best small theatres in the country and one of the most important in London. The great critics of the time came to Q. The best actors, the stars, the writers, the designers all came to the small theatre splendidly placed opposite Kew Bridge Station. Naturally, apart from the Big Names there had to be a school of minions, dogsbodies so to speak, who would hustle about, mend the fuses, call the actors, cart and carry and generally make themselves useful. I was one of the lucky happy band. It was, in those days, the way to the stage proper.

The war was but a few weeks old; life, mine certainly, was in turmoil. Too young at eighteen to join up I was at a complete loss and no-one, it appeared, wanted me. The Old Vic, to which I had recently won a much prized scholarship, had closed down along with all other theatres, cinemas and places of amusement, and I took a bus ride down to Kew Gardens to have a good think. I never got there; the bus stopped outside the yard of the Q Theatre. I looked down at piles of old flats, fireplaces and the backside of a young woman who seemed to me to be painting a large cut-out of a tree. Q Theatre, it would appear, had *not* closed. It was open for business. I left the bus as it started up for Kew Gardens and walked into the yard and asked for a job. Beatie was coming down a corridor eating a cheese roll when I first set eyes on her. Small, intense, hair lightly greying, eyes bright with interest. No, I had no appointment. No, I did not want to act (at that exact moment anyway). I was a painter and could help with the scenery and so on. I didn't know exactly what 'so on' really meant. I very soon found out. Beatie, short of help for a new show they were about to launch, accepted me there and then at seven-and-six a week. Amazed, bewildered, overjoyed, ill with happiness and delight, I dashed off to help the girl in the yard and for the next few months I cut canvas, applied size, splashed paint about, lit the pot-bellied stove in the scene dock to keep warm, and progressed to the Gentlemen's lav with my tin of Brasso and a cloth and, from time to time, waited at table in the club room and got the actors their tea, meals or bottles of beer from the pub alongside. Sometimes, if I was lucky and a Big Star was playing, I could be tipped threepence. I was giddy with joy.

In due course, as I hoped, I was offered a small part. My first line in any theatre was, "Your carriage is outside Mr. Ormeroyd." I was in! Gradually the parts increased as the actors got called up and I was available. Jack and Beatie, at the end of one quite glorious week in which I had played a long role for the first time, called me to their office after the show and gave me the little buff envelope which held our salaries, Mine, this week, contained a pound note and a silver shilling. A whole guinea! Beatie nodded absently as I stuttered my thanks and pointed out that it was the normal fee, so not to make a fuss. But I was on my way, and Q became for me my theatre-nursery. I never forgot, and never will.

Jack, in those days, was understandably showing signs of strain. The war was hitting hard at his actors, audiences were uncertain about the black-out and bombs, but his elegance, his perfect manners, his kindness never suffered. He was a truly beautiful man, groomed, tall, softly spoken, extremely warm-hearted towards those who, like myself, were prepared to die for that squat little theatre near Kew Bridge. Beatie always reminded me of a bright-eyed wren or robin; eager, alert, determined. She never fussed, was always direct, to the point and completely on the ball. She was amazingly unsentimental, which was vastly important in her job; she never missed a trick, and no-one could fool her or, more to the point perhaps, get the better of her. In this amazing partnership she was the heavy, she took up the gun, the knife, even the hangman's rope, protecting Jack at all times, leaving him to concentrate on the business side of things, the choice of plays, the whimpers and boasts of writers. Beatie and he were inseparable, they were salt and pepper, they ran a good ship and we were a wonderfully happy crew.

It is heart-breaking to realize that no such theatre as Q exists today. It was totally unique in that you could, as a budding actor, start off as a menial doing all the jobs available, and there were a great many, and at the same time be in a position to watch some of the greatest actors at work. You could get them their beer, sandwich, aspirin, hear their 'lines' watch how it was done close to. Even in the great companies today like the RSC or the National it is not quite as it was at Q. Although as a member of a company one stays in work, has the chance to watch other actors performing, perfecting, inventing, the general free-for-all that made Q unique seems to me to be lacking. We were all closer somehow. It was never a question of just 'acting'. We didn't just carry a spear, play the maid or the front, or back, of a pantomime horse, we had a great many other things to do as well.

We were sometimes required to prompt (a quite terrifying job!) to change electric light bulbs in the dressing-rooms, in the floats, or wherever they were needed, we sold programmes, cleaned up the Gents on matinee days, carted trays of food to the stars in their tiny dressing-rooms, rang the curtain up or down, served coffee and even ice-creams in the intervals and *still* had our bit to do on the stage. There was no pressure to perform these functions: we just did. It was what happened at Q. I don't know if Beatie ever heard the old saying that the Devil makes work for idle hands but she sure as hell knew what it meant. It you were fortunate enough to start your theatre learning under her wing, and many of us were, then you didn't just laze about being an 'actor'. You got on with learning how the theatre worked from the basement up. Invaluable training that no teacher can possible transmit to a pupil or student.

Discipline, toughness, determination, loyalty and, above all, survival were just scme of the things learned and which are essential for the firm basis of any actor's career for perhaps, of them all, acting is the cruellest and the most fickle career to adopt. If, by some unlucky chance, a player failed this course of training, and some did, they were more or less lost. I don't remember anyone chucking in the sponge at Q surviving to do anything worth watching.

Through that once-familiar pillared lobby, in the club bar with its fat corner sofas, its little tables, its long bar, in those titchy dressing-rooms some of the greatest names of the theatre and the cinema were to be found. Consider; a pretty girl with not a great deal of talent called Vivien Holman, who changed her name to Leigh, started in that theatre. Peggy Ashcroft, Anthony Quayle, Flora Robson, Michael Hordern, Margaret Lockwood, Donald Wolfit and Donald Sinden, Mrs. Patrick Campbell and Joan Collins, Sean Connery and Roger Moore, all of then and *many, many* more started or played there. The list is endless. It does give you some idea of the scope, the range, the breadth of that theatre.

New plays were tried out, went to the West End, or were gently forgotten; new actors and actresses, writers, painters, directors were all given chances there, encouraged, counselled, and allowed to show what they could do. Beatie, with her devastating eye, knew good from dud, possibility from impossibility, determination from ambition. If I write at length about Beatie here rather than Jack it is only because I knew Beatie well and closely, and Jack hardly at all. He was in the sanctuary of The Office, to which I was seldom bidden, and, apart from a first night, one saw him little. His presence, however, was always about. It was Beatie *and* Jack, and so it remained until he died. They brought to their theatre the same love and blinding ambition that they lavished on their family. It was a tightly knit Jewish family and to be admitted into it was a single honour and privilege. One felt secure, brave, courageous and proud.

Passing the site of the theatre today is a saddening affair. Now a hideous block of something or other stands where all the joy and heartbreak, where the laughter and the tears, where the great triumphs and brushed-aside failures took place. Memories are almost, but not quite, obliterated.

In this excellent book they are brought back to glittering life once again, brought back through the words of Jack and Beatie, their daughter Jean and many, many of us who were survivors of that magical place near Kew Bridge and who will always carry with us the crazy, happy improbabilities of Q.

PART ONE

1900 - 1929

CHAPTER ONE - BEATIE

I do not remember the house where I was born, but I do remember my father taking me to kindergarten from our house in Green Lanes near Victoria Park in East London. He was so kind, Mama said, that one day when he saw two barefoot urchins longingly gazing in a confectioner's shop window, pointing at first one cake and then another, he placed his hand gently on one boy's shoulder and asked, "Which would you like?" and gave them money to buy cakes. Another time he gave away his coat to a beggar on a wintry night.

I remember him singing "Hopty-Bopty" and bouncing me on his knee with my brother Victor, three years my senior, on the other knee. Papa had a canary he adored and he was also very fond of our mongrel dog, Gyp. Even though I was very small I was aware that Papa suffered from asthma and that he had poor eyesight.

Beatie's father Bernhard Lewisohn was born in Hamburg on December 28th 1850. He, his brother and two sisters were descendants of Mathias Levy who had been a communal leader in the Schleswig Holstein of the first two decades of the eighteenth century. It was fifty years later that the name Levysohn emerged, modified by some members of the family to Lewisohn.

At the age of thirty five, Bernhard came to England. Shortly after his arrival he was invited to a party. The evening's entertainment was provided by a charming young girl named Lydia Moses. At a loss to know what he would do for a living, Bernhard was delighted to be introduced to the girl's mother, an ambitious widow who ran her own shoe factory in East London. Mrs Moses offered him employment as she needed someone to take care of the clerical side of the business. It seems, too, she was also on the lookout for a new husband and mistook Bernhard's effusive gratitude for romantic intent. It was consequently somewhat devastating for her to discover Bernhard had other ideas. In what would prove an echo in Beatie's life, he had fallen in love at first sight with the entertainer at that first party, the nineteen year old Lydia. Shortly afterwards they were married.

Beatrice Lewisohn was the baby of the family. When she was born in London on November 22nd 1900 her sister Helena was already fifteen years old. Between them were seven brothers: Harold, Norman, Caesar, Leon, Stanley, Ferdinand and Beatie's beloved Victor. She was a tiny child, lively and mischievous. Nevertheless she was shy with others and when first taken to kindergarten was too frightened to ask for the toilet, with obvious results! When she was still very young the family moved to 60 Well Street in London, taking a house on the opposite side of the street to where Lydia's sister Rose and her husband still ran the family shoe factory in the grounds of their own house.

There were horse cabs in those days trotting along the roads. I often walked along Well Street with my little doll's pram. I had a treasured doll whose eyes opened and closed.

Sometimes we were taunted, with rude gestures:

> **".Jew! Jew! Had a bit of pork,**
> **Put it on a fork**
> **And gave it to a Jew boy. JEW"!**

Occasionally we too were horrid, calling back: "Christ face, Christ face!"

Lydia Lewisohn was a remarkable woman, not only managing a large house but eventually running the factory, looking after an invalid husband with a new baby almost incessantly on the way (there had been a tenth baby which died at birth), seldom herself very well. Her granddaughter Nora recalled, "They had a difficult time living from hand to mouth but managed to get orders for the factory from Upsons, Lilley and Skinners and Stead and Simpsons, supplying them basically with the same shoes but finishing off each customer's differently with a bow or a buckle. In order to have enough money to pay the wages Lydia called on her customers on a Friday morning to collect payment for goods supplied that week.

"She enjoyed trying to be a matchmaker and found a German husband for her maid who had no family of her own. They were married from the Lewisohn home and spent their first night there. The unfortunate bridegroom suffered from his stomach all night and had to pass Lydia's bedroom to get to the lavatory. With no lighting in the passage and unfamiliar with the geography of the house, several times he started to enter her bedroom and she fearfully called out, 'Kommen sie nicht herein, Mister.'

"She learned her German presumably from Bernhard. He came from a good Jewish family. Neither he nor Lydia knew more than a few phrases in Yiddish, the common language among the Jewish population of Hackney. Nor were they orthodox. However, they kept up certain Jewish practices, including recognising the Sabbath eve. There was always a special Friday night meal at which all the children old enough would sit at table, presaged by grace before meals sung in Hebrew by Bernhard and accompanied by the elder sons.

"But Bernhard, while being educated, sensitive and artistic was not very strong and not a good businessman, so that the driving force was Lydia. However, with twelve mouths to feed - nine children, herself, Bernhard and a maid, they were always hard up."

One night in February 1906, I was woken and taken into Mama's room. Papa had died. I can still see my mother slowly rocking backwards and forwards in her rocking chair. I was five years old when Papa died. I slept in Mama's room from that night until the day I was married.

There is a feeling in the family that Lydia named four of her children after Shakespearean characters because of her great love of the theatre. Helena was, in fact, the name of Bernhard's mother and their eldest child was probably named in her honour. However, this is not to diminish the fact of Lydia's first love. Had she not married quite so young she would have liked to have pursued the career she had begun by giving recitations at parties. She was very fond of opera and took one son at a time by horse-drawn tram from Hackney to Covent Garden. Eventually it was Beatie's turn to accompany her.

We would sit in the 'gods'. Mama knew all the operas by heart and would sing them through for me beforehand - *Faust* and other popular operas.

When I was very young I was not allowed to go into the factory, but later I was allowed to look round occasionally. Mama used to supervise the bows and decoration of the shoes which gave them their exclusive style. The girls used to varnish the shoes with sponges on bamboo sticks. As they worked they used to sing. Often the song was slow and sentimental and they would drag the sponges lethargically from side to side. Then Mama would break in with a livelier song, perhaps a marching song from one of the operas, and they would join in. Work was speeded up and the orders were completed on time!

After kindergarten Beatie was sent to Lady Hollis School. This was to prove the happiest part of her formal education. Everyone, teachers and pupils alike, were pleasant and, most important of all, there was a large well-equipped gymnasium. Although she quite liked Geography and once got reasonably good marks in French, Beatie was not academically minded. What she loved most of all was sport. One particular time she won three sports prizes.

My mother and everyone used to come when there was a gym display. One year she couldn't come. I stayed with Auntie Rosie and she came along instead. I was so good at gym I climbed to the top of the rope before anyone else and I waved and waved at my aunt.

More than seventy years after, passing an empty gymnasium, Beatie saw the ropes hanging. Only an uncharacteristic onset of discretion prevented her from shinning up one of them.

She was very popular at Lady Hollis, always one of the first to be picked for a sports team. Later she went to the Skinners School which had over five hundred pupils. Lydia felt that Beatie would feel lost among so many and spoke to the headmistress, Miss Newton, with the result that she was transferred to Northfield High School. Unfortunately Northfield didn't have a gym, the sports teacher preferring the more ladylike callisthenics for her very select pupils, but Beatie was to prove a useful athlete.

Business at the factory boomed and so we decided to move. Mama suggested that Victor and I might like to see the new house. Although there were still horse buses in those days she sent us by tram. When we arrived at 151 Upper

Clapton Road we stood peering over the gate. I remembered I was standing on the lowest bar, both of us imagining what it was going to be like living there. Unfortunately the owners spotted us and rapped angrily on the window to send us away.

It was a lovely house and we had very happy times there. Mama purchased several elegant carpets and pieces of furniture from the previous owners. Here we gave parties that became the talk of the town. Victor once brought his whole class from Clerks' College. Mama said that if they didn't break up the chairs then the party had been no good!

We shared happy Sabbath nights, with lighted candles, and occasionally I fried the huge dish of fish for as many as twenty people for supper. After the meal my older brothers' girl friends used to drop in.

Once we went in a brake for a picnic in Bushey Park. I remember a lovely cherry pie. My brother Leon disappeared to take a girl for a stroll. We discovered them later! Caesar had a motor-bike with a side-car. He often took his girl friends on a trip up Stamford Hill. I was longing for a ride. One day he took me along. I loved it, though it was very windy. My brothers spoiled me, but the younger ones also teased me.

When I came downstairs one morning early in May 1910 I picked up the newspaper off the mat. It was all edged in black. The King was dead. There was to be three days of national mourning. King Edward was known as The Peacemaker and was especially dear to the Jewish community to whom he had shown great kindness.

Mama decided to take us to see the funeral procession. On May 20th the King was borne from Westminster to Paddington en route to Windsor. According to the newspaper thunder threatened at dawn but when we left early in the morning it was fine and sunny. We travelled from Upper Clapton by tram and open topped bus to Leon's office in the Edgware Road. The streets were crowded with carriages, horse cabs and only a few motor cars.

We sat at a window with a good view of the long road. The street was decorated with laurel wreaths and purple hangings. There was an enormous well-behaved and darkly dressed crowd, with a few motionless policemen along the roadside. We sat for hours by the window. The procession was a mile long with royalty from all over Europe, representatives from all over the Empire as well as the armed forces. As the procession of men on horseback and carriages moved by the coffin on the gun carriage came into view. There was a profound hush. The veiled face of Queen Alexandra was visible in the carriage following the coffin. Because of my father's having been German Mama was eager for us to see the Kaiser. He was on horseback next to King George, both in uniform with plumed hats. I remember the Kaiser had a long moustache. A leading carriage carried the Prince of Wales, then known as the Duke of Cornwall, later Edward VIII and then the Duke of Windsor. He was in naval uniform. Next to him was Princess Mary, later the Princess Royal. She was attractive although, I believe, she was less popular than the three princes who were with her in the carriage. The dead king's little white terrier followed among the great dignitaries of the world.

In June the following year we witnessed a very different procession. The coronation of King George V remains one of the highlights of my childhood. We waited in anticipation. The distant sound of cheering grew to a crescendo. As the long procession came into view I was spellbound by a vision of fairyland! I was only ten and young for my age. The coaches and horses seemed fairy coaches. It was then, when he was on his way to the Abbey, bare-headed in his robes of white silk and blue velvet that, oh, I fell in love with my prince! I liked him until he died, even when he was very naughty! Somehow he still has a special place in my memory. My daughter remembers nearly weeping when as Edward VIII he broadcast his abdication speech. She thinks that, like Prince Charles, he was a friend to the underprivileged. He had vowed to help the Welsh miners and Baldwin used Mrs Simpson as an excuse to be rid of the Prince, refusing him a morganatic marriage.

The death of Edward VII came as a blow to Victor. His barmitzvah party had to be postponed. He was still in short trousers and he had been studying his Hebrew portion for weeks.

A boy's barmitzvah signalled the onset of adulthood. To some extent Lydia could hardly wait for her children to grow up. It meant that she could begin to see in them the fulfilment of her own dreams of a life in the theatre. When Helena was only a little girl, Lydia taught her various pieces of recitation. She was still in her teens when she began producing children's plays. Around the same time she used to take part in Band of Hope concerts. Lydia, Bernhard and Grandma Moses would go along to see her perform. To their chagrin they had to join in the singing of the Christian hymns. Helena found it hilarious to watch this deputation of her Jewish relatives on the front row singing 'Onward, Christian Soldiers!'

Several of Bernhard's cousins had emigrated to America and had become very rich. One of them, Leonard Lewisohn, had several daughters, among them Julia who had married a banker, Charles Henry, who would later be knighted. On a visit to England, Leonard Lewisohn read in the Jewish Chronicle of Helena's activities and paid a visit on his cousin Bernhard. Helena performed for him and he saw she was very talented, but that she needed tuition. He arranged for his daughter to take her in hand.

Helena's daughter Joan recalled, "Lady Henry asked if my mother would like to live with her at her home in Porchester Gate as her protégée, but my mother would not leave her family. My grandmother suggested she be enrolled at Henry Neville's Academy and this was arranged. Lady Henry said she must have further private education in the West End area. She became a professional entertainer whilst still very young and managed to get a good agent. She had many engagements for Masonics in the West End and also in Concert Parties. At one stage she had one of her own. The money she earned was sorely needed at home. Lady Henry changed her life. Among other things she also gave her many of her own clothes, exclusive designs by Worth, the majority of which she had worn only once."

Eventually Helena was engaged to play in pantomime with George Robey, later Sir George Robey, in a scene with him in which she was cast as a sorceress, performing it with him for two seasons first in Newcastle and then in Birmingham. Subsequently she was offered a Stoll tour of the music-halls but by this time she had become engaged to be married to Johnnie Rundbaken, eventually the manager of Rootes, and retired to Manchester and marriage at the age of twenty-two. By this time Beatie was seven and Victor ten and the way to the stars for Lydia would finally rest with them.

CHAPTER TWO - DREAMS AND REALITIES

LYDIA had already begun. When they were both very young she taught them the same recitations she had taught Helena. The earliest which Beatie could remember was 'Flo's Letter', a precocious piece of doggerel about a child's reaction to a newborn baby brother and a subsequent 'letter to God', which had been the delight of many a Victorian drawing-room.

"Dear God," it concluded, "the baby you sent us
Was awfully nice and sweet
But because you forgot his toothies
The poor little thing can't eat.
So that's why I'm writing this letter
On purpose to let you know
Please come and finish the baby
That's all, from little Flo."

Some of the pieces were very good. 'The Ballad of Lorraine' was excellent. I was able to put together a whole recital from them years later which I performed at the Steinway Hall. Mama often took me out to the local theatre at Dalston, as well as to the opera. Occasionally we were able to persuade Mama herself to recite. She put such feeling into it that she would have us all in tears. Victor and I would perform too. Oh, but he was marvellous. He had such dramatic gifts.

Eventually Lydia decided she had to take firm steps to launch Victor into the theatre. Wearing her 'uniform' of black lace, white gloves and black straw hat with cherries and a veil, she took Victor, with Beatie in tow, to His Majesty's Theatre in the Haymarket for an audition with the legendary Sir Herbert Beerbohm Tree. **"Allow me," she said, raising her hand and giving her charming smile as she moved through the crowd to the door of Sir Herbert's office where she asked, in her best voice, "Will you hear my son next?"** Tree did hear him, performing from W. S. Gilbert's *Comedy and Tragedy*. After the audition Tree said, "Send him to my school, the Academy of Dramatic Art."

Tree's academy, which he had founded in 1904, was in Gower Street where he had taken over two old houses and installed George Bancroft as administrator. It was an unusual and uncharacteristic step for Tree to have taken, as he had always maintained that acting could not be taught. However, he felt there was a diminishing degree of technique in the actors and actresses in his employ and had set about rectifying this regrettable state of affairs, enrolling his eldest daughter Violet as one of his first pupils. No one was surprised when Tree lost interest in his brainchild, preferring to invest his time in other more appealing projects. He continued, nevertheless, to stage benefit performances at His Majesty's to fund the school. In the Spring of 1906 a corporate body had been drawn together to carry both the financial and administrative burdens. Sir Squire Bancroft was elected President, and the Council included Sir George Alexander, Sir John Hare, Cyril Maude, Arthur Bourchier and J. M. Barrie. When it was later incorporated by Royal Charter in 1920, Tree's school became the Royal Academy of Dramatic Art, eventually the most famous and celebrated drama school in the world.

As well as offering Victor a place at the Academy Tree suggested, "Meanwhile he can be in the crowd in my next production." This was good news indeed. Tree was noted for his spectacular productions which would often employ live animals and over a hundred extras. Each extra was paid one pound for his services and this helped Victor through his student days. He remained with Tree's company for two years from April 1913 when he made his first appearance as the Second Officer in *Twelfth Night*. One of Beatie's treasured memories of this period was being in bed at two o'clock in the morning, aware of her mother sitting at their bedroom window watching and waiting for Victor's return from the theatre in the cab which Tree provided. Suddenly there would be the sound of horse's hooves, and then Victor would rush in to share his news.

The rest of the family was not immune to the resident theatre bug. Although the three older boys were busy at the factory Harold had sung in the chorus of *Carmen* at Covent Garden. His daughter Nora pointed out, "He sang with Stedman's Boys Choir at Covent Garden, not so much because of his voice, but rather that he was able to keep the boys in order, no doubt having had experience with his younger brothers." Norman tried to play the violin at family parties. Naturally everyone entertained at these events. The three middle boys all proved excellent mimics. In addition to her work in recitation Beatie also took piano lessons. She proved no musician, but a bout of flu was somewhat alleviated by a visit from her teacher with a bunch of freesias and a prize for general progress. But by now, aided and abetted by Lydia, she had one constant dream.

I attended several dress rehearsals at His Majesty's. I remember sitting behind Sir Herbert in the empty stalls - he was alone in the front of the auditorium - and touching his shawl and whispering, "Mama, I'm touching Sir Herbert!" sometimes he would call out to his wife who was sitting in a side box, "Maud, can you hear?" In 1913 I saw Phyllis Neilson-Terry in a rehearsal of *The School for Scandal* which I loved. Mama continued to take me to the theatre and the opera. I longed to go to the Academy of Dramatic Art, and it was Mama's aim for me to follow Victor there.

But history intervened. The outbreak of the Great War in 1914 meant a collapse in the market for the kind of evening dress shoes the factory was famous for. Orders dried up and they were forced to close it down. Dreams had to be set aside. Her school prize had been her first and last. Thirteen year old Beatie Lewisohn had to be withdrawn from school to learn some useful skill. She was sent to Cissie Goschalk, her brother Norman's sister-in-law, with whom she studied shorthand

and typing. Cissie was appalled by her spelling and taught her the basic rudiments. This was to stand her in good stead when, at the age of fifteen, she took a job in Highbury where her mother had taken a house.

I remember I cycled to work. To begin with I earned fifteen shillings* a week. In the third week there was an extra two shillings and sixpence in my paypacket. Naturally I wondered if it was a mistake and told Mama who said, "Keep it, but ask if they've raised your salary." It was some sort of tally firm. I remember repeatedly writing letters which said, "Dear Sir, In reply to your letter to hand ... at the moment Raleigh cycles are extremely difficult to obtain ... "

Later she worked in a solicitor's office and then had her first taste of theatre management at the Coronet in Notting Hill Gate. She hated it there as she was stuck in an office on her own high up in the building. She suspected that her boss drank. Once she was left with the responsibility of paying the wages, having to pay seventeen shillings and sixpence to herself for the week. She was lonely, with too little to do and couldn't wait for five o'clock to come when she would go to the Aeolian Hall where she received acting coaching from Gertrude Burnett.

In 1916, Mama and I went to stay with my brother Norman and Dolly, his wife, in Springfield Gardens. They already had a son, Bernhard, and Dolly was expecting her second child. I remembered one foggy December night being sent with their little maid to run and fetch the nurse.

There were few telephones in those days. We ran and ran through thick mist. When we got back I remember collapsing on the floor absolutely exhausted and drenched. Soon afterwards the nurse came in to say a baby girl had already been delivered, but there was another on the way! The twins, Peggy and John, always remained dear to me.

She had finished work at the Coronet. Lydia was determined that Beatie should go to the Academy. If she were able to win a scholarship then Bernhard's rich American relatives might help out with her day-to-day expenses. Beatie applied for a place, passed her entrance test and joyfully made her way to Gower Street. After three weeks, like all new students, she was entered for the scholarship. The Academy then had a juvenile section and there were over fifty entrants in competition with her. Over those first three weeks each was assessed by their tutors in speech, acting, mime, dance and fencing. Beatie learned the voice instructions parrot-fashion as this was her weakest subject and ran through the list in her mind when asked questions on it. Among the adjudicators was the exquisitely beautiful actress Gladys Cooper.

After the tests were all over I remember sitting in the canteen, eating a sausage! Suddenly some students bounded up and banged me on the back.

(*75p)

They said my name was on the board, that I had won the scholarship. I couldn't believe it and rushed upstairs. I looked on the board and it was true. There was my name. I was delighted, almost more for my mother than myself. I rushed to tell her, bursting with excitement. She was visiting Raie, Leon's wife. Raie opened the door and told me that Mama hadn't yet arrived. I told Raie instead who seemed quite unenthusiastic. My heart sank. But then Mama arrived and hugged me and said, "Oh, you darling!"

With the scholarship under Beatie's belt, Lydia contacted the American Lewisohns. She had reason for cautious optimism as her late husband's cousins were far from uninterested in the theatre. Oscar Lewisohn had married Edna May, the star of *The Belle of New York*. Adolph Lewisohn had donated three hundred thousand dollars to found the Lewisohn Stadium on the Upper West Side of New York City. The culmination of many years' dreams, it was dedicated on April 12th 1915, and from 1918 was the setting for open-air summer concerts under the supervision of Minnie Guggenheimer, at twenty five cents admission per person. The sprawling athletic field and Doric columned amphitheatre have gone the way of all developments but a commemorative bust of Adolph still stands on Lewisohn Plaza at City College. Lydia wrote and told them how the war had blighted the hopes of her talented daughter. To the delight of both they received a prompt promise of support which covered all of Beatie's out-of-pocket expenses for the duration of her course. One of her tutors at the Academy was Rose Mellor O'Neill.

She used to have me stand in front of the class to demonstrate different moods or she had me acting killing people, strangling them. She had a very dramatic voice "Good ...," she would begin in a very low voice, her fingers running through her touched-up copper hair, "Very good! Oh girls, girls, can't you see? Such soul, such fire, such passion!"

Miss O'Neill would recall Beatie a decade later when she chose her to pose for a series of photographs to illustrate her book *The Science and Art of Speech and Gesture* in which Beatie appeared in a number of fairly fatuous tableaux depicting Anger, Grief, Coquetry and so on. One shudders to think of the number of young hopefuls who felt they knew all about the art of acting from emulating them! Helena and Victor had taught Beatie an audition piece from W. S. Gilbert's *Comedy and Tragedy*, "Who am I gentlemen ... I am an actor." Lydia told Beatie to suggest doing the play at the Academy. She played it there in 1917, elegantly dressed in yet another nearly new gown from the wardrobe of Lady Henry. On another occasion Lydia turned up to see Beatie play Queen Margaret in *Richard III* and was disappointed to see what was apparently another student playing the role. Norman Page had made Beatie up as the ancient crone and she was completely unrecognisable!

While Victor was playing at His Majesty's Theatre, before I went to the Academy, we moved to a maisonette in Highbury New Park. I remember going

out one night to see a Zeppelin in the night sky! I remember one day when I was having French coaching from Mme. Gachet for a part in an Academy production. I was alone with her in the house. Its dear little hall door was always open when the sun shone. Suddenly a shadow fell over the house. A Handley Page aeroplane came down in flames next door and we were terrified. Mme. Gachet started to run upstairs although the front door was open. Then she ran down again and we saw brother Ferdy rushing down the avenue with crowds of people, shouting that Mama had heard that the last house in the avenue was ablaze.

Thankfully we were safe.

I thoroughly enjoyed the First World War! I had the time of my life. There was a boy I was quite keen on. He used to call me his little sausage. Mama trusted me with him, but then I was very young for my age, rather naive. I liked him but I never thought anything seriously about him. He never kissed me. I think once he might have taken my arm - rather forward that, I thought. It's difficult to imagine anyone thinking like that nowadays!

Mama was rather sentimental. She believed in love, that there was only one true mate for everyone. But she had had an early disappointment in love.

Before Lydia had met Bernhard Lewisohn she had been in love with a boy called Louis Levy. Mrs Moses had disapproved of the youth. Together they arranged to run away and be married in secret. Unfortunately Louis told his brother who in turn told their father. Lydia had arranged to meet Louis at the railway station but his brother turned up instead. He proffered her a letter. In it Louis had written, 'May the hand that writes this be dead by the time you read it.' Lydia was disgusted that he had been so foolish as to let his father tell him what to do. Later she was invited to recite at the party where the newly arrived Bernhard was a guest. More than thirty years later history was to repeat itself. Beatie was invited to a Hanukkah party at Miss Chapman's in Golders Green. She was asked to recite and chose to perform a piece entitled 'I Don't Care'. Part of the assembly that evening was someone who had been staying with Miss Chapman whilst his family was evacuated to Brighton to avoid the Zeppelin raids. He was a tall, dark, rather shy young man who would, eventually, change Beatie's life. His name was Jack de Leon.

CHAPTER THREE - ENTER JACK

BEATIE was twenty months old when Jack was born. Though they both came from families which today would be considered large - Jack had four brothers and three sisters - and both would lose their fathers during their early years, their backgrounds could scarcely have been more different.

Jack was born on August 12th 1902 in Colon on the Atlantic side of the isthmus of Panama. Not many miles distant was the capital, Panama City. Jungle covered the mountains. His sister Delia, with whom he shared a similar devoted closeness to that which Beatie and Victor enjoyed, recalled their idyllic childhood. "All I can remember is growing up by the sea. My grandmother and aunt lived with us. My grandmother had her own little place at the side. All of us, except my youngest brother, were born there. I recall the carnival time with music and dancing in the streets. It goes on all night. The people with their national costume all wear gold ornaments, with a little fish at the bottom. The fish is the symbol of Panama. There is some religious significance. We had quite a few servants, nurses, little black boys, mostly Jamaican. That's where I heard all the Bible stories about Jesus and the holy women which started my interest in mysticism. That was something Jack and I shared, together with a love of mystical poetry."

Michael de Leon, Jack's father, was born in Jamaica though his antecedents originated in Spain. He went to Panama as so many did when the Panama Canal was being built. A lot of Saphardic Jews emigrated from the Virgin Isles and Jamaica to Panama at this time. It was a time of hope for them. It was there he met his wife May Miriam Maduro, twelve or thirteen years his junior. At one time Michael ran an ice-making business locally with a partner but then had started an import-export concern with an American partner in New York. The business is still flourishing today. The couple set up home with May's mother and her first cousin Sarah. Sarah had been left an orphan when she was very young and Mrs Maduro's people adopted her. To add to the insecurity of her origins she was jilted by the man she hoped to marry and became a tough, embittered old woman who terrorised the de Leon children. The children born in Panama numbered Delia, Jack, Roy, Herbert, Evelyn (Evey), Aminta and Stanley. Michael very much wanted his children to be educated in England. He was, after all, a British citizen. A fire had destroyed all the papers connected with his origins and Cordelia de Leon, his mother, had to swear in front of the British Consul in Cincinatti that her children had been born in Jamaica.

Delia, the eldest, had been sent to Jamaica at the age of eight to begin her schooling at a boarding establishment run by three English ladies. The family moved to England in 1911 taking residence in Lambolle Road, Hampstead, London. It was from here that Michael commuted between his business interests in Colon and New York, on which trips he was usually accompanied by his wife. Minta's daughter

Pat has pointed out, "It's extraordinary that each of my mother's generation in the family felt they were unloved and neglected as children. Several have told me that they thought they were the only one no-one cared for, that they had been rejected. Each was surprised later to learn the same thing from one another. It is only in later life that they have got to know each other. In the family home there was an inability to communicate, they never talked to one another. None of them had much of a relationship with either parent as they were always away, and little of a relationship with brother and sister because they were sent away to boarding school."

In 1913 Evey, Minta and Stanley accompanied their parents on a trip to New York where Michael had offices in Bridge Street. They had taken a house on Long Island and it was here that Michael the eighth child was born. In October of the following year, back in Lambolle Road, Michael senior had an attack of pleurisy. "All the younger children had gone out," continued Pat. "In fact, they'd been sent out of the house. They knew their father was ill but obviously hadn't been told how seriously. They came back laughing and talking and old Aunt Sarah interrupted them saying, 'You *wicked* children, laughing like that when your father's just died.' My mother, for one, felt this whole experience had a devastating effect upon her life and future psychological development."

May de Leon, at the age of thirty eight, like Lydia Lewisohn was left a widow with a large family of young children to bring up. Without Lydia's robust warmth, her middle class reserve served only to fragment the already isolated family. The experience of sitting shivvah in the orthodox Jewish tradition after Michael's funeral managed to further traumatise the children, as it still can to youngsters to whom the implications are not fully explained. However, for the first time many of them felt they had a real home. At least their mother was not constantly setting off for other parts, but was now permanently in London. There were financial problems. Michael had died intestate. The businesses were sold off but, as this coincided with the outbreak of the war, the family lost out. However, part of Michael's capital was set aside to be paid to each of the children when they reached majority, several thousand pounds each and quite a considerable sum in those days. The family moved to Compayne Gardens in Hampstead. "My first memory of Jack," recalls his sister Evey, "is of him entertaining we younger children with his puppet theatre. Even in those early days he was excited about the theatre. He grew to be the tallest in the family, very intelligent and charming. He and Delia were the closest because they were the eldest." After early education in Brighton Jack was sent to University College School in Hampstead. Stanley recalls, "Up to the age of ten I was in the nursery. There was eight years between Jack and myself. I only have one recollection of him during that period. That was when he was at University College School in the OTC and he came into the nursery in his soldier's uniform." Delia continued, "He looked wonderful in his uniform, he was a very handsome young man with a beautiful speaking voice and great charm. He could sing beautifully too. In fact he was very varied in his talents, with the most receptive brain."

At the Hanukkah party which he attended shortly after he left UCS he was immediately attracted to the tiny young woman who stood up to recite. The latter part of her recitation ran thus:

"I saw him since reading a letter
He took out a soft tress of hair
It clung to his hand like a fetter
But I laughed and said 'I don't care.'
When I opened my window this morning
His wedding bells rang on the air.
I thought of *her* happiness dawning
I couldn't say 'I don't care.'
For over my memory came stealing
My laugh and his look of despair
And I cried with my senses all reeling
God only knows how much I care."

He was enchanted by her early gaiety in the poem, moved by the powerful ending, and made up his mind to see her again.

How fortunate he thought himself to spot her at a dance at Hampstead Town Hall. He had escorted his mother and sisters there to celebrate Delia's eighteenth birthday. Having searched for the hostess he asked her to introduce him to the young woman. His description, imbued with a lover's observation, produced an introduction to the wrong girl. However, eventually he caught up with Miss Lewisohn. By this time her dance card was all but full and he had to wait until after supper to dance with her.

But this was just the first of many evenings.

I remember one particular evening. It was a party at the de Leon's house in Compayne Gardens. They were all assembled in the drawing-room, one after another of the guests entertaining each other. I was at the one end of the room and Jack was at the other surrounded by all his intelligent friends. Someone else was playing and he was singing. The song was 'If I Might Only Come to You' a very sentimental song.

If ever there are single moments which shape great events this was the beginning of Jack and Beatie. He spoke to her mother and then Lydia conferred with May. Jack was far too young, it was decreed, for marriage. He must wait until he was at least nineteen. The two of them prepared to wait. Beatie was still at the Academy and Jack had to earn a living somehow. How was the problem. To begin with he followed in his father's footsteps.

My first operation was in the import trade. Panama hats arrived from my uncle by the gross. Then followed in quick succession purchases in great quantities of

German and Czech toys and fancy goods, pencils and pianos. Unsaleable to the trade as the Mark collapsed, I embarked on their retail disposal during two successive Christmas seasons by leasing temporarily a dozen or so empty shops. Thus rid of dolls and teddy bears, trumpets and clarinets, I was free to answer an intriguing advertisement to call upon the short story writer Louise Heilgers. She received me reclining on a divan in a darkened room near Kew Gardens Station like an Elinor Glyn heroine.

The result: my abortive entry into the publishing business. I installed myself in offices opposite the Palace Theatre, registered 'The Star' Magazine Company and paid for the preparation of a dummy copy. For three months I waited for the lady's share of the agreed two thousand pounds capital. I waited in vain, and eventually retired from the venture with a chocolate box beauty (in colour) as the competition cover of my single dummy copy of 'The Star', and the magazine rights in a short story by H. de Vere Stacpole.

These, together with a quarter's rent, had reduced my rapidly dwindling bank balance by some three hundred pounds. But I had committed myself to the Cambridge Circus offices for one year, so I acquired a few gross of silk stockings to occupy the floor space and finally pay my rent. Within two months my brother Roy decided, for some mysterious reason, to enter the wholesale stocking business. He acquired my stock and the remainder of my office tenancy. I departed to think.

This led me to the discovery of Windwood Read's Martyrdom of Man. *The title and the author's name were both appropriate enough. I devoured Read's frenzied writing and decided the time had come for me to follow my true calling. My life must thereafter be devoted to reading and study. Why as a result of this decision I should have embarked on a Max Pemberton course of Journalism and Short Story Writing I have no idea; yet that is just what I did.*

At the end of 1922 I suddenly developed an interest in law. My resolution would not be broken if I devoted the next five years to reading law! Within three months I fluked my way through the Law Society's Preliminary Examination, and a month later settled down in Chancery Lane Offices of Indermaur & Brown (as an articled clerk) to continue my course of reading.

CHAPTER FOUR - JACK AND BEATIE

MEANWHILE, back at the Academy, Beatie had crowned her training by winning the Silver Medal. The climax of the course was the Public Performance at the Globe Theatre on April 15th 1919, adjudicated by Marie Löhr, Sir Squire Bancroft and Sir Johnston Forbes-Robertson. Beatie appeared in a mime sequence in which she had to strangle the one other actress from behind, and as Casca in a scene from *Julius Caesar*. However, her most notable appearance was as The Daughter in Norman Page's production of Rupert Brook's only play *Lithuania*. It was a gift of a part for Beatie. For much of the early part of the action she had to sit on a stool with her back to the audience, in a gruesome setting with the glow of the fire on her, slowly turning her face over her shoulder at the appropriate moment with a telling look.

It was a wonderful part, not many lines. She was surly, but beautiful, and I had a colourful but shabby costume . At the end of the play I had to commit a murder for money. I climbed slowly up a high step-ladder to the loft where the wealthy stranger was sleeping and then, offstage in an attic, I murdered him to the sound of horrific bangings. The play finished when I came down the ladder. It took quite a bit of rehearsing the getting down. When first I did it in rehearsal I came down breathing very heavily, down, down to the audience breathing hard, breathing hard. But Norman Page quite rightly stopped me. He said, "No, I want you to come down quite differently. Absolutely limp. No emotion." And I did it that way; spoke my line slowly; my hand opened and the hatchet fell to the floor; "They'll put me in prison"; and the curtain came down! I was enjoying it too much the other way, overacting. But Norman Page wasn't having it. He was right.

After the long applause and after the final curtain there was a long wait while we took off our make-up and changed. Some of us went to the stage-door to see the results and we waited and waited. Finally the whole family and I went to Lyons Corner House and had tea and cakes without knowing the results. Then a group of students came in and one came over and thumped me on the back and said, "You know you've got the Silver Medal." Irene Ward and I had the same marks but because she was a little older she was awarded the Bancroft Gold Medal.

I had been quite a success in the part in *Lithuania*, so much so that Constance Collier, who was a really great and famous actress then, wanted me to appear with her in the play at the Coliseum and then to tour. Unfortunately she was offered another part and the tour fell through.

Shortly afterwards Beatie was offered a part in a film, *The Sign of David*. There were many long breaks as the cameramen waited for the fine weather. It rained for several days. The other actors sat around playing poker. Not Beatie, she couldn't waste a moment. She used the time to practise her movement. The film earned her the princely sum of seven pounds ten shillings a week. At the end of a day's work she had the treat of being met at Waterloo Station by Jack. Unfortunately the film was never released. It was to be her last work as an actress for Beatie for some time. She grew unaccountably shy of large audiences. Had she managed job after job to begin with she might have learned to take it in her stride as other young actors do, but this was not to be. Her idol at the time was Madge Titheradge. She longed to tour in a Titheradge part but sadly none came her way.

She did perform an excellent recital at the Steinway Hall. Jack asked his mother to get him a bouquet for Beatie. She went to Selfridges flower department but the bouquet was not good enough for Jack. Back it went and he selected his own. He never came to visit Beatie without flowers. He wrote at least two letters every day, long romantic letters. In those days there were postal deliveries at 7.30 in the morning, then one at midday, one in the afternoon and one in the evening. The first and last post always brought a letter from Jack and sometimes he would turn up with one he had written at lunch time.

Staying with the family at Compayne Gardens at this time was Jack's cousin from Panama, also known as Evey. "I came to England from Panama when I was nine and a half," she recalled, "all very excited because I saw snow for the first time! Granny Maduro met me at the station with Nurse Lomax. I was very shy of them all. There was Delia with her hair parted in the middle like a fierce Indian, and then Jack appeared. He was instantly my hero. He was very handsome and outgoing and intelligent. I was like a tomboy. I had run wild in Panama. I couldn't even tell the time. Jack took me in hand and taught me. One day he told me he had met a beautiful lady at Miss Chapman's and that he wanted to meet her again. Eventually I was to meet her too. She *was* beautiful. I remembered the way she dressed. I used to copy the way she behaved. They made the loveliest couple." Jack's sister Evey continued, "When Beatie first saw Minta and myself outside school, or so she told me later, she nearly broke off the engagement because we looked so terrible! Minta was the ugly duckling who turned into a swan. Delia and I took a back seat. Whenever my brothers brought friends home they always fell for her. She was beautiful with enormous sex appeal."

When I first saw Evey and Minta one of them had glasses on and they had on their school uniforms with ribbed stockings. Oh, they looked awful. They were very dowdy and I didn't like the look of them at all.

I went often to Compayne Gardens and became quite a member of the family. Naturally I eventually became fond of Evey and Minta despite that first meeting! There were always sixteen to lunch on Sundays. Aunt Sarah was a wonderful cook. Sometimes we played tennis nearby. And Jack and I used to go to dances. He used to sit at my feet.

"While Beatie and Jack were courting," recalled Nora, Beatie's niece, "they were the talk of Golders Green because they were frequently seen spooning in the back row of the local cinema, the Ionic. About that time I acted at St. Edward's Hall, Golders Green, taking the part of Fairy Rosebud, rehearsed by Beatie. She asked my mother to make me up, but Beatie scolded her for putting lipstick all over my rather large mouth. The performance was given by her to raise money for the building of the St. John's Wood Synagogue which was eventually built and was opened in September 1922. My father, Harold Lewisohn, was a founder and a plaque bearing his name appears on the building. Reverend Livingstone came from Bradford to be its first minister, in time to marry Beatie and Jack."

The waiting time had passed and Jack and Beatie were married on August 30th 1921. Both Eveys, Minta, Delia and Beatie's nieces, Peggy and Joan Rundbaken and Peggy and Nora Lewisohn were bridesmaids. There was a dinner followed by dancing for over a hundred guests at Frascatis, a wedding gift from Beatie's older brothers. Leon's son Bobby recalls a splendid table with a special meal for the children.

My mother romanticised about married life, but I think there was something lovely in it. I did adore my husband, all our lives together. There wasn't a single day of our married life when I didn't see him. There was something special about Jack and Beatie.

My mother had been living in a rented house in Garrick Avenue but moved out to live with her sister. Jack bought it. It was repainted and made delightful for us. Here, after a honeymoon at the Royal Bath Hotel in Bournemouth, we spent the first years of our married life, and here on October 14th 1922 our only child, Jean, was born.

I was anxious she should not come on the thirteenth and was out walking that very day in the sun, full of beans, when visitors arrived horrified to find me not in my room. I just made it to the fourteenth! Jean was born at 12.45 am. My husband and mother were nearby. I heard later that Jack had been lying on the top of the stairs listening. Within two weeks I was wheeling her out in her pram in an Indian summer. Neighbours and nurses wheeling their prams admired her huge brown eyes and curly hair and dainty clothes. She was an adorable baby. Three years later when we moved to Richmond she would dance on the lawn to the tune of 'Virginia', daintily holding up her skirt.

But there was to be another move before the move to Richmond. The first plan may considerably have altered the eventual course of their lives. A theatre was advertised for sale in Inverness and serious consideration was made by the young de Leons as to whether they should buy it and run it. Instead they made a move which caused somewhat less of an upheaval. Beatie wanted to teach Drama. Delia was interested too. She had trained in elocution under a Miss Sergeant and had gained her LACA gold medal. Victor too was interested. After working with the

Tree company he had gone on to the Old Vic. Here he met Sybil Thorndike, then the leading actress in the company. In subsequent years he would work frequently with Miss Thorndike and her husband Lewis Casson. Beatie asked Sybil, together with Dennis Neilson-Terry and his wife Mary Glynne, to be patrons of their new school, the London Academy of Dramatic Art, at 59 Finchley Road, a house known as 'The Towers'.

What a house was this 'Towers'. A Victorian Gothic monstrosity, with a dozen stone steps leading to its massive front door, four internal staircases and a great parqueted drawing-room giving access to a wide balcony ten feet above the tennis court and garden.

We quickly transformed this large room into a little theatre. It seated a hundred and twenty and the tiny stage led into a passage and down one of the staircases into a six-roomed basement on the garden level. Here were the dressing-rooms and the living quarters of our married couple staff. We lived on the first floor beneath two ludicrous towers with staircases winding up to nowhere. In this house The Dramatic Academy flourished and I gave private elocution lessons in my spare time to juvenile students.

"59 Finchley Road was a magical place for children," recalled Peggy, Beatie's niece. "There were cellars and an attic to explore. Every Christmas and on Jean's birthday there was a huge, wonderful party." Peggy was one of Beatie's pupils. During this period Beatie presented *The Banishment of Evil* at the Golders Green Hippodrome in aid of the waifs and strays with a cast made up of her pupils. Peggy played the Princess and her brother Bernhard was a goblin.

The bare-footed fairies were almost naked save for a flimsy drape of delicately coloured butter muslin and garlands of flowers.

"At the beginning of the play," continued Peggy, "the curtain rose on a woodland scene with all the little fairies lying on the ground about to be woken. As the curtain went up one of the fairies began to cry. They had to bring the curtain down again so she could be taken off! I felt very superior because I didn't cry."

Within seconds we re-started and the atmosphere was again captured. For the finale we all sang, "We leave the sunshine to the flowers" with elaborate gestures, gradually walking backwards and waving to the audience at the end. Then, as the applause increased we ran down to the front of the stage throwing flowers and streamers to them!

As well as training students the large house was put to other uses by Beatie, already displaying the managerial skills which would stand her in such good stead in after years. On Saturday afternoon teas were served and there were two monthly balls. She also managed to persuade a reluctant Jack on to the boards. In one particular end-of-term production of Stephen Phillips' poetic drama *Paolo and Francesca* he was the hero to Beatie's heroine, with a supporting cast of siblings, Delia as

Lucretzia and Victor as Giovanni. But, as it transpired, the London Academy was only to be a stepping stone.

My mother-in-law was the real culprit. I would never have made this discovery had I not set myself the task of explaining how I could have been such a young imbecile as to have plunged to my own destruction with a whoop of joy.

As I could not assume that I had once been utterly egocentric and devoid of rational thought, even at the age of three and twenty, a scapegoat there had to be; and what better scapegoat than one's mother-in-law?

My mother-in-law certainly led me to believe that I was capable of performing the impossible, so should I have doubted her judgment when her judgment was so flattering to my young ego? However I was no more responsible for the inanity of my first decision than a spoilt infant careering into a forbidden wood inhabited by a multitude of sheep and goats, a few isolated serpents and rare birds of prey. The climax came in the Spring of 1924. It was no accident, the opening of my Sunday Times at a marked page; no accident that Mama turned our morning topic to the obvious need for another Everyman Theatre the other side of London. Dear me - the very thing! A few hundred pounds would convert this delightful hall at Kew Bridge! How nice to have a theatre near the river ...

Beatie

Jack

The Lewisohns - Beatie on her mama's lap

Harold, Norman, Caesar, Leon, Stanley, Ferdy and Victor Lewisohn

May and Michael de Leon

Jack, with brother Roy (left)

The de Leon brothers - standing
(left to right) Herby, Michael and
Stanley; seated Roy and Jack

Lydia   Helena

Jack and Beatie's wedding-day. The bridesmaids standing (left to right) are Peggy Rundbaken, Minta, Evey, Joan; seated are Delia and cousin Evey Maduro; on the floor are Peggy Lewisohn and Nora

CHAPTER FIVE - KEW AND Q

*My grandmother's chauffeur drove us to Kew that very afternoon; Mama, Beatie
with our two year old infant Jean, Delia and myself. The old Mercedes rattled
past the derelict building adjacent to the Star and Garter, and I caught a glimpse
of its curious elevation, set back some fifty paces from the main road.
In Kew Gardens Delia entered into the conspiracy; we had virtually pooled our
resources and made the decision before we returned home that night.
The next afternoon I played truant from Chancery Lane, and having arranged
with the Estate Agents concerned to look round the advertised Prince's Hall,
once again trekked out to Kew Bridge with the family.
Soon we were all inside the ramshackle shed, threading our way through
thousands of feet of discarded film, obsolete film studio lamps and stands,
photographs, newspapers, account books, dust, dirt, cobwebs, and a mass of
broken-down film settings. Amid this scene of confusion my heart sank lower and
lower until I escaped, speechless with humiliation and disappointment.*

The ramshackle shed had a mixed history suggesting that everything had been tried
there and nothing had succeeded. It had been a beer garden in the 1880's, then a
swimming pool. In the early days of World War One it tried to cash in on the roller-
skating boom and became a roller-rink. It was converted into a dance-hall when
the fashion faded before, oddly, being converted back into a rink. Its next
incarnation was as a cinema before it was taken over by Walter West as a studio
for his Broad-West Films. It had been here he made many of his Henry Edwardes
and Chrissie White silent films. *The Sign of David* had been a Broad-West
production. When the company had gone into liquidation the lease had reverted
to the brewers whose beer garden had originally occupied the site: Fuller, Smith
and Turner.

*Next morning the Castles in Spain had re-materialised. Timidly, yet undaunted,
I commenced negotiations. Within a month my mother, Delia and I had
undertaken the responsibility of a long lease of the Prince's Hall, Kew Bridge
Road, Brentford, Middlesex.
Very soon came the first great shock. Into my strange new world materialised
hitherto unknown officials representing mysterious all-powerful County Coun-
cils. They wanted plans, they demanded exits where no exits existed, they insisted
on a new roof, a new floor, panic bolts and encased wiring, gangways and
passages of specified width, emergency gas lighting and exterior lighting. My
horror soon turned to bewilderment, and my bewilderment to resignation. In a
few weeks we had contracted to spend five times the amount which, in our
childish fancy, we had assumed would have been sufficient to turn the Prince's
Hall into a workable theatre. Mama's hundreds were multiplied tenfold. Too late
to turn back, we had to swallow the pill and start a system of family borrowing*

which continued in its harassing uncertainty for years. Week by week we watched, at times fearfully and at times in a fever of excitement, the growing walls and the shaping of the plans.

Bricks and mortar were all very well but there was the artistic side of the theatre to consider. Lydia Lewisohn's idea of creating a theatre in the mould of Hampstead's Everyman was excellent. Although something can be gained of a play's worth by reading it from the manuscript page, no-one can be certain how it will perform in front of an audience without the full creative process which transforms the play into a living thing. Then, and only then, when all the compromises have been made and all the possibilities examined and the work is exposed to an audience can the play be judged. It was for this purpose, the trying out of a new play before an audience, that the Everyman existed. Many plays would fall by the wayside, but a select few would find their way to the West End and theatre history. Even the ones which flopped taught their writers some of the pitfalls to be avoided in the future. Try-out theatres were the backbone of the English theatre in its golden age.

Although Beatie to a small degree, and Victor to a larger, knew something of the working of the theatre, Jack had no experience at all, nor had Delia whose own money supplied the major part of the initial investment. He knew it was essential to find someone of greater experience to guide them through their early days. Milton Rosmer, a fine actor who had trodden much the same path as Sybil Thorndike with Miss Horniman's company and Ben Greet's American company had recently appeared in her greatest success *Saint Joan*, agreed to meet the new theatre proprietors at The Towers.

To Delia and me he was a great theatrical celebrity. What he must have thought of our ingenuous first conversation I never asked him, but I can well imagine. Nevertheless he accepted a contract as Production Manager of the new 'Q', whose name was the first of his many constructive suggestions.

At Rosmer's suggestion Jack engaged Keith Moss as Business Manager despite the fact that his most notable credit was as manager of a cinema in Swiss Cottage which had been a failure. Jack recognised in him a similar enthusiasm to his own and a number of good ideas. One idea he would eventually put into practice was The Spotlight Casting Directory which is still the mainstay of casting directors today. *I remember vividly the first clash of ideas I had with Moss. Of course I knew I was right, therefore he must be wrong. It was in connection with the ticket booking system. He maintained that the only satisfactory system was the one then, and still, in use in almost every theatre in the country - a book of numbered and dated tickets specially printed for each performance.*

In my simplicity I averred that if the theatre was only half full at any performance the wastage of the remaining half of the tickets was typical of the incompetent business organisation in the theatre world. In consequence I devised a new system under which books of consecutively numbered tickets were to be issued instead, maintaining that although this method involved the filling in of a date, letter and number on each ticket sold, it avoided the wastage of even a single piece of paper.

I gloated over Moss in triumph when the tickets began to sell by the hundreds and the system seemed to be working magnificently. The fact that the nightly cash return rarely corresponded to the amount in the till was to me by no means the ominous sign it should have been. But I was to repent at no distant date.

The opening night was originally scheduled for September 1924, but then it was changed to October, then to November and finally the doors were opened to the public on Boxing Day. The play chosen for the event was not a new one. In fact the new enterprise was originally advertised as 'A Bright, Cosy Theatre for the presentation of successful WEST END PLAYS.' The opening play was Gertrude Jennings *The Young Person In Pink*, directed by Rosmer. The only star name in the company was that of Sydney Fairbrother recreating her original role of Mrs Badger, the drunken charwoman. Naturally she stole the show. One of the original policies of the management was that Delia and Beatie should perform whenever possible to save on salaries. It was Beatie who appeared in *The Young Person in Pink* and it was, of course, her professional debut.

The part did not suit me and I was terrible. At the Academy I had played mostly in classics. Marie Hemingway, the second of Claude Rains four wives, was also in the cast.

The theatre was animated on the opening night. We had a trio playing in the auditorium led by Delia Morris, a cellist friend of Delia's.

Every seat in the theatre had been sold, and outside was a seething mass of people agitating to gain admission. Uniformed attendants had been instructed by Moss not to open the doors until he gave the signal. I had hidden myself, on the verge of tears, in my corrugated-roofed office off the main corridor. Milton Rosmer was still in the middle of his dress rehearsal, while simultaneously the act drop, late in arriving, was being placed in position.

It must have been about ten minutes before the curtain was due to rise when Moss burst into the office with the news: "We've got the curtain fixed: Rosmer's going on with the rehearsal with the curtain down, and we're letting the house in. **We've already found twenty duplications."**

I hadn't the vaguest idea what he was talking about, but followed him out to hear the fag end of an angry conversation between a murderous-looking patron and the timid fireman. The position suddenly became illuminatingly clear. Every seat in the house was already occupied and an uncountable number of infuriated ticket-holders were left seatless and stranded, fuming in the congested entrance and foyer. In the midst of this crowd was my mother-in-law, my sister and a score or more members of my family.

I cannot remember what I did. I know two uniformed policemen seemed to appear from nowhere, but I like to think I succeeded in quelling a bloody riot by placating the mob and returning with profuse apologies the money they had paid for their duplicated tickets.

I saw the remainder of the play standing at the back of the theatre. At the end of the performance Rosmer and Moss entertained the cast in my office with many bottles of whisky, for which, presumably , in due course I was presented with a bill.

Jack's law studies were in abeyance. Instead of Beatie testing him on his Latin, she now needed testing on her lines. Besides, he had grown disillusioned.

The world of Statutes, legal precedents and copper-plate written parchments originally fascinated me. The text books of Gibson and Indermaur had kept me occupied when I was not in the Chancery or Divorce Court enjoying the privilege of sitting on the Solicitor's Bench. I gradually began to appreciate that the success or failure of these 'Equity Cases' rested on subtle distinctions between judgments of recorded cases dead and buried for generations.

It must have been twelve months after my entering into Chancery Lane that I made the devastating discovery: Solicitors rely on Barristers and justify this reliance by the ancient custom that Barristers, not being paid by the litigant, cannot be held responsible in law for negligence and bad advice, whereas the Solicitor risks being brought himself into the Courts by his fee-paying client.

To my youthful mind this was a monstrous state of affairs. There was I, embarking on a profession that took refuge under the silk gown of a colleague to cover up his ignorance of the law and his fear of the consequence of his ignorance. From that moment I lost interest.

As the curtain swung down on one part of his life and another was rung up, Jack could have no inkling that not many months hence the two areas of his professional life would become unavoidably linked and he would be called upon to summon everything he had learned of England's legal system.

CHAPTER SIX - THE CZARINA AFFAIR

THE ADRENALIN stimulated by the events of the opening night would not be quelled so Jack picked up a manuscript that had arrived in the post to help himself unwind. In the early hours of the 27th he had made up his mind that this would be the next play presented at Q. This was to be a theatre of new writing, and this was an exciting new play. Next day he instructed Rosmer to begin rehearsals immediately. The wiser professional courteously pointed out that he could not start rehearsing a play until he had obtained the performing rights from the author or his agent. "And there is, of course, the question of the actors," he added. Instead he began rehearsing the proposed second play, *A Message from Mars*.

I was in a thumbnail gem of a part as Polly. The presentation was a great success and the snow storm aroused wild applause. Jack was always keen on effects. Eventually Strand Electric installed a splendid lighting board.

Feeling himself put down by Rosmer, Jack summoned his energies, his sister and his Business Manager to make sure the third play of the season could be the new play he wanted produced. In his memoirs Jack noted that within a week the contract was completed, the script and parts typed, a cast secured and that the new play opened on January 23rd 1925. An accurate check of his records would have shown that the play would not open until February 9th. This would suggest that Rosmer was right and these things took longer than Jack might have thought, and memory had blurred the edges. The third play of the season was in fact, a comedy by Stanley Houghton entitled *The Younger Generation* which was preceded by a curtain-raising performance of *Lithuania* with Beatie in the role she enjoyed so much at the Academy. This was originally advertised for a week's run, possibly in the hope that Jack might have the new play ready. In the end *The Younger Generation* played for a second week. It had been the original policy that plays would run for two weeks. In fact it was on that basis that Rosmer had agreed to join the venture. He felt it was the only way to get the true value from rehearsals and performance. However the box-office receipts proved this to be a luxury the theatre could not afford. The returns were scarcely sufficient to warrant a one week, let alone a two week, run. They didn't have far to look for the reason. As the critic of the Richmond & Twickenham Times noted in his review of *A Message From Mars*, "one's enjoyment of a really good presentation (was) marred by the absence of local people." The indigenous theatre-goers seemed to prefer the inconvenience and cost of a journey to the West End rather than sample the dubious delights of the new little theatre next to Kew Bridge. News had doubtless also circulated that you might find someone sitting in the seat you'd paid for.

Leonard Merrick and Michael Morton's *The Fraud* was the new play presented on what Jack liked to call the first real 'First Night' of Q. A distinguished audience and most of the London critics were present and the cast included Dorothy Dix, a leading West End player, Gerald Ames, Franklyn Bellamy and the supposed illegitimate son of Edward VII, Morton Selten. The splendid cast was not enough to draw the local audience and the first new play proved the last to be staged for a two week run as part of the theatre's regular policy. As a result Milton Rosmer regretfully withdrew his services though he would be back at Q on numerous subsequent occasions.

Six months later perhaps the title of this premiere production would echo ironically down the corridors of Q.

The next new play followed three revivals and was Lennox Robinson's tragicomedy *The Round Table*. The Irish dramatist and newspaper critic took a bow after the first-night performance as authors would continue to do at Q. In his speech he referred to "this rather absurd little play of mine," which assertion was greeted by cries of "No, no!" from members of the audience. The critic of the Richmond & Twickenham Times noted, "We were rather inclined to agree with the author." However absurd, it was snapped up by Bronson Albery and Howard & Wyndham for production in the West End. This was the kind of response Jack and Delia longed for as Q could only benefit from transfers, or the West End production of plays originally produced at the theatre.

Delia had already made her debut at Q in Walter Hackett's *The Barton Mystery* but was to win acclaim for her performance in the Lennox Robinson play. "*The Round Table* proved the most enjoyable play I ever did," she recalled. "I played what could only be described as the conscience of the character played by Dorothy Dix. Sybil Thorndike and Lewis Casson came down to see it and Bronson Albery bought it for Sybil to do in the West End. Sadly, my part was also recast. The West End notices weren't as good as the ones we got at Q. The critics thought it miscast." She had played in *The Barton Mystery* under her own name. The name 'D. de Leon' was also linked to Jack's in all publicity as the theatre's management.

Delia had been closely involved with me throughout, but her several stage appearances brought on nervous hysteria during rehearsals, culminating before the first night (on most occasions in the presence of our family doctor to administer sedatives) in the oath of renunciation. "Never again," said Delia, but never again was invariably followed two or three weeks later by: "Well, perhaps just this once more ..."

She played as Delia Delvina, and the name became a family joke.

Only a matter of days after *The Round Table* had opened at Wyndham's Theatre Jack was approached by a gentleman called Claude Yearsley who suggested he try out an English adaptation of Melchior Lengyel and Ludwig Biro's play *The Czarina*. Some weeks later Jack met Hans Bartsch who controlled the English performing rights and agreed upon a contract for the production. Bartsch was returning to the Continent and indicated that should the play warrant a transfer then all further arrangements were to be made with Yearsley.

Reginald Denham, whose production of Ernest Vajda's *Fata Morgana* with Jeanne de Casalis in the leading role had recently completed a successful run at the Ambassador's Theatre, was engaged to direct the play. (Denham would eventually become a leading Broadway director but is now mainly remembered for his co-authorship with Edward Percy of several thrillers, particularly *Ladies in Retirement*.) In the cast were Dorothy Dix, Leslie Faber, Henry Kendall, George Relph, Victor (now the veteran of four Q productions) and Beatie.

During the action of *The Czarina* I was involved in an exciting scene. The Czarina (Dorothy Dix) was jealous and in a violent temper pushed me roughly to the floor, apparently knocking me out. She had to look at me, cursing me and saying "How dare you! ... How dare you!... *I* am twenty-six." The biggest laugh came because the audience thought I was unconscious, and I sat up like a Jack in the Box and said, "Twenty-*EIGHT*".

The play opened on June 22nd 1925. "During this period," recalled Delia, "there were queues around the theatre on first nights. The critics came, evening dress was worn, and it was all very exciting." The play was a huge success ("Miss Beatrice Lewisohn makes a charming Annie Jashikoff, her 'big scene' with the Czarina being a fine piece of acting") and Jack prepared to present it at the Hippodrome, Golders Green, under an agreement signed by Claude Yearsley on Hans Bartsch's behalf which gave Jack the right to take the play to the Lyric Theatre after a week at Golders Green.

When he arrived at the Hippodrome on the morning of Monday July 13th, Jack was greeted with a bombshell in the shape of a letter from a firm of solicitors informing him that he had no rights in the play and that if he opened at the Lyric he would do so at his peril. When contacted, Yearsley seemed unperturbed and promised immediately to cable Bartsch. Jack spent a nightmare week. Eventually a writ was issued on behalf of Hans Bartsch with Notice of Motion for the following Monday July 20th.

It is quite clear in retrospect that in my youthful ignorance and eagerness I took for granted far more that I should have done, but it is not clear whether Yearsley exceeded his authority knowingly or whether he, too, assumed his right.

A Leader was briefed over the weekend and simultaneously with the transportation to and setting up of scenery at the Lyric Theatre on Monday the twentieth, the advertised day of the play's opening, I listened in awed silence to the arguments placed before Mr. Justice Eve by Mr Clayton, K.C., for Bartsch and Mr Gover, K.C., for me.

I had so often sat in these courts, dispassionately following the arguments and legal quibbles, but now for the first time I was vitally concerned in the issues, so concerned that I was quite unable to listen objectively and could only fume at the stupidity and unfairness of the whole procedure.

At one o'clock the Judge pronounced against me. The injunction was granted and my heart sank as the world seemed to topple before my eyes. This just could not happen to me! I saw the situation as a horrible injustice, to be fought without thought of consequences.

We were still at the Golders Green Hippodrome while the production was being set up at the Lyric. We decided to rehearse. During one of the scenes I was not involved in I was sitting by the Stage Door high up, anxiously looking out of the window, specially concerned because I was the boss's wife. I was waiting for my call to come back to the stage when I heard the newsboys crying, "Theatre closed, show can't go on." I felt devastated.

Jack demanded an appeal. Application was made, the matter further discussed and it was arranged that production of the play might take place subject to Jack's paying the then not inconsiderable sum of two hundred and fifty pounds to Bartsch's solicitors.

In a crowded car, with Eric Barker of The Evening News standing on the running board, we drove from the Law Courts to Shaftesbury Avenue. On our way the evening papers hoardings mocked:

FIRST NIGHT ABANDONED

'CZARINA'

INJUNCTION GRANTED

This was the last straw, even if Eric Barker did succeed in a Stop Press contradiction later that night. Publicity may rarely succeed in the theatre in transforming success into failure, but when millions of readers of the three London evening papers are informed with great headlines that a play will not be performed, only a fool could hope that audiences will queue up for a cancelled opening. I was just such a fool, and the anti-climax of my success in failure was despair.

The first night nervous tension reacted on the cast; the empty house reacted on the critics; and a potential success became a "tiresome historical satire."

James Agate, the influential critic of the Sunday Times, thought it "musical comedy without music ... Personally, I found the entertainment tiresome and would have welcomed a ukulele. Twelve ukuleles would have been better."

Apart from all the distress of the legal action this was a disappointing time for Beatie. *The Czarina* marked her debut in the West End.

The run lasted one week, but repercussions on Q and myself were not so quickly over. The episode cost nearly £1,000, plus almost twice this sum on the production and week's run which of itself was well in excess of the capital. Not one of the Subscribers, including Veyzey-Strong who had been a partner in the venture from its inception, contributed a pound towards what was to me and Q at that time a calamitous drain on our resources.

The irony of the whole episode only became apparent on the day the play was withdrawn. A cable arrived from Ludwig Biro, one of the authors, informing me that Hans Bartsch's interest in the play had expired some time ago, and that performing rights had reverted to the authors. Maybe I could have joined them in a claim against Bartsch but I had had enough.

Jack's solicitors in the legal action had naturally been Indermaur and Brown. He was still officially bound by articles to Fisher Brown Jr.

For nearly nine months I had been away from the office on 'holiday', but in running Q during these months, with the knowledge of Fisher Brown, we had both been parties to an 'irregularity'.

Front page publicity brought the situation to a head. I received an official letter informing me that my absence would no longer be countenanced, and I must either return to Chancery Lane or relinquish my articles.

I surrendered my articles, forfeited my premium and redoubled my concentration in an effort to save Q from premature demise. I had burnt my boats; for good or ill I was in the theatre.

CHAPTER SEVEN - THEATRE OF CONFLICT

REGINALD DENHAM, in his autobiography, *Stars In My Hair*, recalled, "The Q Theatre ... was something quite new, and its growth as a try-out theatre was very rapid ... This theatre was in essence an off-shoot of Sunday night play-producing societies, which also 'fagged' for commercial managers, the difference being that directors and actors were paid a small sum by Mr de Leon, which was a godsend to out-of-work actors, even though it did little more than cover expenses ... We would rehearse at Q two weeks (the two weeks rehearsal period was later reduced to one week) and play eight performances, and usually most of the London critics would come to the opening nights. A direct result was a new crop of shoe-string managers who could raise just enough money to pay Mr de Leon to allow them to put on a show at his theatre. If such a play happened to be received well by the Press, it would inevitably transfer to the West End, because more money would be forthcoming from theatrical financiers who were standing by to jump on to a good thing that someone else had been clever enough to discover for them. It was a good gamble for the shoe-stringer and many hits were born that way."

Whether Michael Hogan and Donald Macardle would qualify as 'shoe-stringers' it was under just such an arrangement that they presented *The Odd Man* in association with Jack at Q on August 24th 1925. Q became front-page news yet again when the authors of the play, St. Clair Scott and Caswell Garth, staged a protest at certain changes Hogan and Macardle had made in their play of which they did not approve, by walking out in the middle of Act Three, making it perfectly clear why they were leaving. Controversy was in the air, it seems. Q first-nighters found the back of the auditorium lined by a squad of uniformed police when they attended the next first-night! The police were called when the theatre began to receive numbers of anonymous letters and cards threatening to tear down the theatre if *Taffy* by Caradoc Evans was allowed to open. Never, at any point, did Jack seriously consider abandoning the project, but calling in the police certainly seemed to be justified. The play treated rather cynically on Welsh village life and angered a certain section of Welsh nationalists.

"Many well-known people, including Mr. T. P. O'Connor MP., were in the audience," reported the Richmond & Twickenham Times. "As a precaution against scenes, police were kept in the background, but unfortunately were not needed. The audience generally gave the play a good hearing. One or two Welshmen sitting near the writer exhibited a good deal of excitement, and some passages were lost in moments of hysterical laughter, and again when one fervent Taffy smothered his head in his arms and groaned in agony as though suffering from excruciating stomach pains, but generally speaking all was well until the final curtain fell. Then the storm broke. The Welshmen got on their feet and booed and shouted themselves hoarse, whilst other sections joined in loud applause. The appearance of the author was the signal for a fresh outbreak, and it was some minutes before Mr Caradoc Evans, who faced his critics unflinchingly, could make himself heard. Then he expressed gratitude on behalf of the management and of the players for the reception given to the play, and for the kind appreciation of the play itself. 'I am grateful also,' he added, 'to you, my people, who have left your little businesses - (laughter) - to come here to bear witness to the truth ...' (Voices: Why don't you produce the play in Wales?) Mr Evans: 'We have conducted this meeting tonight in the manner of the Welsh - (a cry of 'Liar!') - in the manner of the Welsh riotous prayer meeting. Let all men and women depart with new sins in their hearts.' A further burst of cheering, mixed with booing, greeted the close of the speech. This was followed by the Welsh element fervently singing 'Land of My Fathers', the Welsh national anthem, whilst although the hour was late little groups remained outside the theatre for some while after abusing the author and praying for a chance to 'get at him'.

"These Welshmen could not have spent much time in bed, for early next morning Mr Evans received a score of vitriolic anonymous letters and dozens of furious telephone calls. The people on the phone announced their intention of tearing the Welsh author and playwright limb from limb. The letter-writers said the same, only in more concentrated rage. Mr Evans merely smiled at them, however, and in an interview related how one man had rung him up and said he was going to shoot him, but he was still waiting for the shot.

"'I am undeterred by my noisy critics. I intend to take *Taffy* to Wales with me before the end of the year. There is very little in the play to which one can take exception, not even a Welshman. I have been nothing like so severe as I could find it in my heart to be.'"

The critics had turned up in force. Words like 'genius' were freely bandied about, some doubts were expressed as to Evans' view on his compatriots, but a generally favourable opinion of the play was expressed. Within a few days a transfer to the now defunct Royalty Theatre in Dean Street was arranged.

By the opening night, September 21st, public and private threats had reached formidable proportions.

I was understudying and prayed not to be called. Apart from anything else I had not really had time to polish my part.

Not even the presence of a squad of police could prevent an outbreak which half-way through the second act led Caradoc Evans to speak from the stage.

He faced the infuriated section of the audience, vainly attempting to appeal to their sense of decency, only to be greeted by the throwing of missiles and the breaking loose of pandemonium. The evening-dress audience in the stalls naturally began to take themselves to safety by precipitantly leaving in the middle of the play. The furiously indignant Welsh section, having served their purpose, also left the theatre, and before the few brave stayers-on, a dejected Caradoc and

a more than dejected family of de Leons and Lewisohns, the cast half-heartedly continued the performance until the curtain finally fell to the sympathetic cheers of the few.
Next morning's dramatic criticisms were virtually non-existent. Sensational reports of
RIOT IN LONDON THEATRE
were undoubtedly responsible for the amazing indifference of theatre audience to a very remarkable play. A hundred or so brave or curious Londoners constituted the second and third night audiences, but **Taffy** *had died on its first night of resurrected life.*
Jack was not having much luck with his West End transfers. *The Czarina* had lasted but a week, and *Taffy* closed after four performances. The handful of other plays which were taken to the West End by other managements paying Q a percentage, such as *The Round Table* and *Adam and Eva* had not made much impression either. The second play after *Taffy*, *The Life Line*, was similarly taken up by another management. Even the great star Dame Marie Tempest could not help it to a substantial run. An interesting sidelight occurred in the Q presentation of the latter play when the local critic opined, "it is to be hoped that the cordial reception given to it by a fairly large 'house' - despite counter attraction - will encourage (the Q management) to attempt something more pretentious in the near future." How words change their meanings!
When the coffers seemed to be getting too disastrously low, Delia was commissioned to do a fund-raising round of the family. They were to help the theatre in other ways too. "When Jack started the theatre," his sister Evey recalled, "he said to me, 'If you take a secretarial course you can come and work for me.' So I rushed through a course and I went to work at Q. While I was still on the course he put me in the box-office which I hated. When I graduated to the office and there was a new play I would take the script home and type out each actor's part. Along with everyone else I was prevailed upon to put my inheritance into the theatre but I had just married Harry Wolff and we only had enough to live on."
Jack and Beatie now had a new family home at 200 Kew Road within walking distance of the theatre.
I was able to rush home to lunch and supper, spend a few minutes with my chatty infant, slip on my badly fitting dinner jacket and return to play host to managers or critics, to greet the few regulars whose faces had already become familiar; to work out methods of advertising, to continue casting, or just to hang around looking on.
Beatie often played in our productions--
(Apart from those already mentioned she had appeared with Jack Esmond in *Eliza Comes To Stay*, Maugham's *The Land of Promise*, *Tilly of Bloomsbury* with Marie Ault and Reginald Denham's production of *The Man From Toronto*)

--she had great talent for mimicry and a sense of humour : but Jean, her mother and her home remained the first call. Invariably Beatie and her mother spent Monday and Saturday nights at the theatre. Mama would sit in the draughty entrance watching the animated audience trooping in: enjoying the spectacle of a full house, or preparing her re-iterated complaint (if the audiences were sparse) that I wouldn't advertise 'big'.

Nine months into its first year Q was already a well known and much publicised institution whatever Lydia might think. There was a considerable number of regular first-nighters and now that first nights happened on a weekly basis the theatre's income improved. However, the gap between the income and the outgoings were perpetually worrying. Several fund-raising ideas occurred. The father of a young man who had written a play suggested that he would invest a small sum of money if Jack produced the play at Q. Jack at first balked at the idea but the gentleman remonstrated that had he wished to enter his son into any other profession his payment for 'Articles' would have been readily accepted; this method would cost him far less than supporting the boy for months or years while he continued filling notebooks with unspoken dialogue and theoretically constructed dramas. The payment was made and the play produced, the first of many others thus initiated. Towards the end of 1925 Jack obtained a bar licence and leased the bar franchise for a substantial weekly return.

Such subsidy was necessary because apart from domestic success there was failure after failure in transferred productions. Jack decided to stage *Conflict*, a play by Miles Malleson. Malleson is mainly remembered today as the double-chinned bumbler in many character roles in films, such as Polonius in Laurence Olivier's *Hamlet* and Chasuble in *The Importance of Being Earnest*. Now forgotten is that he was an excellent teacher of actors, an accomplished director and an imaginative playwright. His new play, according to the local critic, dealt "with the struggle between a Socialist and a Conservative - a theme which has many possibilities and which has been written, in this instance, with great thought, intelligence and observation."

Alfred Butt offered Jack the chance of presenting *Conflict* at the Queen's Theatre. He would receive a two per cent profit royalty and participate in any sale of the film rights. After a successful run at Q which opened on November 30th 1925, the play opened at the Queen's on April 7th the following year, with a cast including Colin Clive and Isabel Jeans, under the direction of the author. It was immediately acclaimed a 'smash hit' and the jinx on Q transfers seemed to have lifted. Not so. Within a month the play was forced to close, along with virtually every other West End production, a victim of the General Strike.

It is impossible to recapture the excitement or the mental anguish of those months of apprenticeship, for that is all they could have been. I had plunged into the deep waters of theatre finance and adventure unprepared and inadequately advised.

Or maybe in my young arrogance I rejected advice but I watched and learned. I learned at a high price, but the lessons to be learned in the theatre are so manifold that one continues to purchase experience over the years until one's judgment is sharpened to the recognition that experience can carry one thus far and no further. Then intuition takes over. And there still remains the unpredictable, unforeseeable combination of circumstances which, when added together and conspiring in your favour, are spelled L-U-C-K.

Fortune, as fortune has a habit of doing, was to change, at least in the prestige in which Q itself was held. José Levy, the manager of the Little Theatre, a club theatre in John Street, Adelphi, took one of the Q plays, T. C. Murray's *Autumn Fire*. Its star was Una O'Connor who would eventually make a name for herself in the many eccentric character roles she played in Hollywood during the thirties and forties after travelling to California to appear in the screen adaptation of Noël Coward's *Cavalcade*. Levy was often at a loss for suitable attractions for his theatre. His expenses were low and he was able to offer sharing terms which made it possible to transfer a play from Q with no more risk than a second week at the mother house. The stages were also identical and virtually no adjustment of scenery was necessary. Not unnaturally the players were delighted to make a further week's money.

The association with Levy led to Jack's meeting Arthur Bourchier. It seems the celebrated actor-manager needed little persuasion to try out an Eastern melodrama which Jack had given Levy to read. He opened at Q for an unprecedented three week run in Achmed Abdulla and Robert Davis's *The Prince's Harem* on May 17th 1926.

For Delia it was a red letter night. She played with Bourchier and decided 'never again' for the Nth time. Dr Coldstream coped successfully, with syringe I fear, on this auspicious occasion.

However nervous Delia might have been, and it is probable that Jack exaggerated this, enjoying a joke at her expense as a brother might affectionately do for a treasured sister, her performances continually found favour with her audiences. "Miss Delia de Leon adds to her reputation," observed the critic of the Brentford & Chiswick Times - in addition to the roles already noted Delia had earned praise for her performance in Ralph Stock's *South of the Line* with Milton Rosmer, Dame May Whitty and Raymond Massey in the cast - "with a clever study of the spirited and passionate little native girl, Musk Drop."

"I had to play a strong-minded female," recalled Dame May Whitty a decade later, "very masculine about the clothes and very pith-helmet about the head, and I had a predilection for some strange animal of the beetle variety which I insisted on eating. The property man was much exercised as to what to provide that would look dark and beetley and repulsive. We tried chocolates, charcoal biscuits - oh, dear, those biscuits! and finally decided on French plums cut into small pieces. They were very well cast and looked their part, but I've had a strange feeling about French plums ever since. Also I had to smoke a cigar and as I don't smoke at all, there was another difficulty to be overcome. Looking back on the record of Q's work, I think we must all be grateful for this sturdy little organisation which has battled its way along in the teeth of failure and disappointment and has achieved so much."

Bourchier's appearance at Q had far greater repercussions than the local interest resulting in a capacity week's business. The appearance of a famous actor-manager in a Q try-out was news and provided headlines in theatrical gossip columns. More than this, the example once set could be accepted by other star artistes who so far had hesitated to risk the cynicism of brother artistes. "So-and-so must be hard up for a job to fall back on a Q try-out." Bouchier's appearance at Q during the second year of the theatre's activities added exactly the element which had so far eluded me.

Within a few months Malcolm Keen, Heather Thatcher, Alfred Drayton, Gwen Ffrangcon-Davies, Godfrey Tearle and a host of others had added this illusive 'prestige' to the Q try-out.

CHAPTER EIGHT - ASK BECCLES

WHILST the theatre's jinx was still exerting its dampening effect on Q's fortunes the normal 'the show must go on' policy was suspended when, on April 5th 1926, the matinee performance of *The Wrong Number* had to be called off and the audience's money refunded. It seems a rat had gnawed through an electricity cable and all the lights went out! Jack must have thought that even the animal kingdom was against him. However the Bourchier success and, two months later, the successful transfer of the first of a series of plays by Cyril Campion served to raise his spirits. Campion's play, written in this instance in collaboration with Edward Dignon, was *Ask Beccles*, a fairly standard and old-fashioned detective story which caught its audience at the right moment. The critics were in accord. When the play transferred to the Globe on July 20th 1926 with its original cast intact, James Agate wrote, "Clever Mr. Jack de Leon, that what you think today at Barnes the West End managers so often think tomorrow." A slight error in geography did not diminish Jack's exhilaration.

The opening night of *Ask Beccles* at Q coincided with the opening night of Jack's first West End venture entirely independent of Q. During the run of *Autumn Fire*, Una O'Connor did a Sunday night try-out of Kate O'Brien's first play, *Distinguished Villa*. Jack was attracted to the play, acquired the rights and presented it at the Little Theatre. However he chose to attend the Q opening of Campion's play. *At last I began to believe in myself and my future in the theatre. The original nebulous policy had taken shape and I had stumbled on a feasible direction.* This direction involved an extremely adventurous policy which resulted in the introduction of well over *one hundred* new plays in the three years 1926-28. Many were presented and immediately forgotten but others followed the fortunes of *Beccles*. The play ran for one hundred and forty three performances at the Globe Theatre, considered a fairly good run in those days, and did a further four weeks' business at the Comedy Theatre. For two or three years the play continued to be performed on tour or in repertory theatres and the authors netted a small fortune. Q's weekly losses were somewhat reduced while the royalty cheques continued to arrive.

Although, as Jack correctly pointed out, the Bourchier play made it respectable for notable actors to play at Q, several had already braved the ridicule of peers. Apart from Dame May Whitty, her husband Ben Webster had appeared at Q, as had Jean Forbes-Robertson (who would become the theatre's best loved Peter Pan), Louise Hampton, Haidee Wright (Queen Elizabeth in the West End and on Broadway in Clemence Dane's *Will Shakespeare*), Colin Clive (who would play the title role in Hollywood's Frankenstein films), Hay Petrie, Angela Baddeley (very late in life an international star as Mrs Bridges in television's *Upstairs, Downstairs*) and

Martita Hunt (later immortalised as the definitive Miss Havisham in David Lean's film of Charles Dickens' *Great Expectations.*)

In the wake of Milton Rosmer's precipitate withdrawal as Production Manager, two distinguished members of the profession had taken over as directors-in-chief. Robert Atkins had acted with Tree, Forbes-Robertson and Benson, before appearing at the Old Vic and Stratford Memorial Theatre. He had been responsible for the British premiere of *Peer Gynt* and had recently toured with his own company. His prodigious knowledge of Shakespeare stemmed from his having acted in every one of the plays.

Bob, round-faced, burly, with his methodical stolid approach, rarely laughed. When he did, because of his slight deafness, his laugh was loud, his temper quick and fiery, and to many people frightening. The theatre to him was serious and of tremendous importance.

In 1933 Robert Atkins would join forces with Sydney Carroll to found the Open-Air Theatre in Regents Park.

The second new member of the production team was W.G. Fay, the founder of the Irish Company and later the manager of the Abbey Theatre, Dublin. He came to Q after extensive experience working both as actor and director in America and Dublin, and in the West End.

W.G., short, slim, mercurial, with typical Irish humour, light-heartedly approached every production, brushing aside obstacles and problems with an inconsequential chuckle, taking the least line of resistance whenever possible. The theatre to him was just a jolly good joke and a pleasant way to earn a living. **He was a dashing man. When he directed me in one of my favourite roles in** *Eliza Comes To Stay,* **he helped me so much. He was so patient.**

This contrasting pair complemented each other and provided a stable pool of resource for the theatre until 1927 when each moved on to pastures new, Jack, by this time, with their example behind him, feeling more able to take on greater artistic responsibility himself.

The infusion of celebrated actors meant publicity for the theatre.

Thy Name Is Woman *by Neil Grant created something of a stir. Heather Thatcher, who had already established herself in musical comedy, was making her first appearance in a straight play. This attractive be-monocled, sophisticated comedian was at this time in special favour with an influential newspaper baron, and it was rumoured that a 'must' reposed on many Fleet Street desks. Despite an extraordinary spate of publicity and elegant performances from Heather, Norman MacKinnell, Gerald Ames and Hay Petrie, the comedy failed to pass the fifty performance mark at the Criterion Theatre.*

Another performer who brought her publicity with her was Fay Marbé, an American musical comedy star.

This lady had recently succeeded in her action for damages (for loss of publicity due to non-appearance) against a well known London management who, having contracted for her to appear in a West End musical presumably decided that the risk of an action was preferable to the fulfilment of her contract.
Miss Marbé had received over £3,000 damages so, naturally, the press turned up in force when she opened in *A Disturbed Night* at Q. The Richmond & Twickenham Times recorded, "Possessed of an excellent voice, she sings several numbers very cleverly and also dances well. As an actress she reveals powers well above the average of musical comedy stars, whilst her personal beauty is enhanced by the wearing of many sumptuous creations, including a particularly striking pair of gold pyjamas." Jack was less impressed.
Fay Marbé was dark, thick-lipped, soignée and self-assured. Her legs were reputed to have been insured for some fabulous sum, but her acting talents proved of the flimsiest and confirmed the judgment of the unfortunate West End management. The Indian Maharajah who on occasions arrived with her provided the clue to the royal coat-of-arms emblazoned on the luxurious Rolls which brought her nightly from the Savoy Hotel to Kew Bridge.
Another actor drawn to Q at this time was the excellent and underrated Claude Rains. Born a Cockney, he began his career as a call-boy, dresser and subsequently an Assistant Stage Manager at His Majesty's Theatre. He later told Flora Robson that he used to walk round Trafalgar Square late at night after his stint in the theatre practising his 'aitches'. Eventually he became a well known West End actor and a respected teacher at the Royal Academy of Dramatic Art. His enduring fame was founded in a film in which he made no more than a few fleeting seconds' appearance as his recognisable self and that was in the title role of *The Invisible Man*. Dame Flora also recalled his telling her that he was afraid of stardom. A successful Broadway appearance as the Chinese peasant farmer in *The Good Earth* resulted in a lengthy period of his being out of work. His success in *The Invisible Man*, where it had been his beautiful speaking voice alone that had caused his celebrity, led to more film roles in which he made more substantial appearances but audiences stayed away and the option on his contract was dropped. Subsequently he found himself a comfortable niche as one of Hollywood's most respected character actors. At the time of his conversation with Flora Robson he had made an enormous success in a supporting role in one of his several films with Bette Davis (who always championed Rains as her favourite fellow player). He was actually terrified that this might signal the end to his career! Fortunately it didn't and he continued to illumine films in the supporting capacity he preferred. When he played at Q it was in an indifferent melodrama by Ben Fleet and Clifford Pember entitled *Before Men's Eyes*. Jack recalled that he 'electrified' the audience nevertheless. His co-star was one of the most respected actresses of the time, Gwen Ffrangcon-Davies. Sixty-two years later, when in her ninety-eighth year, Dame

Gwen proved to television audiences that not only was her talent undimmed but that giving a moving portrayal of Shakespeare's Juliet was not the prerogative of the young. A distinguished trio was completed by Felix Aylmer, later knighted for his services to the profession and to British Actor's Equity, the play being directed by Norman Page.

A very special recognition of Q in the pantheon of British theatre was conferred when Edith Craig directed E. L. Shute's *The Price*.

The once great and lovely Ellen Terry visited the Q for the first and, I believe, the only time. Dame Ellen at the age of eighty was nearly blind and a very frail old lady. The pathos of greatness in decline can be almost unbearably poignant. We had tea in my office, but I remember nothing of one of England's greatest actresses except her shrivelled weakness.

I remember going to see a performance by Ellen Terry when she was very old. When Mama and I arrived we were stopped at the entrance to the theatre by a lady selling bunches of red roses for the audience to throw at the end. When the curtain rose Dame Ellen was seated centre stage at an oblong table facing the audience, wearing sombre attire. Her daughter was seated on a form facing towards her. We realized later this was so she could prompt her mother. She was about eighty but seemed older. I paid little attention to what she was saying because I was fascinated by her. I remember her frail face ... her lovely hands ... When she rose to the final ovation roses were showered upon her from the gallery, upper circle, pit, boxes and all over, on to the stage. As Mama was still stage-struck we went to the stage-door which seemed illumined. Ellen Terry was already in her carriage with the window open and people on all sides hailing her. The horse was pawing the ground. My mother went to the open window and said, "I remember when you played Juliet." We all waved her off, she smiling and waving all the time as the carriage moved away.

Another performer whose celebrity now survives mainly for supporting roles in films was Elsa Lanchester. Her career parallelled the stellar career of her husband, Charles Laughton. Her striking face and eccentric personality were not star material but she would nevertheless create an icon in cinema history as the *Bride of Frankenstein*. She appeared in the second play by Brenda Girvin and Monica Cozens to be performed at Q. *Cautious Campbell* was as charming as the co-authors' first play, *Miss Black's Son*, which had been performed by Hermione Baddeley and Louise Hampton. With Miss Lanchester in *Cautious Campbell* when it played at Q in November 1926 was Mary Merrall and the two were joined by Leslie Banks and Edward Chapman when the play opened at the Royalty Theatre on July 26th 1927.

Mrs Ethel Whitty, who would feature notably in Q's history, entered into an agreement for the acquisition of the touring rights before the transfer. The consideration was £500, plus a further £500, in addition to the usual author's royalties, should it be presented in the West End. This method of capitalising Q's profit royalty served also as a means of capitalising the London production.

Unfortunately Mrs Whitty was wickedly advised by her solicitor who, she told me months later with tears in her eyes, had embezzled large sums of client's money, including her own, and was then serving a prison sentence.

Just before the play opened in London Mrs Whitty issued a writ against me for the return of the £500. On the advice of my solicitors I counterclaimed for specific performance of the contract. For the second time in under two years I found myself an unwilling litigant, but on this occasion the issue was much clearer. Mrs Whitty's counsel argued that the document she had signed did not constitute a legally binding contract and she had changed her mind and no longer wished to proceed. The judge did not have to decide this issue as Mrs Whitty, transparently honest in the witness box, admitted under cross-examination that she had in fact signed the actual agreement I had submitted, but under the influence of her solicitor had destroyed it after starting the action. On this fact the judge passed judgment in my favour on both claim and counterclaim.

At this juncture Mrs Whitty admitted to me privately that all her capital was in the custody of her solicitor and unless he paid out she would be in difficulties. I destroyed the original document and entered into a new agreement with her on a profit royalty basis. The initial payment was invested and lost in the London run, which added one more failure to my continually growing list.

I was still resilient enough mentally to recover rapidly from setbacks and disappointments. The pattern of failure was not then sufficiently apparent to overweigh the vainglorious sense of success consequent upon publicity and the awareness of the theatre's growing prestige.

A further major setback was just around the corner and it came from an unexpected quarter. St John Ervine, the theatre critic of The Observer, as respected a voice of the theatre as Agate, published an attack on the system of subsidising plays for try-out productions at Q in The Author, the official organ of The Society of Authors.

J. T. Grein, benevolent and respected doyen of dramatic critics at the time, with understanding and sympathy restrained me from closing the theatre and surrendering to what then seemed to me the will of the very group of people I had believed I was most serving.

It was J. T. Grein who sat for hours in my office going through authors' contracts and running accounts and who drafted a letter to St John Ervine offering to disclose all the facts and figures to disprove the calumny he had launched against my sister and me.

St John Ervine's integrity was unassailable, but that he should have acted so violently on the information of a single disgruntled individual, with no attempt to see confirmation or explanation from the persons attacked, was strange enough, but to ignore my offer of complete disclosure of every relevant fact was, and still remains, inexplicable.

J. T. Grein, despite this added insult, proved his generosity of spirit by giving me his wife's new play **The Lonely Road,** *to try out in an effort to establish publicly his disassociation from the views expressed by St. John Ervine.*

It was J. T. Grein alone to whom I could expose my youthful pain and disillusionment, and his encouragement and sage advice served Delia and myself in our need.

The Author was limited in its circulation and, as Grein pointed out, if its readers continued to offer plays to Q, as in fact they did, was that not proof that they rejected Ervine's views and still considered they were being well-served. An issue, however regrettable, that might have died a natural death was, however, intensified by a sensation-seeking journalist who decided to bring it to a wider public through the pages of The Weekly Dispatch.

"Somewhere in the suburbs of London there exists an institution known as the Q Theatre," wrote Gordon Beccles. "The laudable object of its promoters is to produce the plays of dramatists whose work hitherto has been neglected by West End managers ... There is a picturesque legend that a long caravan of managers traipse down to Kew every Monday evening with pockets bulging with bullion and contracts in their eager hands, ready to implore actors and authors alike to grace their more exalted stages ... The theatre is run by Mr J. de Leon and his sister Miss de Leon. Let me say at once that Mr and Miss de Leon are probably animated by a sincere affection for the theatre, and that they may be possessed of an unfailing flair for spotting the virtues of plays whose strange beauty and unusual stagecraft escapes the notice of their coarser brethren who amass fortunes in the West End theatres ... (But) they have to live - even as other managers.

"I have before me a copy of a contract offered to the novice playwright who aspires to have his ewe lamb produced by the worthy de Leons. Clause 5 of the contract is sufficiently strange. It states that the author shall pay the de Leons the sum of £150 as 'a contribution towards the expenses of production and running' of his play. It is a largish sum for a youthful and struggling author. But this does not exhaust the income of the de Leons in this arrangement. The contract provides that they shall have sole and exclusive right of production. In return, they vouchsafe to the author royalties on the following scales:-

25% over £200 up to £300
33½% £300 to £400
50% all over £400

Thus, if gross takings of a successful week at the Q be £400 (after the deduction of Entertainment Tax) Mr and Miss de Leon pay over to the author the sum of £58. 6s.8d. But that payment has a ghostly air, for the author has already handed over to the de Leons the sum of £150. So, to meet the expenses of that successful week,

ON Q

Mr and Miss de Leon have the sum of £491.12s.4d. (the original £150. plus their share of the takings, £341.13s.4d.) whereas the unhappy author, in whose brain the so successful play was conceived, is actually mulcted in a loss of £91.13s.4d. ..." There was more. Jack responded by letter and Beccles pontificated further. For brevity, here is part of Jack's reaction as recorded in his memoirs.

Poets and writers have for centuries contributed to the cost of the publication of their works where no publisher has been willing to accept the risk. In several well known instances poets and writers have deliberately chosen to be their own publishers. Dramatists have invested or influenced the investment of money in London productions for centuries. Shakespeare himself was the first. If a dramatist disapproves of this system then surely he refrains and waits until he finds a theatrical management able and willing to undertake the full responsibility.

The deal offered should be fair and just, taking all the circumstances into account, but who is to decide on its fairness and justice? Surely the parties concerned, provided they are both aware of the whole circumstances and background.

Could the reader assume (from the article) that Mr Beccles was aware that the terms of the contract in question were all inserted in ink, thus clearly disclosing to him that the terms were in fact applicable to the particular contract in his possession and may or may not have ever applied to any other contract?

As the kindly author who handed his or her contract first to Mr St John Ervine and then to Mr Beccles still remains anonymous I am unable to identify the play concerned.

Jack then proceeded to list the contents of the nineteen contracts in his possession entered into during the first half of 1927, the likeliest period from which this situation might have arisen. However, it seems to have been a much older grudge as, among them, there didn't seem to be a contract providing for a subsidy of £150. Indeed, such a contract was a rarity.

Mr Beccles ignored any loss to the Q. The fact, of course, was that the loss to the author was no loss in its normal sense, but a sum invested to establish a 'property' which presumably proved unsaleable. I had personally paid Messrs. Indermaur and Brown considerably more than £150 in respect of my apprenticeship. Could I or anyone else be justified in exposing Indermaur and Brown to calumny and ridicule because of my change of mind, lack of ability or perverseness?

Jack was incensed that The Weekly Dispatch did not publish his letter in full. Any attempt to ask Beccles for a retraction or an explanation in print, or a justification of his stance was blocked as Beccles declared the matter closed. The repercussions for Q continued. As a result of this added publicity the number of new plays received began to diminish, depressing an already deeply demoralised Jack. Then a sour footnote was added. José Levy nominated Jack for membership of the

42

Savage Club. He was turned down. It transpired that the complainant was St John Ervine. Twenty years later Ervine managed to subdue his qualms about Q, entering as he did into a new play agreement with Jack when his play, *Boyd's Shop*, was tried out.

CHAPTER NINE - LIFE WITH THE DE LEONS

"MY FIRST RECOLLECTION is of sitting on my mother's lap, stroking her face, as she sang a lullaby that my Aunt Helena had, apparently, sung to her children," recalled Jean de Leon. "She sang, 'Oh she was a beautiful girl, A booty, booty boo.' I remember my father lifting me up and hugging him. I adored my father, but he did have a prickly face. He was dark and his facial hair grew quickly and by the evening it was very prickly. He always wore dark suits, was a very serious person but with a lovely smile. He was always kind and generous to me.

"Our house" was always full of music. There was a radiogram with gorgeous scratchy records and a Steck baby grand piano. My father was not a great pianist, but he played with *enthusiasm* ... He had a lovely voice, but not so good an ear as my mother who could sing coloratura. He used to sing ballads like 'Two Eyes of Grey' and 'Drink to Me Only With Thine Eyes', Schubert's 'Serenade' and 'Impatience'.

"We had a dog called Peter. What a personality he had! Half retriever, half spaniel, with a long wagging tail and a white shirt front.

"Then there was the garden. I loved the garden. The second of my bedrooms was my favourite. It was a back bedroom, adjacent to my parents' room. Out of the side windows there were lilac bushes, purple and white lilacs. They belonged to the neighbours but they were quite friendly and said, 'Pick as much as you can reach.' The perfume of lilac still enchants me. Through the other windows I could see our garden which was just the size of a a tennis court. I could look out on the almond tree in the Spring and down the side of the garden, there was a big white cherry tree to which later I wrote a poem which begins:

> The tree is ready now for confirmation
> Whiter than snow it waits the blessing
> Of old Father Sun.

"I remember Christmas and having to sleep in a cosy little bed next to Mummy's and Daddy's big double bed. Mummy filled the stockings beautifully. I remember the anticipation. A tangerine in the toe - a real tangerine, not like the stupid little things you get nowadays.

"And lying in the garden in summer! All those rose trees. Both my parents were fond of roses. We'd lie there on a Sunday and sometimes there appeared, in the passage by the dustbins, as many as a dozen unexpected guests. They had come to tea after a walk in Kew Gardens. When I was older I would quickly bake a batch of scones or fairy cakes."

"It didn't matter how many arrived at 200 Kew Road," recalled Jean's cousin Peggy, "and, believe me, many people did regularly, everything would come out of the larder. Anything that Beatie had was yours."

"In a sense she was part of our generation," Peggy's twin brother John continued. "Where others would treat we children to the occasional ice-cream cone, Beatie would treat us to ice-cream sundaes. And she would always manage to pack away five or six of them herself."

"She always had a good appetite," interjected Leon's son Philip, "and a great appetite for life. She loved life and was always full of life, always very interesting to listen to. She had a great sense of family which she obviously got from her mother who was, to my mind, the great matriarch."

"When my grandmother and Auntie Beatie and Uncle Jack used to come and visit us," added Peggy, "I might be out and walking down the road on my way home, you knew they were there! You could hear the conversation half way up the street."

"They all used to talk across each other," Peggy's husband Nick recalled. "I remember one occasion vividly. There were about half a dozen conversations going on in the room. Beatie was sitting next to her mother and talking to my father-in-law, Norman. They were discussing, of all things, the price of teas in hotels. They were talking quite animatedly. Grandma who was sitting next to Beatie kept saying. 'Beatie, what are you talking about?' She was a bit hard of hearing. And Beatie said, 'It doesn't matter, Mama,' and they would carry on with the conversation and then, 'Beatie, what are you talking about? Beatie, I'd like to know.' Eventually Beatie said, 'Mama, we're discussing the price of teas in hotels,' and she said, 'Well why bother me with that?'"

"200 Kew Road was run by Granny Lewisohn," Harold's son Anthony observed. "This meant that Beatie and Jack were free to go to the theatre. She was always complaining that they never told her anything. I used to visit them almost every weekend. Every Sunday before lunch it was a ritual that Jack would sing a song. I must say he had a rather poor singing voice and he couldn't get the notes at all. But he would do his best. He couldn't really play the piano, but he would accompany himself."

"I would say that he had a nice voice, but a poor ear," interposed Jean. "He had a nice voice but he just couldn't sing," continued Anthony. "His speaking voice was amazing. A bit larger than life, but a fine voice. There was nothing false or forced about it - there was nothing false about him."

"I remember one occasion when, as a family, we went to lunch at 200 Kew Road," recalled Philip's brother Bobby. "We sat at table with Beatie and Jean; Jack whom we had not yet seen on that visit, was called from his study. He entered slowly, face buried in a book, placed the book on the table, continued reading it without once looking up while he ate his meal, uttered one phrase during the meal -'Good rice'- did not remove his eyes from his book throughout and when he had finished picked up the book and left the room still deeply immersed to return to his study. The occasion was often referred to by my late parents and the expression 'Good rice' made us laugh for years afterwards. None of us took Uncle Jack's behaviour as rudeness. He was such a sweet and charming man that the thought never occurred." "Jack, at home, varied between being enthusiastic and elated, and being extraordinarily depressed," continued Anthony. "Before dress rehearsal on a Sunday, after lunch, he would lie down on this long black velvet pouffe they had, looking absolutely miserable, with his head in Beatie's lap, always with a bottle of bay rum and he would have a white handkerchief, pour bay rum on to it and swathe it round his head, looking as though he was going to die! Beatie would sit behind him, stroking his head, trying to while away his cares. He had many failures in his life and he would feel every one of them. Beatie, on the other hand, was full of vitality always and would always be there to encourage him to get on with the next thing." "My mother dedicated her life to her family and Drama in that order," added Jean. From August 1926 Beaties's name appeared less frequently in Q cast lists. The reason was no disenchantment with the stage, but that she was needed at home. "Not long before my fourth birthday," recalled Jean, "I had a bout of whooping cough and I was taken to Littlehampton for the air. There, as I was told later, I had pains in my leg. Anyway I couldn't walk. My mother called in a doctor who told her I was just being naughty. Can you imagine, a child not wanting to go out on the sand, wanting to stay in the bedroom on holiday? Later they discovered there was an epidemic of infantile paralysis in Littlehampton. How ironic that my parents had taken me there to recuperate.

"They took me to a Mr Elmslie who immediately dropped everything and put plaster of Paris on my leg. I can still see him. He was a jovial, round-faced person. I remember he had a rather round tummy, with a watch chain. The front room became my bedroom and I was kept in bed for six weeks. Eventually when he removed the plaster it felt as though it was someone else's leg.

"There was a nice masseuse lady, Miss Phillips, who used to make bunny-rabbit faces at me. I find I still make the same faces to amuse young children! Miss Phillips lived in. I used to have electric treatment with pads against my legs. I still love the fragrance of Johnson's Baby Powder and Pears Soap and it goes back to those days. Then came a further masseuse, Miss Shepherd, who was the daughter of a canon. Her name was Ruth. Later I called her Truth, and I knew her right up to her death. She was a lovely lady with long hair in plaits and a fringe. She taught me the Lord's Prayer in Kew Gardens. She was a very good masseuse. And I loved her very much.

"I had to learn to walk again. Of course, at first they took me out in a pram. But then they took me out along Kew Road. They tried to walk me from tree to tree - I always loved trees and there were benches near the trees. My leg felt terribly weak. They took me into Kew Gardens where I fed squirrels, especially one we called Joey. I was in a wheelchair on and off for over a year. Of course, everyone spoiled me."

She tried not to let her problems with her leg spoil her fun.

"I remember parties with games - blind man's buff. And sliding down the stairs with Anthony on a tray, so I must have been quite daring. There was a put-you-up bed. I used to walk, precariously, along the back of this bed, very naughty with my leg. When I fell, as I almost always did, I used to catch hold of the bell cord and break it. Cousin Geoffrey mended it for me. There were always crowds of cousins. The house was always full. I did have some times alone and occasional lonely times. Sometimes it's good to be alone. With not being very good at sport I had time for reading, and I was always an avid reader."

In fact, Jean never let her leg be a handicap. On meeting her today one is so taken by her charm and intelligence that her manner of walking is a mere afterthought. **I will never forget Jean's courage throughout her illness. she was so brave for such a little girl. Later I presented a short season of plays at the Royal Court Theatre in aid of the Orthopaedic Hospital. It was my way of saying "Thank you" to everyone who had helped Jean. Sometime later I was invited to be a Life Governor of the Hospital. For many years I organised flag days. Burlington House, Piccadilly, was my stand.**

As Anthony has stated, Lydia Lewisohn ran 200 Kew Road. "Granny usually wore black or lavender colours," recalled Jean, "always with white gloves when she went outdoors. She didn't think too much of clothes, of purposely making up and dressing for men, She had a charm from within. Like Beatie, a smile from the inside. She was a very extrovert person, in fact a bit overwhelming."

Mama never quite got over not being allowed to go into the theatre. She could never tell even the simplest story without wringing from it every last bit of drama, terribly melodramatic! She would often have Victor and me in tears, she could be so moving.

"On the occasions she would come round and visit us at our house," recalled Philip, "we would always have to recite something. My forte was 'The Charge of the Light Brigade!'"

"She was a most gracious woman," added John, "and gracious in the regal sense. She was more like a duchess than the mother of a large family. She used to sit in the vestibule of the Q Theatre, bowing graciously as people went by. I'm sure the patrons thought they were being received by the Queen. She was a remarkably well-educated woman, not so much by orthodox education but by self education."When she died in 1939, Jack, as part of his tribute to her would write, *'She lived and died heroically.'*

Mama really believed that she had discovered George Eliot. To her the massive and artificially contrived **Daniel Deronda,** *with its mysteriously attractive hero unaware of his Jewish origin, was the greatest masterpiece in English Literature.* Lydia was convinced it would make excellent theatre. Failing to enlist an indifferent Jack as a collaborator she turned to Lily Tobias, a novelist acquaintance of hers.

As the ponderous and heavy-handed Victorian dialogue was transplanted into a script to become the spoken word I must confess I became more and more despondent. Sooner or later I knew the transparent assumption on Mama's part that the play would be tried out at Q would have to be faced.

The work was completed, but I still remained unconvinced. Mama's obsession was unassailable, and when she embarked on a campaign of canvassing famous Jewish personalities for promises of support I surrendered.

To my surprise Ernest Milton, Barbara Everest and Nancy Price accepted the parts offered them, though they had been influenced by Mama's violent enthusiasm. George Owen undertook the production, much to Mama's disgust. But we could not persuade any established West End producer to accept the arduous and difficult task.

Naturally Lydia's favourite actors, Beatie and Victor, were in the cast. A distinguished, mostly Jewish, audience cheered the first night performance on February 14th 1927. The critics were respectful of George Eliot and praised the industry of Mesdames Lewisohn and Tobias, but felt the play "remained only a sincere and honest effort to uproot off-shoots of a formidable work of art and transplant them into the shallow confines of a stage play." Whatever its failings it packed the theatre at every performance, but no offers were forthcoming from London managements.

Mama was bitterly disappointed and could not rest until she had persuaded Sybil Thorndike to appear in Nancy Price's part at a special charity Sunday performance (at the London Pavilion) organised some time after.

Then she accepted the inevitable; but for the rest of her life she was convinced **Daniel Deronda** *could have succeeded in the commercial theatre.*

CHAPTER TEN - INTRODUCING NOEL DOON

LYDIA was not the only member of the household with literary aspirations. Beside her, there was Noël Doon. Doon wrote in collaboration with Jack Celestin. Doon was not his real name, neither was Celestin his. The latter was really called Jack Donohue, but everyone, to add to the confusion, called him Steve.

He stalked into the auditorium one day as a dress rehearsal was about to commence, with his head erect and his chest thrown forward.

"Don't mind, Jack if I sit through the rehearsal? I'm writing for The Era."

"Can't you come to the first night?"

"Sorry old chap. You see, it's too late for the paper. They must have my few lines by Monday. You haven't by any chance a cigarette?"

I gave him one - and a light. On and off for the next twenty years we maintained a curious and mentally stagnant writing partnership.

The first fruits of their partnership grew out of a casual conversation concerning a minor controversy of the day, the occasion when thriller writer Agatha Christie had mysteriously disappeared. A nationwide search discovered her living under an assumed name in a Harrogate hotel. There was a suggestion that it had all been a publicity stunt. From these few thoughts emerged their first collaboration, *The Man at Six.*

The play was premiered at Q on January 16th 1928, with Martin Lewis, Arthur Pusey, Victor Lewisohn and Marie Ault in the cast. Came the time for the authors to take their customary first-night bow and Martin Lewis stepped forward. The Richmond & Twickenham Times reported that "at the last curtain the principal player said, 'The authors wish to remain funny names in the programme.'" At the time the play attracted scant more attention than *Daniel Deronda.*

The name 'Noël' is obviously an anagram of 'Leon', but where the 'Doon' came from has been obliterated by the sands of time. However, the next occasion it would emerge was neither a collaboration with Celestin or Donahue. This time it was with Warren Fawcett. Warren Fawcett was, in fact, two people, one male, one female.

Marion Fawcett was only just over forty when I first met her in 1926, but she seemed to me then, and still does, an ancient, unshakeable monument. She had a vast store of repertory and professional experience in every aspect of theatre. About the beginning of 1927, 'Fawcie' asked me to read two or three plays for which she had been offered partial finance if try-out productions could be arranged. At the same time she naively informed me that the plays were quite unactable, but she would be perfectly willing to undertake the 'play doctoring'. The repercussion of this was that we started a play doctoring association which opened up a new line of activity as far as I was concerned.

Late in 1927, Fawcie waded through the two or three dozen pages of illiterate handwriting which had been submitted as a complete melodrama by a simple-

minded and simple-hearted blacksmith from the Midlands. I think it must have been the pathos and Fawcie's sentimentality which influenced me to decipher the almost illegible pages. But it was the submarine under-water setting which captured my imagination.

I wrote to the author, whom I had then not met, and suggested that he might like me to rewrite and develop the play, utilising the basic idea, which at that time was certainly original - smuggling off Malta by submarine. The author readily agreed and Fawcie and I settled down to a collaboration on what was to become virtually a new play.

Contraband by Noël Doon and Warren Fawcett was tried out at Q on March 12th 1928, and it was acquired by Daniel Mayer Company for London production. Audiences were very enthusiastic, particularly when it came to the second act curtain and the submerged submarine was wrecked by explosives. It was so realistic that the audience roared their approval. Frank Vosper and Gwen Ffrangcon-Davies were secured for the West End run which survived five or six weeks at the Princes Theatre.

For my part my only satisfaction was the pleasure and comparatively large financial reward obtained by the little blacksmith who appeared in London on the first night, dressed in his Sunday best, enjoyed the spectacle of the composite authors' name on the bills outside the theatre, noticeably incorporating his own - Warren.

Fawcie's activities at the Q were multifarious. She flustered and flurried, but still remained a tower of strength in an emergency. She came to the rescue as director when I was stranded; she stepped into the shoes of character actresses when they were ill; she plodded through part after part, extracting laughs by the very speed and seriousness of her approach, by the shape of her figure and the stolidness of her walk; she waded through unreadable scripts; was business manager for a time; and undertook on my behalf the presentation of a series of 'highbrow' plays at the Theatre Royal, Huddersfield, for a summer season in 1928.

It was during this season that Delia Delvina played Sonia in Chekhov's *Uncle Vanya*. Delia had by this time made her West End debut. Directed by the interestingly named Benrimo she had played in Martin Flavin's romantic psychic drama *Children of the Moon*. When it was presented at Q, the Richmond & Twickenham Times reported, "Q achieved fresh distinction this week. It produced a new play that was already booked for town merely on the strength of its being done at the Q. Such is fame! ... Miss Delvina and Miss Miriam Lewes thrill the audience with one of the most emotional, poignant and powerful bits of acting ever seen at the Q." When it transferred to the Royalty Theatre it sadly played for only eight performances.

Perhaps it was Jack's and Delia's gratitude to J. T. Grein that led to the introduction of Sunday night plays. Grein's wife was interested in taking charge and it was under her supervision that Ion Swinley and Victor played in *Pelleas and Melisande* and Delia and Victor appeared in Ibsen's *The Master Builder*.

Since our last roll-call of those leading actors who made the journey to Kew Bridge can be added the names of Dame Lillian Braithwaite, Jeanne de Casalis, Violet Vanbrugh and Marie Löhr. Barry Fitzergerald who would go to Hollywood and eventually win an Oscar for his performance in Leo McCary's *Going My Way* also appeared. The roster of directors was added to by Sir Nigel Playfair who directed *When Adam Delved* by George Poston. In the cast was a twenty year old Peggy Ashcroft.

For one particular new comedy at Q Jack agreed that the production could be supervised by the master of sophisticated English comedy, Sir Gerald du Maurier. However, in terms of prestige, the great feather in Q's cap would be provided by a legend of the theatre.

A producer, whose name I have mercifully forgotten and who shall be called X, mentioned to me that Mrs Patrick Campbell was at a loose end and wanted to play in **John Gabriel Borkman.** *Apparently I was sufficiently courageous to ring and ask her if she would consider appearing at Q. Her immediate reaction escapes me now, but she invited me to call on her for tea the next afternoon.*

If it took courage to telephone, it needed valour to approach the lioness's den. Mrs Patrick Campbell had acted opposite the greatest actors of her day, a day which had all but passed. She had never been easy to get along with and in old age the kindest adjective was formidable. This held true both on stage and off. She had recently played Mrs Alving in Ibsen's *Ghosts* and in the long scene where Pastor Manders usually holds the focus, she had drawn the audience's attention back to herself by hanging a complete set of curtains.

Sir John Gielgud, who played the role of Oswald in the same production and would later befriend her, summed her up thus: "Brilliant, impossible, cruel, fascinatingly self-destructive, witty (especially when she had a foeman worthy of her steel - Herbert Tree, Bernard Shaw or Noël Coward), devastatingly unpredictable, she despised people who were afraid of her, would patronize an audience if she felt them to be unsympathetic, and made fun of her fellow actors it they failed to provide her with inspiration."

As for her wit - of a fellow actress she said, "Her eyes are so far apart that you want to take a taxi from one to the other," of Noël Coward's dialogue, "His characters talk like typewriting," and when she was playing in one of her most celebrated roles in *The Second Mrs Tanqueray* opposite Sir George Alexander, "Tell Mr Alexander I never laugh at him while we are on the stage together. I always wait till I get home."

I was admitted to the Pont Street mansion by her daughter, Stella, and immediately led upstairs to the vast front drawing room.

Mrs Pat was nearly as vast as the room; she enveloped it and the chair on which she sat in regal dignity.
"How nice of you to call," she began. "Sit down and tell me all about the cast. Who is going to play Mrs Borkman?"
"But, I ..."
"No, my part is Ella Rentheim. And who will play Borkman?"
"I though of Victor Lewisohn, my brother-in-law."
"Why not - he was with Tree. Has he a fine voice?"
"Yes - I ..."
"Well, that's all right. Now, Mrs Borkman."
"What about Nancy Price?"
"Do you think I could manage *Miss Price? Is she strong?"*
"I - well ..."
"I'm sure I can manage Miss Price. What do you think, Stella?. Mr deeLee-on is dying for a cup of tea ..."
I had risen; a painful flush had also risen from my neck upwards. Mrs Pat went on: "Open the window, Stella. Mr deeLee-on is suffocating in here!" Stella opened the window and left us alone.
"You know, Mr deeLee-on, Stella and I live in this great mausoleum all on our own. We just can't afford to move into a smaller place. We are appallingly poor. How much are you going to pay me?"
"Well, I thought ..."
"And we have no car. How do I manage ... all that way out in the country?"
"I'll send my car ..."
"How very kind of you. It'll be so much easier - taxis are so fabulously expensive. Well, that's settled. You pay me £50 and send a car."
Stella brought in the tea and poured while her mother continued a fascinating and frightening one-sided conversation.
I escaped, with beads of perspiration trickling down my crimson forehead and under my sodden collar.
Rehearsals, out of deference to the great lady were held not 'all that way out in the country' at Q but on the stage of the St James's Theatre.
Mrs Pat greeted X and the cast as long lost relatives. She arrived with a collection of penny exercise books into which she had copied her part in a large firm hand. Before the end of the first week's rehearsals X walked out and Mrs Pat introduced Y to take over the direction.
She explained in the presence of the whole cast, and Y: "It's no good having a director who wants to direct. We are getting on very well, don't you agree? Miss Price doesn't need any direction and Victor will let me help him." Then, to Y: "You go out front and we'll start with Act Two."

*I disappeared and only returned five days later when the comedy was replayed
with Z taking over from Y.
On the Thursday before opening night I received my final summons.
"Mr deeLee-on, the position is serious. We open next Monday, and here we are
without a director."
"But, Mrs Pat ..."
She whispered loudly enough to be heard at the back of the St. James's gallery:
"It's no good, Mr deeLee-on, I can't be directed by a man who smells."
"I'm ... But ..."
"There is only one way. You go in front and tell me if Miss Price is masking me."
And so it happened. From that moment Mrs Pat never let me out of her sight until
the curtain rose on the opening performance.*

During the final days of rehearsal, one lunchtime Mrs Pat took Jack by the arm as
they were leaving the stage, telling him that unless he wanted her to starve, he
would have to give her a pound. Jack surrendered a pound note though he left
himself with only small change. "Isn't it abominable to be so poor?" she said.
"You must be very rich, with a lovely theatre, always packed." Jack breathed
deeply to prevent what might result in hysterical laughter. As they passed through
the stage-door Mrs Pat released his arm. She was looking pityingly at the stage-
door keeper. "Poor man. He looks so hungry," she said, and handed him the pound
note. "Oh well," she added, "now I suppose I must starve - unless you'd like to
buy me a sandwich." They had sandwiches at a nearby pub, Jack keeping his eye
firmly on the price-list.

*Before the dress-rehearsal, Nancy Price got in first about the colours I should
use in the spot batten which held the lights that lit the individual actors. She liked
Pink; Pink was such a glowing warm colour and so good for the women's faces;
would I be sure and use Pink? I did.
The rehearsal started. Mrs Pat's first entrance came. She gazed upward at the
light batten, came forward and looked straight out into the darkened auditorium,
"Mr deeLee-on, what is the meaning of this? Pink, pink, everything pink. If Miss
Price desires to look like a salmon I do not. We'll all have some coffee while the
electrician changes the colours."
For the first time Nancy held her ground. Mrs Pat simply stalked off the stage
with: "When you've settled your differences we'll carry on with the rehearsal."
Even in those distant days I must have had some embryonic quality of tact, for
the matter was settled, and both Mrs Pat and Nancy Price were satisfied. I
readjusted the spot positions and changed the colour of the spots covering the
area in which Mrs Pat moved to straw. When she returned only her spots were
on. She looked up and beamed: "Now, isn't that much better? Don't you think
so, Miss Price?" The switches were reversed and Nancy paced the stage and was
also content. The rehearsal recommenced with both colours alight.*

Mrs Pat was a wise old bird, and she said no more, but meticulously kept in the straw. Where difficulty occurred in the overlapping of colours she out-manoeu-vred Nancy, forcing her into the detested straw. Long before the rehearsal was over Nancy was wise and demanded the necessary readjustment of the offending spot position. So two great artists compromised in silence and kept their distance. The first night - October 15th, 1928 - was sensational. No one cared about pinks and straws; Mrs Patrick Campbell was on the stage.

Everyone, not least the impoverished Mrs Pat, hoped for a transfer to the West End, but no theatre was forthcoming. By way of consolation to all concerned Jack brought the production back two weeks after it closed for a further triumphant week.

CHAPTER ELEVEN - MY Q IS VILLAINOUS MELANCHOLY

THE EPISODE with Mrs Pat had served to raise Jack's flagging spirits. Indeed, he recorded in his memoirs that previously Q was almost at its lowest ebb. Mrs Pat's agreement to play left him feeling he was walking on air. However, when she was taken ill before rehearsal got under way and it had looked as though the whole project would have to be cancelled, he recorded "the world went black again." Such episodes were enlivening, but beneath and behind it all there was a continuo in a minor key of frustration, disappointment and disillusionment.

The County Council, always the bane of his life, had made repeated demands for the rebuilding of the dressing-rooms and offices. Both Delia and he were reluctant to further embarrass their family by begging for more money.

Everything they had previously borrowed had been given in the shape of loans. A loan must eventually be repaid, and none of these advances had been repaid. When the theatre had shown a small profit, as it had done in the first six months of 1927, it was still insufficient to cover the losses of 1926. But the County Council were insistent, the dressing rooms must be rebuilt or the licence would be withdrawn. To accomplish this the theatre would have to close for at least a week, something Jack would have preferred not to do. However, somehow the money was found and the theatre closed its doors for the first time on June 23rd 1928, to re-open eleven days later. In a programme note Jack attempted optimism.

The effect of wet paint on the human mind appears to be akin to the starting again feeling that one gets after a particularly exhilarating seaside holiday. One's mind, clogged with the accumulated cobwebs of a whole year's mental strain and anxiety is swept clean and becomes vigorously alive with renewed aspirations. All of us engaged in the conducting and running of this theatre, not only now return from seaside holidays, but return to the smell of wet paint. Here, there is a double effect operating; abundant incentive to start afresh and put in more and better work than we have ever put in before.

The programme note was deemed necessary because the auditorium still smelled of paint when the theatre re-opened on Saturday August 4th with no visible explanation for the public as dressing-rooms are always in that invisible hinterland where audience and angels fear to tread.

It was vitally important to keep the public happy. The previous March Jack had installed a panatrope which, in his own words, he ingenuously described as, "the latest musical invention, a combination of wireless and gramophone. Thus patrons will be entertained during the intervals by the world's finest bands and orchestras." This was presumably in response to the reaction expressed by the correspondent of the Richmond & Twickenham Times on his first encounter with the innovation. He wrote, "In place of the choice entr'acte music for violin and piano that used to charm the patrons, an amplifier of gramophone records filled the little theatre on Monday with a variety of sounds. We hope it is only an experiment." It wasn't intended as an experiment; it had been a means of saving money. The initial outlay on equipment and gramophone records would soon be forgotten whereas a weekly wage bill for musicians would be always with them. Eventually Jack would again attempt to please his public. The following February, as the same columnist recorded, the panatrope was silenced and a piano, violin and 'cello continued to charm the patrons.

Although Jack had begun to write for the theatre he still felt his place was in the manager's office or in the foyer. During the early days at Q the inner sanctum, the creative centre of the theatre's work, where directors directed and actors came to terms with the roles they were to play, was beyond a self-imposed perimeter which he refused to cross. His curiosity had recently begun to get the better of him but he still felt ill-at-ease inside the doors of the rehearsal room.

I had developed the habit of attending one or two rehearsals of every play: at first just to see what was going on, and later to be fascinated by the mechanics of the production; by the humility or vanity of the author; by the ingenuity, the tact or lack of tact of the director. I listened and for the most part remained silent and embarrassed.

Occasionally my opinion on a point in the script would be asked. This only added to my embarrassment and crimson'd my cheeks. I was quite convinced that a female artist noticing the effect on me during my first visit would sit in wait for my second in order to purr a question I could not answer, "What does Mr de Leon think? Is it better like this ... or like this?"

The differences were marked enough, but whether I had any opinion or not I was too self-conscious to fraternise or participate in public discussions. As the beads of perspiration rose on my forehead I would quickly and boorishly withdraw, like a guilty child, hoping that the colour had not spread upward from my neck to become visible to a gaping crowd.

Without any background in the theatre at this stage Jack still felt like a duck out of water. In fact his interest was seriously flagging. An article under the heading 'Brilliant Work at Q' published in The Art World, gave a temporary lift but new resolution was rapidly forming in Jack's mind.

It is, perhaps, important to remind ourselves that at this juncture Jack was still only twenty six. At the time of *The Czarina* injunction he was twenty two. It was two days after his twenty fifth birthday that Gordon Beccles had launched his attack. A young man with ambition can generally find the resilience to bounce back after most set-backs, but when each obstacle surmounted reveals a tedious progression of further obstacles the toll on someone who has not yet achieved a settled emotional maturity can be profound. There had been no settled time in his life, no time "to stand and stare". Even on the domestic front, his beloved daughter had suffered a cruel illness. As a result, any joy he might have derived from watching her daily meetings with life was compromised by premature worries as to what her future might hold. Both Jean's and Beatie's courage were coping with that particular crisis, but his helplessness at work must, bitterly, have reflected his helplessness at home.

It is little wonder that he needed to call a halt and, temporarily at least, shed some of the mantle of responsibility. As if on cue his former courtroom adversary Mrs Ethel Whitty offered to take over the theatre for a minimum period of one year on behalf of St. James's productions.

After **Thérèse Raquin,** *in which Nancy Price's terrifyingly realistic performance of the paralysed mother motivated a transfer to the Court Theatre, Ernest Raymond's devastatingly tragic and superbly written play,* **The Berg,** *was the second and alas the last worthwhile play of 1929 for which I was responsible. It opened at Q on Monday March 4th, with a cast including Godfrey Tearle, George Relph and Beatrix Thomson.*

I must have watched the first performance of this overpowering play with mixed emotions, for by then I already knew that this was my last production at Q. The instantaneous success and spontaneous cheers of the audience were momentary compensations, and the arrangements for a transfer to His Majesty's Theatre proved an immediate distraction and created a new interest.

On Saturday, March 17th, 1929, my sister and I departed from Q with no intention of ever returning.

The one year away from Q stretched into two. Mrs Whitty went and others less competent followed. The theatre dwindled into a sad shadow of its former self, then closed, lying dark for months on end. Finally Delia and Jack came to a regrettable but irrevocably decision. Q must be sold.

However they reckoned without an energy that had thus far been largely untapped. And it lay closer to home than either of them realized. If anyone could save Q, it was she.

Cue Beatie.

PART TWO

1929 - 1934

CHAPTER ONE - CUE BEATIE

LIKE HELENA and Victor before her Beatie spent a great deal of her time training other actors. Even before she entered the Academy she had directed groups of amateurs in shows for charity. After her graduation and the onset of stage-fright which deterred her early acting career, it had seemed the only way forward if she was to remain in the theatre. Perhaps her career lay in her directing abilities. Thus, on her marriage, the London Academy had been inaugurated at 59 Finchley Road. When Q was born and Beatie was gradually weaned back into enjoying acting again in the more comforting surroundings of a family theatre, she did not let this part of her life go. Eventually it was her amateurs who performed the special season at the Royal Court Theatre in aid of the Orthopaedic Hospital. There were occasional Saturday matinee performances at Q. Finally Beatie felt they had achieved a sufficiently high standard to warrant a full week in the theatre. Thus she presented *My Lady's Dress* by Edward Knoblock the week leading up to Christmas 1928.

"All my life I had wanted to become an actress but with no private income this was, in 1926, considered out of the question," recalled Joan Kemp-Welch, "so I was training to be a teacher at the Froebel College. In my spare time I joined Beatie's Dramatic Society. How I loved it! I vividly remember working on *Comedy and Tragedy* with her. Then, one day an actress playing in the professional company at Q fell ill, and Beatie asked me if I would like to take over her part in *The Kingdom of God*. What excitement! What a chance! Then, miracle of miracles, Peter Godfrey, producer of the famous Gate Theatre, came to see the show and offered me a year's contract at his theatre. Of course I accepted at once and, instead of becoming a teacher, I became an actress. So it is thanks to dear Beatie that I have spent more than sixty happy years in this wonderful profession of ours."

We built an asbestos-lined studio near the scene dock. Here I developed the amateur dramatic society, working nights and some weekends. This became the nucleus of the Q Repertory Players and would instil new life into the theatre.

Early in 1931, Jack and Delia met to decide the fate of Q. The final tenant had absconded several weeks before the termination of his agreement. If they were to put the scenery, seating and lighting up for auction, together with the lease of the theatre they might be able to raise enough to repay their discharged loans. In due course this "Famous and long established theatre at Kew Bridge, together with furniture, fittings, scenery and Good Will" was offered for sale by auction. It was withdrawn after the first and only bid - a mere £300.

Beatie intervened. Why not open the theatre with a season of plays performed by her amateurs? She invited them all, together with their relatives and friends and Jack and she outlined their plans. For the first time Jack made an appeal for public funds. Some five or six hundred pounds was raised in units of £5. Everyone pitched in to help with re-decorating the rather shabby looking theatre.

Such were the Q Repertory Players, a gay and brotherly band with myself as elder brother, and Beatie as elder sister.

Mr Gobel, a keen drama enthusiast, who was a clerk at the head office of the Swiss National Bank, came on Fridays and Saturdays at first to help with the circularising, which gave me the idea of asking for his assistance in the box office. He agreed to help but would accept no payment.

Somewhat older than me, with a long nose, a tidy mind and an unbounded enthusiasm which belied his phlegmatic personality he worked at the accounts and at his exquisite graphs of the weekly expenses and receipts. I will always remember the invaluable help and encouragement he gave my wife during my fits of depression or my violent bouts of enthusiasm, when directing, writing or lighting I let the whole burden of 'front of house' problems and money worries fall on her less experienced shoulders.

The play chosen to open the season was Bayard Veiller's *The Trial of Mary Dugan*. It was part of the new policy that the larger parts should, where possible, be played by more experienced players. For the arduous title role Beatie chose a former pupil of Victor's who had been a professional actress for two years. Her name was Daphne Odin-Pearse. "I fell ill," she recalled, "and the doctor would not let me rehearse. I sat in bed and, though I was very ill, I learned every word of that enormous part. He allowed me to go to the dress-rehearsal in a taxi with a blanket round me." She was word perfect but the people playing with her were all over the place, missing cues and fluffing lines. This was the price of inexperience. Having got used to someone reading in at every rehearsal the timing and dramatic intensity was different with the actual actress newly among them. As a result, nervous tension was running high on opening night March 9th 1931. It seemed the elements were against them too. Unusually for March the streets were deep with snow and there was a keen frost. Would any kind of audience turn out? Relieved to have the de Leons back at their theatre the small, loyal core of local supporters was swelled by the relatives of the players. It was a capacity house.

I had always taken charge of the stage-management myself for the amateur shows. I stayed in the prompt corner and opened the curtains and operated the lights. I was very proud of my production of *The Trial of Mary Dugan*, and, for once, I tore myself from the prompt corner, made sure there was someone to take over my responsibilities and went into the auditorium. There wasn't a

single seat left so I had to stand at the back. It was a great success and I remember feeling proud of the ovation.

The Brentford & Chiswick Times recorded, "Beatrice Lewisohn has grappled with considerable success with the difficulty of handling a large company on the small stage ... Daphne Odin-Pearse gave a sensitive and moving performance."

Again we started weekly production, mainly of old plays. I supervised the casting as I was to do for all of the revivals and many of the new plays from then on, and took charge of the day-to-day running of the theatre. For the first few months Jack supervised the stage-management and the scene painting. Also he was always in charge of the lighting. He was very good at that. When the curtain went up on _Old Heidelberg_ (the play that inspired the operetta _The Student Prince_), Jack got a round of applause for all his twinkling lights.

We started a training scheme for stage-management. We charged a small premium and guaranteed several months' work with a salary. A lot of people got an excellent training that way. We also took on acting students who, generally, had had some previous experience. They also paid a premium - fifteen guineas for the men, twenty five for the women; there were always so many more women wanting to join up than men!

One of our acting students at this time was Anthony Quayle.

Sir Anthony Quayle, a much underrated man of the theatre, would go on to put the Royal Shakespeare Company on the map, later in his career making sure good theatre was still getting to the provinces with Compass. "Of my days at Q," he wrote shortly before his death in 1989, "my recollection is mainly of an atmosphere that Jack and Beatie created, a very happy and encouraging one for a young fledgling like me."

If the Q Repertory Players at the outset were substantially 'Amateurs' the members were at least devoted to the theatre, and love compensates for a multitude of technical faults and elevates talent to the status of competent professionalism.

It must now be apparent that the beginning of a metamorphosis had taken place. My wife had ousted me from my 'business' desk and permitted me to indulge in my growing urge to participate actively and continuously in the 'artistic' side of the theatre. Up to this point in my youthful frenzy I had watched, occasionally advised, frequently revised virgin scripts and collaborated on play writing; all made possible only by escape from the real problems of management and the perpetual harassment of finding the wherewithal to meet the rising costs.

This changing state of mind had no doubt been partly the cause of the initial despair and temporary abandonment of Q in the summer of 1929, and I was now permitted to flourish more or less free from the distasteful 'front of house' responsibilities lifted from my shoulders by my wife.

Beatie's impediment of youth never troubled her. She was already the mother of an eight-year-old schoolgirl, and never added to her troubles by being concerned either with her youth or later with her age. In fact, as all who know her must by now have realized, she is the eternal feminine counterpart of Peter Pan.

CHAPTER TWO - DENNIS, MARY AND DONOHUE

The years between had not been idle ones. Despite his inability to run Q Jack still believed, in the Spring of 1929, that his forte was theatre management. With funds invested by Ida Molesworth, an actress-manager friend who had scored a success with the West End presentation of *White Cargo*, together with yet more cash from his long-suffering family, this time including Granny Maduro (*who was intimidated and enlisted for the first time*) he took a lease on the, as yet incompletely built, Duchess Theatre. The builders promised to be out by November.

Ida Molesworth suggested that, in the interim, she would back the West End production of the Noël Doon and Jack Celestin opus, *The Man at Six*, "provided," she added, "that you can get Dennis Neilson-Terry and Mary Glynne." It just so happened that Jack had run into the celebrated theatrical couple who had, of course, been patrons of the school at The Towers, at a performance of *The Berg*. The play, about the Titanic, had transferred from Q to His Majesty's Theatre to overwhelming critical acclaim and complete public indifference, closing after a disappointingly short run.

Dennis Neilson-Terry was to become one of Jack's most valued friends. His name united two theatrical legends, his father being Fred Terry, brother of Ellen, and his mother the celebrated Julia Neilson.

In 1929, Dennis was thirty-four - tall, thin and somewhat ungainly in his movements. His features, too, were thin, and he was very short-sighted. His voice lacked the resonance usually associated with his romantic name. Yet he had charm, grace and humour, sometimes a biting humour, and women found him wholly attractive. His original personality and inborn sense of timing more than compensated for his lack of vocal quality. Almost invariably he chose parts which perfectly fitted his idiosyncrasies and the indefinable queerness suggested by movement and voice. He was seldom required to impersonate a character other than the stage character he had made his own.

In her book, *A Pride of Terrys*, Marguerite Steen expressed the Terry family's view of Jack's new friend and his wife. "Dennis Neilson-Terry," she wrote, "should have played Shakespeare, Ibsen and Chekhov; should have lent his great talents to the oncoming British dramatists. He had all the qualifications - and he knew it ... He played for safety, played claptrap, for the sake of an extravagant young wife, who thought nothing of spending a hundred guineas on one evening gown, and two idolized children, whose least whim was to be gratified in the most expensive fashion. As for Mary's pretty frocks, Dennis got as much pleasure out of them as their wearer; he liked elegant women, and little blonde Mary chose and wore her gowns admirably ... 'Ten guineas for a bloody ribbon!' exploded his father, when an unpaid bill of Dennis's boiled to the surface of the chaos left after his death." Mary Glynne was the daughter of a North country doctor and had known Dennis from childhood. Eventually they had played together in Sir George Alexander's production of *The Aristocrat*, falling in love onstage and off. She had a quiet, genteel beauty and is now mainly remembered for her charming performance as Miss Trant in the original film version of J. B. Priestley's *The Good Companions*. Noël Doon decided to bare all to the theatre world and become plain Jack de Leon, playwright. The initial subterfuge had clearly been an attempt to retain some dignity as a theatre manager, not wishing to be seen as a dilettante in any sense. It is clear from his memoirs that he had no particular pride in his work as a thriller-writer. Steve Donohue had more to hide as he had a regular day job with the Ministry of Pensions, so Jack Celestin remained Jack's partner in crime.

The Neilson-Terrys were charmed to be asked to do the play, the roles in question suiting each of them perfectly, providing no conflict for their regular audiences who preferred to see them in familiar guises. Sir Alfred Butt had offered Jack the Queen's Theatre. Jack, used to performing under pressure at Q, had the play cast and rehearsed and facing opening night within an incredible two weeks, Easter Saturday 1929.

We were so excited reading the evening press headlines that we narrowly missed having a serious car smash outside Kew Gardens Station.

The play itself wasn't exactly a smash either, but made a reasonable profit which was considerably supplemented when Dennis and Mary, immensely popular in the provinces, took it on a Number One tour.

Later *The Man at Six* was filmed. Directed by Harry Hughes for BIP, with another celebrated theatrical couple Ann Grey and Lester Matthews in the leading roles, it was released in August 1931.

As a postscript to this episode, Jack was paid £50 for 50,000 *"hastily strung together words"* in the form of a novel, a version of *The Man at Six*, which was published by Collins as part of their Sixpenny Detective Series.

The unfortunate young lady in my Regent Street office simulated enjoyment in the typing of this blush-making effort.

Jack chose a war play, *Tunnel Trench* by Hubert Griffith, to open the Duchess. Cast in the leading role was Brian Aherne. Victor (who had also been in *The Man at Six*) was one of many others in the cast. A promising young actor was given what was considered a gift of a role as Aherne's younger brother. One day Reginald Denham, who was directing the play, took the actor to one side and told him, "I'm sorry, but I've regretfully come to the conclusion you're not right for the part. It's just that you're ... well, not believable as Brian's brother, you can't help being emotional and ... well Welsh. Of course, if you want to stay, walking on and understudying ... I'm so sorry." Upon due consideration the too Welsh Emlyn Williams agreed to the more menial casting.

The theatre had just been built. It wasn't until we went for a run through that we realized that there were no dressing-rooms.

The play opened on November 25th 1929. "On the first night," wrote Emlyn Williams, "the audience began to cough." It closed within a few days. Jack rushed in a revival of *Typhoon* with Dennis Neilson-Terry in the leading role. Whether the audience coughed much on opening night is unrecorded, but it shared the same fate as *Tunnel Trench*. To try to save the situation Jack made matters worse by prematurely reviving *The Man at Six* with Dennis and Mary contributing their salaries. This made a hat-trick of failures in the opening six weeks of the new theatre. Jack surrendered the lease to Arthur Gibbons. Feeling himself under obligation to Dennis and Mary, Jack looked about for a suitable vehicle in which they could tour, thus recouping some of their personal losses. Noel Scott appeared at the right psychological moment with a thriller called *Traffic* which would guarantee the favour of the Neilson-Terry's provincial audience. Off they went on the tour early in 1930 with plans to arrive back with it at the Lyceum Theatre in the summer.

Jack, left to his own devices, decided to stage his second West End collaboration with Steve Donohue.

In the summer of 1928, Jack had made the decision that crime quite possibly could be made to pay, and set about writing a crime thriller, titled after the detective's name, *Justin Masters*.

For two weeks I scribbled feverishly the most nonsensical crudities, before the unexpected arrival of Steve, who had decided to spend a week of his holiday at my expense.

I certainly had no objection, except perhaps that Justin Masters must temporarily suspend his hair-raising adventure in a gas-filled chamber, for we had been discussing a vague idea for another and more human thriller.

Our method remained consistent throughout our partnership. First came the idea and vague plot; then for a month or two, meeting occasional evenings and most weekends, we developed the plot in detail scene by scene, with interminable good humoured argument. Each scene had to establish this and that, and had to be so long and no longer; each entrance and exit had to be reasonably contrived; each scene and each curtain was devised. Until the entire play had been constructed and synopsised in this manner we never settled down to write. It was a poor way to 'create a work of art', but these plays were 'technical achievements', constructed brick by brick remote from artistic endeavour.

Anyway, **Justin Masters** *remained unfinished, typed and buried away and the synopsis of* **The Man in the Dock** *blossomed instead. I still look upon this as the best of our collaboration. The fact that we both made considerable sums from English and American royalties and a fabulous film sale to Fox Films via the Shuberts of America, is entirely incidental.**

*(It was filmed as *The Silent Witness* in Hollywood in 1932, directed by Marcel with Lional Atwill and Helen Mack in the cast.

Wallace Geoffrey's brilliant performance as the villain of the piece is my one outstanding memory of the Q production on November 26th 1928.
Noël Doon and Jack Celestin were again conspicuous by their absence on stage on the first night though the local press rumoured the former to be "a London theatrical manager." The Brentford & Chiswick Times said of the play that it was "a melodrama which is likely to appeal to those who like a sensational story and one not too critical of facts." The co-authors re-worked the last act and after a second try-out at another theatre it had its West End premiere as *The Silent Witness* at the Comedy Theatre in April 1930, with half the capital provided by Wallace Geoffrey. It had settled in for a comfortable run when *Traffic* arrived at the Lyceum on July 30th.
The run of *Traffic* began well and Jack made a good profit but business began to peter out. Jack and Steve had a new comedy thriller, *House of Danger*, which he gave Dennis and Mary to read.
To be fair to Dennis in view of the situation which subsequently arose, I must record that he was horrified at the shoddiness of the plot and the inanity of the dialogue. Yet we were on a sufficiently friendly footing for him to suggest a bargain to which I readily acquiesced. If they played in House of Danger *I agreed to work on the script of a draft version of George Preedy's novel,* The Rocklitz *and eventually present it in London with Dennis and Mary.*
The day after rehearsals began, the play's director let Jack know that the Neilson-Terrys were not proposing to come to the next day's rehearsal. They had realized that this was greater claptrap than even they would consider appearing in. Jack drove to see them in a raging temper. Eventually he prevailed upon them to attend the rehearsal and managed to induce Steve to take a three day holiday from the Ministry.
We kept awake, scribbling and arguing all through two nights, imbibing strong coffee and champagne. Fortunately this kept us away from the theatre and I was entirely oblivious of the distress which Dennis and Mary and, presumably, the rest of the cast must have experienced as the typed pages of 'muck' were delivered to them morning and afternoon. I was too mentally and physically exhausted at the end of this fantastic and ludicrous effort even to enquire what was happening at the theatre. I must have slept for a day and a night before facing that ordeal. Whatever had been said or thought in my absence was certainly not disclosed on my return. Dennis and Mary were resigned to the inevitable. It was only their friendship which could have made it possible for them to proceed with those rehearsals and face a first night audience.
The play opened at the Lyceum on November 8th 1930. The audience laughed and clapped in the wrong places. I hid myself. The next day's notices reflected he derisive reception and the play was withdrawn on the following Saturday

week. Yet I think it ultimately enhanced rather than detracted from our friendship.

Jack worked with Marjorie Bowen, whose historical novels were written under the name of George Preedy, on the adaption of *The Rocklitz*, which recounted the association of the Countess Rocklitz with Johann Georg of Saxony. It was to be only the second costume play Jack presented, the first having been the ill-fated *The Czarina*, and it was also to be the most expensive production he had, up to that time, presented. It opened at the Duke of York's on February 4th 1931, with an outstanding cast supporting the Neilson-Terrys which included Lawrence Anderson, Roland Culver and Felix Aylmer. The critics, almost unanimously, dismissed it as "Wardour Street history." The play survived but a few performances.

Jack was able to put all this behind him as he rolled up his shirt-sleeves and devoted himself to the renaissance of Q. The physical effort, the novelty of the situation and the eager enthusiasm of the 'gay and brotherly band' all had a restorative effect on him. This helped him set aside his disappointment when *The Bandits* which he had toured with Dennis in the cast with some success, failed at its Garrick Theatre opening on June 15th.

Early in their friendship, obviously conscious of his family's disillusionment in the direction of his career, Dennis had asked Jack to find him a good part in which he could really test his mettle. Thus far he had only been able to present him in plays his family despised. However, he was able to make reparation.

A short, tense, tragic little play by Lord Lathom, entitled Fear, *had come his way. Quite obviously no commercial management would have taken the risk of producing such a play with Dennis in London.*

They came to Q, played with semi-amateurs and triumphed. The play was his, despite Mary's moving and sensitive performance. He held his audiences in horrified silence as in a twenty minutes soliloquy towards the end of the play his mind visibly disintegrated.

But for Dennis the play had to be seen in London and luckily the Little Theatre was then available.

Incredible as it seems now we ventured with this horrific subject two weeks before Christmas, and thereby performed two miracles. The first and least significant: the play survived without losing money until Dennis and Mary embarked on their final tragic South African tour; the second and more important: Dennis was for the first time recognised by critics and audiences as a real actor.

When the play closed Dennis and Mary took *The Man at Six* on a tour of South Africa. On July 14th 1932, Dennis died at the age of thirty-six. With Jack's help he had been able to prove to his family and the theatre world the actor he truly was.

CHAPTER THREE - METAMORPHOSES

IF A METAMORPHOSIS was taking place in which Jack was evolving from a business man into an artist, some things would never change.

"Jack presented an extraordinary figure in the theatre," recalled Anthony Lewison. "The norm was to look sophisticated or casual or avant-garde, but Jack always presented himself the same way, in a black jacket, waistcoat and striped trousers, whether it was seventy degrees or not, looking absolutely anomalous in a theatre situation. Very tall with a shock of black, wavy hair, I remember him constantly checking the time on the ever present watch with its gold chain. The black suit and striped trousers were perhaps held over from the time he was studying to be a barrister. He really was a barrister manqué. He had that sort of investigative mind, a natural feel for the dramatic and an arresting voice. And so he always dressed as a barrister, but there he was in the theatre!"

Apart from any evolution in Jack himself, the entire character of Q had undergone its own metamorphosis. Gone was the almost desperate search for prestige that had been ever present before 1929. With casts made up of amateurs as well as professionals, no great stars were going to venture down to Kew. Apart from Dennis Neilson-Terry and Mary Glynne who came for a specific purpose, the calibre of leading actor to come to Kew in the year 1932, for example, was of the order of Basil Gill, Sam Livesey, Louise Hampton, Dorothy Dix, Roland Culver, Robert Speaight, Iris Hoey, Ion Swinley and George Skillan. Fewer new plays were presented - in the same year a mere twelve were tried out, contrasting with forty new plays in 1927 and only three revivals. This proved more popular with local audiences who ventured to new plays with trepidation, feeling more comfortable with the tried and true. Beatie, flexing a business muscle she never knew she had came up with a membership scheme. Members of the Q Theatre Club were entitled to a concessionary half price ticket, at a cost of ninepence. This was instantly popular. Whereas the de Leon and Lewisohn families had only been plundered for cash in the past, now they were plundered for personnel. Anthony was cast in *The Two Mrs Camerons* and *Mrs Wiggs of the Cabbage Patch* ("I was aged about eight or nine and I was on stage throughout the play. The setting was a very poor sort of room and I was on the bed and had one line to speak. I remember falling asleep and missing my only line ...!") His cousin John was cast in *Young Woodley*. Herbert de Leon appeared in Komisarjevsky's exciting Christmas production of *Robin Hood* and his sister, Minta, became a regular member of the company. The result of all this was a much more relaxed, happy-go-lucky feeling for the theatre. This is not to imply that Jack and Beatie did not try to set a very high professional standard. How embarrassed they must have been when the local press reported of the eighth production of the new regime, *Interference*, "some of the players seemed a trifle uneasy and disturbances 'offstage' did not improve matters."

Nevertheless the whole new charisma of Q lay in the warm, family atmosphere they created.

Play after play was produced with the expenses varying between £100 and £200 and box-office receipts not far short of expenses. Not far short, but short enough for debts again to begin to accumulate. The entire receipts for the first year were under £7,000 and the outgoings just over £6,500. Yet no more than a mere pittance had been withdrawn from the fund which resulted from Jack's appeal to the friends and relatives at that first meeting.

The time was filled with a new satisfaction. I had been active where my activity had been a joy. After directing a series of commonplace revivals I ventured with **Julius Caesar, The Merchant of Venice** *and* **Hamlet.**

Q's Shakespearean productions are remembered by many as a golden period in the history of the theatre, yet they numbered only ten and took place only in the years 1932 and 1933. "They were very impressive," recalls Anthony. "Somehow Shakespeare at the Q Theatre always seems to be well produced and acted with dignity," wrote the reporter for the Brentford & Chiswick Times.

Of Jack's production of *Julius Caesar* the same writer commented, "The mounting of the play was excellent, the design being on the lines of the Cambridge Festival Theatre productions. In other words it was austere, but very effective. It comprised the use of a raised platform, a sky backcloth, giving the same effect as a diorama, and a silhouette of pillars. This set sufficed for a surprising number of scenes, and was altered cleverly by the use of curtains." This allusion to Cambridge and the brilliant work of Tyrone Guthrie whose innovation in production design, together with the performances of his cast of unknowns which included Flora Robson and Robert Donat, would influence the production of Shakespeare for decades to come, was praise indeed.

Hamlet *proved my Waterloo. With a cast including Miriam Lewes as the queen, Thea Holme as Ophelia and my brother-in-law Victor Lewisohn as a well spoken Hamlet, I struggled to infuse what I naively assumed to be a new conception, only to realize too late its violent inconsistency with Shakespeare's text; wore myself out physically and mentally setting and rehearsing the scene and light changes all through Saturday night and Sunday before starting at midnight the dress-rehearsal called for seven o'clock. In the early hours of the morning I collapsed, with the rehearsal half finished - humiliated, defeated and hysterical.*

With the aid of aspirins and my wife I must have slept it off by nine o'clock the next morning, for I remember embarking on a simplification of scenery and scene changes, which were more or less complete by the time the cast re-assembled in the early afternoon. We got through the rehearsal and opened that evening to an audience of a dozen or so grown-ups and a few hundred teenagers. My 'ghost trick' did not work; I sweated blood, but no-one seemed to care or know, except the Ghost impersonated by Dennis Elliot-Watson and Victor who, as Hamlet, should have heard: "I am thy spirit/Doom'd for a certain time to walk the night ..." looking for a sign of the 'spirit manifestation', waiting to see the dim eery head as he exclaimed: "Oh, heaven." But the wrong head *glowed on the wrong side of the stage, and Hamlet looked heavenward as the ghostly head rose from the depth behind his back.*

Perhaps it was more effective that way! At the time I was in no state to realize that the true effect must ultimately depend on stimulating the audience's imagination or, better still, on the hypnotic power of the actor playing Hamlet.

The transition back to a fully professional theatre was gradual. Naturally this was accompanied by a gradual upward trend in running costs. But more new plays were tried out and several transferred to the West End. One such was *Crime on the Hill*, the latest play from the pens of de Leon and Donohue, which was set in a coroner's court. It tried out at Q on October 3rd 1932, and transferred to the old Shaftesbury Theatre (devastated by bombing in World War II) on April 24th the following year. To Jack's disgust Sir Nigel Playfair had pages of the script onstage with him and *read* the coroner's pronouncements at each performance.

Cyril Campion, the author of *Ask Beccles,* came up with a delightful play, *Trust Berkely*, which also transferred. Jack directed two new plays, his first attempt to direct unproven scripts, *Times Fool* by Farquhar Sloan, largely rewritten by Jack, and *The Silent Menace* by H. St Barbe West, which starred Anne Grey and Lester Matthews.

Wallace Geoffrey, the actor who had capitalised the production of *The Silent Witness* for the West End, came up with a play of his own, *Third Degree*, which he wrote under the pseudonym of Geoffrey Pulling. He appeared in it at Q with Sam Livesey, who also directed it, on November 14th 1931.

The late John Maxwell, then Managing Director of British International Pictures (who had made the film version of The Man at Six) *came down to see this play. At the end of the performance I introduced myself and offered him a drink. I have never met a Scotsman who acted on impulse, but Maxwell listened to my criticism of the play he had just seen and my suggestions for adapting it to the screen. He made no attempt to interrupt me or offer any comment on my remarks until unsmilingly he put the apparently pointless question,*

"Have you ever written any film scripts?"

"No ..."

"Would you like to?"

"Very much."

"Very well. Come to Elstree tomorrow afternoon - 3 o'clock."

That was all. We shook hands and he left the theatre without another word. That night I hardly slept. Beatie tried to anticipate my disappointment by assuring me that it would all come to nothing, yet somehow I knew my analysis of the development of the play in film terms had impressed Maxwell.

Jack was hired to work on some scripts that other writers had given up on. To some extent this was calling on his already proven talent as a play doctor. He was paid £500, was able to work at home and continue his activities at Q. There is no record of any on-screen credit for his work in films, apart from adaptations of his and Celestin's plays, so it would seem that script doctoring was his contribution to the cinema.

A play whose title, *Gay Love*, would have another connotation today was presented at Q on February 20th 1933 and would transfer to the West End. Along with Margaret Bannerman, Muriel Aked and Richard Bird was a voluptuously beautiful actress making her first appearance at Q.

I adored Enid Stamp-Taylor. We shared the same sense of humour. Like me she enjoyed a glass of champagne in the morning and we would take one in my office. She would show me the bracelet or necklace she had received from her latest admirer. She would be talking to one man on the telephone as she waited for another to arrive! Oh, she was delightful.

Two weeks later saw the premiere at Q of a play "by an anonymous author." Shortly before Q had risen phoenix-like from the ashes of its former self, Jack had found an interest which became an obsession. Delia had been reading *The Hound of Heaven* by Francis Thompson. Tom Kealy, at the time Q's press representative, had happened upon her in the foyer of the Comedy Theatre with the book in her hand. Thirty years before he had met Thompson and related the tale to a fascinated Delia. It seemed the perfect subject for a play.

She bought Everard Meynell's biography of the poet, read it and passed it on to Jack.

Immediately I knew that here was a tender theme, appealing and dramatic and whether I ever wrote the play or not I must temporarily break from my 'thriller collaborator', and spend every hour I could get away from the theatre reading, studying and thinking only of Francis Thompson. I devoured every life and commentary I could find; read and re-read his essays and poems; spent half days with Delia at the British Museum searching for contemporary reference and a contemporary background, until gradually the play took shape in my mind.

Beatie and I rented a furnished flat in Woolacombe in the county of Devon for our summer holiday, overlooking the long stretch of golden sun drenched sands where day after day I sat and wrote, while Beatie played sand castles or cut trenches to capture the rising tide for our enchanting little daughter.

Each day I read aloud scenes I had drafted; each night fair copied and revised; and every two or three days posted the finished scenes to my sister for her comments and criticism. Before our holiday was over Delia arrived in Woolacombe on her way to a spiritual centre. As she walked through the field towards the farm, she carried the second act of the first play I had written from the heart, without tricks, contrived situations or self-conscious 'funny' lines. I knew it had beauty

and tears, for the beauty was Francis Thompson's and the tears flowed from the
image of the Ann he had conjured up in my imagination as I read the lines which
had decided me to embark on so delicate an enterprise:
    "She passed, oh brave, sad, lovingest, tender thing!
    And of her own scant pittance did she give
    That I might eat and live!"
She was a prostitute as all the world knows.
The first draft was finished by the time he returned to London. However, he learned
to his consternation that the Lord Chamberlain, who in those days had to be
satisfied that a new play would not offend what was considered the sensibilities of
the public or contravene any legal requirement, would not consider issuing a
licence unless Jack first obtained the approval of Wilfred Meynell, the literary
executor for Thompson. Meynell suggested he motor down to 'Greatham' near
Pulborough in Sussex.
In the vast library I read aloud to the man - then in his seventies - who had
befriended the poet in his greatest need: whose wife Alice Meynell still enchants
me with her delicate poems, and two of whose daughters (also among my select
audience) I knew already in my imagination from the many exquisite Thompson
lines dedicated to their childhood I had so recently read and re-read.
I only got through the ordeal - resurrecting in the minds of these friends
memories of the joys and sorrows of their association with a sensitive soul who
had walked among them - by the good will and understanding which they
vouchsafed to me. We were all silent at the end; they with their memories and
I moved perhaps by my own reading of 'my Ann' and 'my Francis', for that was
how Wilfred Meynell described my characterisation of the poet. I accepted it as
fair comment from the man who perhaps alone in the world really knew the true
Thompson. Anyway, the permission was generously given.
Though he was far from ideal for the role, Dennis Neilson-Terry was Jack's
original choice. Even before Dennis's death, however, Jack had already approached John Gielgud. They lunched together at the Cafe Royal. In turning down
the opportunity Gielgud said that he wanted to follow his current success, *Musical*
Chairs, with a comedy role. The role he chose, far from the comedic, was Richard
II in *Richard of Bordeaux*.
With Gielgud, *Francis Thompson* would have been presented at the New Theatre
by Bronson Albery. Jack was bitterly disappointed. He arranged for the play to be
tried out at Q.
The play was sensitively directed by Sir Nigel Playfair. The Playfairs invited
the three of us to their lovely home on the embankment at Hammersmith. The
room was animated with theatre celebrities. I remember Jack sat on the floor,
leaning against my chair. He often preferred to do this despite his long legs.
"I was to have played the child Rosie," recalled Jean. "My father had even

rehearsed it with me. However, I was seven months short of my eleventh birthday. Though my cousin Anthony had been allowed to appear at Q during the semi-professional days a recently enacted law forbade children from performing after eight in the evening. I was heartbroken when the role went to Nova Pilbeam. I was not allowed to see the whole play but remember a scene when Ernest Milton as Thompson turned and looked out of the window at the back of the stage, saying the words, 'And lo, Christ, walking on the water not of Genesareth but Thames.' The words still haunt me half a century later."

I was amazingly lucky with the director and cast. For many years the Q stage had not been graced simultaneously with so perfect a company. But it was Mary Glynne who was to prove a revelation.

Until then Mary had been to me Dennis's wife - an attractive and competent support, and in some respects a hard and disappointed personality. As Ann she underwent - at least in my eyes - a metamorphosis well nigh incredible. Her exquisite tenderness, her deep understanding, her brave sense of humour transformed her into a creature of angelic grace. If she had permitted I would have knelt in silent adoration, for she was the Ann of my creation.

For Jack, at least, Mary was no more the vain, empty-headed creature that had offended the pride of the Terrys, than her late husband had been an artistic wastrel. The play opened at Q on March 6th 1933 in a blaze of publicity to a packed and distinguished audience.

I hid, on the verge of tears, until Bunny Bannerman discovered me and pushed me into the darkened auditorium. She sat on the steps, holding my hand, trying to keep me calm and quiet, for how much of the play I can't remember. Ever after that she always called me 'The Hound of Heaven.'

The majority of the audience witnessing Jack's distress that evening can have known nothing of the reason. Lest the work be diminished by an unnecessary comparison with the thrillers he had written with Steve Donohue, Jack had decided to present *Francis Thompson* as the work of a playwright who preferred to remain anonymous.

"The anonymous author of *Francis Thompson*," wrote W. A. Darlington in the Daily Telegraph, "has performed a very rare feat. He has written a play about a man of genius which is interesting as a play, and not merely because it is about a man of genius.

"The story of Francis Thompson's rescue from starvation by a street-walker in hardly better circumstances than himself, who kept him, fed him, cared for him, and then slipped quietly out of his life when recognition came his way, makes a fine romantic story ... Ernest Milton, who is probably the best interpreter we have of the feckless, unpractical artist, plays Francis Thompson with great feeling. Mary Glynne plays the prostitute heroine with sympathy, understanding, and a very real command of pathos."

The critic of the Brentford & Chiswick Times added, "The author ... has written the story with such vigour and with such truth that it is impossible not to be impressed by the sincerity of the theme, although some of the dialogue seemed annoyingly repetitive and, at first, too straightforward for chaste ears." The latter was, of course, a backhanded compliment.

The Press was full of compliments for the play and everyone expected the offer of a theatre for an immediate transfer. Unfortunately, all the West End theatres had firmly established successes, *'except the unfortunate unsought-after Royalty, off the beaten track in Dean Street.'*

Jack was disappointed, but quite apart from the usual low state of finances he was loathe to admit defeat. The acceptance of the despised Royalty which was offered on the usual sharing terms seemed to him the height of ignominy. However, Ernest Milton, realising that should the Q run, which had been extended for a second week, close before a transfer had been announced, it might mean the dissipation of a cast he considered should be kept together, offered to introduce £500 capital if Jack would accept the Royalty proposition. As there seemed no alternative, he agreed. Playfair had previously warned him that he could not be involved in any transfer of the play as he had another commitment and so it was left to Jack to supervise it. Apart from the frenzied readjustment of the scenery, and the consequential changes to the actors' moves which had to be worked out, a composer friend, Norman O'Neill had offered to write linking music. The rehearsals of the music and the cast and all the other adjustments had to be accomplished within four days. *Yet the thing had to be done, and with hammering and sawing, Norman's gentle insistence on time for his own rehearsals, Ernest's almost hysterical demands for the exclusion of James Agate from the first night and Mary's unforgettable encouragement, somehow I survived those four days and nights.*

Agate had demolished Milton's Othello and Shylock the previous year. But what could Jack do when the uninvited critic turned up anyway on opening night other than let him in? As he took his seat, Milton's wife, Naomi Royde-Smith, flew to Jack's side, imploring him, "Please, for God's sake, don't tell Ernest. He'll throw a fit!"

It was after a heartbreakingly disappointing performance, only partially the result of Ernest's unaccountable slowness of pace and interminable pauses in the middle of sentences during which his mind appeared to be wandering a million miles away from the character he was representing and which he had so brilliantly represented during the two weeks previously, that I discovered he had actually seen Agate enter the auditorium after the curtain had risen. The result was catastrophic.

The Royalty Theatre dressing-rooms were under the stage; the 'star' room situated in the centre of a square around which the other dressing-rooms gave access to an intervening passage. My arrival in this Hades was greeted by a hushed and awestricken cast, stretching around the locked dressing-room of Ernest Milton's central sanctum, from which blood-curdling screams were emerging. Ernest's hysterical voice was recognisable. "How dare you? You had no right! It was all your fault! You knew he was there! You should have told me! It wouldn't have been such a shock!" Naomi's protests were inaudible. suddenly in a deathly silence we heard a thud, a scream: "Oh God!" and Ernest burst open the door, shouting: "My wife has had hysterics! Naomi's fainted! Get a doctor - for God's sake get a doctor!"

And so ended the first London performance of Francis Thompson.

Mary alone remained calm. Less than three weeks later the play was withdrawn: not before James Agate had written perhaps one of his most incomprehensible notices, the final lines of which were: "You ask me, is this a good play? There are some straight questions that cannot be given straight answer. I have expressed my opinion to the best of my ability and the baffled reader is at liberty to draw what glib inference he may."

Yet another failure. Jack could be forgiven for thinking everything he touched turned to lead. However, as is so often the case with an artist, it is the process and not the product which is important. Though his pockets were almost always empty at the end of his ventures, in the case of *Francis Thompson* his soul was inestimably the richer. In his realization of this, Jack's metamorphosis was complete.

Beatrice Lewisohn - actress

Victor

Delia in Panamanian national dress

Minta

Mrs Patrick Campbell at the
time of her Q encounter

Beatie, with an unidentified fellow player,
in the unreleased film*The Sign of David*

The Man At Six by Jack de Leon and Jack Celestin, with (left to right) Victor Lewisohn,
Dennis Neilson-Terry, Mary Glynne and Arthur Pusey

Two Q beginners.

Vivien Leigh (left) at the time of her Q debut   Margaret Lockwood (right) at the height of her career

Rising above it!
The two Hermiones,
Baddeley and Gingold,
with Walter Crisham
and regular Q actor,
Henry Kendall (right)

Mother and daughter.
Beatie and Jean

Jean, with friends   The de Leons afloat, summer of 1939

CHAPTER FOUR - TWO FAMILIES AND THEIR FORTUNES

JEAN'S EDUCATION had begun. First of all she went to a local preparatory school.

One day I had a telephone call from the headmistress, Miss Knight. "It's about Jeanne," she said. For some reason she called her Jeanne. Apparently there was a boy, a good looking boy, a curate's son. He had kissed Jean. She was nine at the time!.

"I can remember him," recalled Jean. "His name was Peter. Miss Knight thought she must let my mother know immediately! Two years later my parents decided they would like me to go to St. Paul's. My mother was advised that I was not up to the exam, that I wouldn't get up the stairs, that I wouldn't stand a chance. But I did, despite confusing Sir Robert Peel with John Peel in the General Knowledge paper!

"When I went to St Paul's I was withdrawn from prayers. I had not been brought up as a Jewess although Granny Lewisohn took me to synagogue once or twice. During morning prayers I sat in our classroom with another Jewish girl and a Catholic girl from my form. I didn't like being withdrawn - no-one asked me if I wanted it. My father saw to it that I had a wide religious education. He never subscribed to a conventional religion. Throughout his life he believed that all conventional religions and institutions eventually betrayed their founders' intentions. Much later in life I studied comparative religion for my Open University degree."

A quest for the meaning of life, if necessary beyond the conventional, was a de Leon trait. Jack's mother had been brought up in the Jewish way but, according to Delia, none of her children were brought up in the Jewish religion at home and she didn't keep Jewish feasts. However, a friend recommended a Jewish boarding school in Brighton presided over by a kindly person called Jacobs. He taught Jack chess among other things and to the end of his life Jack loved to visit the place where the school had been. Anthony Lewison recalled, "After the death of her husband Mrs de Leon at first sought consolation in spiritualism but Stanley's Evey brought her into Christian Science and, after experiencing a healing, she came to feel that spiritualism was a wrong pursuit and completely abandoned it as she became a lifelong Christian Scientist. Jack never seemed terribly interested in such organisations; it all swept over him. He was much more of an individualist. He had to have his own form of mysticism. He was constantly trying to discover the meaning of everything."

"Granny de Leon's Christian Science was central to her character," commented Jean. "She was petite, very gentle with a pale complexion - she hardly wore any make-up. I remember she was more easily shockable than Granny Lewisohn. If Granny de Leon saw a low-cut gown on television she would cry out, 'Look at that bosom!' Her mother, Granny Maduro was a lovely woman, Jewish, but not particularly orthodox."

Granny Maduro was very very generous. She would take the jewels off her fingers and give them to me. One she gave me was a black pearl surrounded by diamonds. Her cousin Sarah was a different kettle of fish. She was rather cross looking. When I first knew her she didn't like me, but we got to like one another well enough later on.

"I always liked her," continued Jean. "She may have looked grumpy but she had a heart of gold. She should have been a career woman except she was needed to look after her kitchen. There's nothing worse for a career woman than that. She used to sit in a rocking-chair, old and short-sighted, swinging backwards and forwards, crocheting. She crocheted wonderful bedspreads for nearly all the women in the family. When I visited her in the Nursing Home in Ealing towards the end of her ninety year life she was listening to the schools programme. I learned later that she could not read and was probably dyslexic. Aunt Sarah dominated the entire household."

"Granny Maduro was great fun," added Pat Gribbin, Minta's daughter. "She loved to play bridge and would trump her partner's aces! Granny May (de Leon) was a very tense, anxious woman; very earnest with a strong sense of duty. She had a slight nervous twitch in one eye, and had several depressive breakdowns." "She was quiet and gentle and perhaps a little naive," Jean continued. "Despite having had so many children she had a tripping walk with tiny feet. She could never get shoes small enough and often had them sent from America. She was dutiful, unhistrionic, undemonstrative and very generous. She believed in the value of silence. I never heard her say a bad word about anyone in her life. I've seen her agitated and I've seen her weep. She had a sweet smile but she didn't laugh a lot. When she did laugh it became almost a hysterical laugh. She painted, quite nicely, but always copies of other people's paintings. She adored my father and was particularly fond of Delia who remained unmarried. She loved all her children." Michael her youngest child joined a friend who was interested in becoming an Estate Agent. Together they set up a firm in Potters Bar where Michael's brother Stanley had his own law firm. "Up to the age of ten," recalled Stanley, "I was in the nursery. Then I went to boarding school, only coming back for holidays, and not always then. So I was an outsider to the rest of the family. I only really got to know Jack from first night visits to Q. He was the cleverest and best in the family. I had the greatest admiration and respect for his achievements." Stanley went into the law Jack had quit and became a solicitor. Beatie's nephew Anthony Lewison was eventually articled to him. Stanley fell in love with and married his cousin Evey, the tomboy whom Jack had taken in hand and taught to tell the time. Like many other members of the family she was prevailed upon to appear at Q. "I played the maid in a gangster play and had to shoot a gun!" At the onset of World War

Two, Stanley and Evey were without a home and Jack came to the rescue by storing their furniture at Q. "I watched week after week," added Evey, "as more and more of my furniture made an appearance on the Q stage!"

"In retrospect, "Stanley suggested, "I feel Jack's weakness was that, unlike other theatrical entrepreneurs, he didn't keep his personal financial affairs separate from his theatrical ventures, but involved his own finances and his family's in the risk. This is a lawyer speaking in hindsight, of course. All the family looked up to him apart from Minta who lost money. She felt very bitter about this."

Minta had sunk most of her inheritance in Jack's ventures and it had all been lost. Eventually she had received some reparation but she felt so let down and hurt that her feelings for her brother were never quite the same again. Nevertheless in many ways he remained on a pedestal for her and towards the end of his life he received several warm and loving letters from her.

Minta, the great beauty of the family, was a charming and sophisticated woman of the world. She had made a mistaken early marriage to Herbert Toledano. "I didn't have an easy ride with my mother," recalled her daughter, Pat, "because she didn't love my father. She was pregnant with me when she was eighteen. They divorced very early. Granny May and Granny Toledano were first cousins, so there was a lot of tension when the marriage broke up. My mother was a very affectionate person, very demonstrative. But she, herself, felt that she had been shown no affection as a child, and her mother's reserve seemed like rejection. It was only later in our relationship that she learned to show affection to me. When I was about six, my father sent for me to come to Panama to be with him. But it proved to be only a ploy to get my mother back."

By this time Minta had followed Jack into the theatre, via the Royal Academy of Dramatic Art where she was a contemporary of Rachel Kempson, later Lady Redgrave. She would perform in some fourteen Q productions between April 1931 and November 1935. When she appeared in *Interference* on April 27th 1931, in a cast which included Anthony Quayle, the Brentford & Chiswick Times recorded, "Aminta de Leon had some difficult dramatic work which to a certain extent she carried out successfully." Four years later they were to credit her with "poise and personality, the possessor of a good voice." Sadly there seems to have been no review of her most ambitious piece of work when she was cast in the title role of Shaw's *Saint Joan*, a role her RADA contemporary Rachel Kempson would play at Q twenty years later. Minta would retire from the stage and marry solicitor Glyn Barton. "She lived in a fine house in Holland Park full of antiques, pictures and a cello," added Jean. "She was an accomplished cellist and would prove a good friend to me."

Her sister Evey, whom Jack had recruited for the Q offices in the early days, also had a daughter, Valerie, from her first marriage. She met her second husband, Christopher Carley in Jamaica. From a Quaker family he had emigrated to South

America only to have to make for the West Indies when the ship he had taken was diverted from its destination due to rioting. Deciding to stay he took a degree in engineering and became chief engineer for a telephone company in Jamaica. When he retired he settled with his wife in Andover.

Evey recalled her brother Herbert, "He had a beautiful baritone voice. He studied singing in Milan. Then he went to Germany before returning to England where he married a Czechoslovakian. He found that he couldn't make a living as a singer and support a wife. It was a beautiful voice but it wasn't big enough for opera, more suitable for small concert halls. He broadcast a great deal. We used to listen to his lunchtime concerts."

Herby turned to his brother Jack for help. Jack cast him in the play Dennis Neilson-Terry had toured, the Mexican melodrama entitled *The Bandits*.

As a Mexican guard I fear he was comic rather than menacing.

As has already been noted he appeared in Komisarjevsky's production of *Robin Hood* in the singing role of Allan-a-Dale. Jean recalls his performance as a delight.

Eventually he surrendered to his need to earn a living and with his Czech wife opened a theatrical agency under his wife's maiden name, Erika Wilka. Crowds surged round agents' offices in those days and Herby specialised in film crowds. Why an agency and why crowds I imagine he didn't know himself. We do things and start things from little seeds implanted when and by whom we do not know. He was too straight and kind and gentle for such a barbarous undertaking. Soon he was divorced and the firm became Herbert de Leon Ltd. and the crowds dispersed.

In their place came Margaret Lockwood, Viola Keats and Greer Garson. Greer Garson was captured by Hollywood. Herby negotiated her contract and then handed back to her the agency agreement which over the years .PA would have permitted him to live in affluence. The ingratitude of the one is only compensated for by the gratitude of another.

Margaret Lockwood owes Herby much and, despite his lack of that streak of hardness and indifference to human feeling usually a concommitant of business ability, he served her as personal manager over the years as no-one else could have done. To her credit she has recognised this service and not transferred her allegiance and agent's commission as so many others have done.

"Herby de Leon," recalled Miss Lockwood shortly before her death, "was such a sweet, kind man. I have never met a kinder." He had one son, Antony, who died young of multiple schlerosis. Having bought out his brother Jack's surplus hosiery stock in pre-Q days, Roy de Leon developed a large wholesale stocking business aided by his wife Eda and settled in a charming house in Horseheath, Cambridge-shire. They had three children, Gloria, Michael and Marilyn.

When Delia was young she had two clear ambitions, one was to be an actress and the other was to come to an understanding of God. Having fulfilled the former through her involvement with Q, she was to devote the rest of her life to the latter. "I used to read a magazine called Everyman which was edited by C. B. Purdom who eventually became a great friend of mine," she recalled. "In it I read a letter written by Meredith Starr in which he said he had been running a centre for the last two and a half years at East Challacombe, North Devonshire, having been to the East where he had met a great spiritual figure who had told him that if he were to find a place and bring the right people there he would journey to England.

"It was at this time that Jack was working on *Francis Thompson*. I went down to Woollacombe where he and Beatie and Jean were on holiday, on my way to Combe Martin. It was there I first heard about Meher Baba."

C.B. Purdom has written, "The question for every man and woman is, 'What is the meaning of life?' All religions provide answers to the question, and their teachings are intended to enable their followers to experience the truth of what they say. None the less, people remain unawakened, dissatisfied and confused. Meher Baba is not the founder of a new religion, nor a teacher, but an Awakener. He is witness to the reality of a man's being. He has chosen not to speak or write, but by gestures has 'spoken' from his own reality, which he 'declares' to be God.

"Meher Baba was born in 1894, in Poona, India, of Persian parents. At nineteen years of age he became conscious of God, and after seven years' contact with five Perfect Masters realized his own existence as God and the true existence of all men.

"In the disenchantment of our lives Baba's silence speaks of Knowledge, Power, and Bliss in the consciousness of Divinity, which cannot be proved, but accepted, changes our lives."

"I remained at the centre for three weeks," continued Delia. "While I was there a cable arrived saying that Baba was on his way, that he was sailing in the same ship that was bringing Gandhi to Britain. I had to return to London. Baba only stayed ten days at the centre and then came to London himself. An appointment was made for me to meet him. However, Baba had expressed an interest in going to the theatre and a box had been booked at the Coliseum where the operetta *White Horse Inn* was playing. He was told there was a surprise for him, and it transpired that I was to be the surprise. In a sense that came as a shock to me. I had imagined our eventual meeting would be a very solemn occasion, that I would fall weeping at his feet! But there we were in a theatre where a jolly musical was being played! (Strangely enough, there is a Hindu legend that the most destructive age of all will be heralded by an avatar on a white horse.) I was taken to the box and there he was in Western clothes, with his long, flowing hair. He had gone into silence and communicated, at that time, by means of an alphabet board. The first thing he 'said' to me on the board was, 'It is not chance that brings you here.' Every single one of us who had been at the centre that summer became friends of Baba. It was as though some strange destiny had drawn us there.

"I then went to see him the next day at the house in Kensington where he was staying. Jack went with me, and Minta and my mother. Jack was a potential mystic, but it was a side he didn't develop.

"Part of Baba's technique, for want of a better word, was to break one's set patterns of behaviour. A group of us, myself, Minta and several others, including Princess Matchabelle who ran the American perfume concern, set out for India. We were shot up to Kashmir and we stayed on the river. Then Baba said that plans had to be altered and he shot us back to England."

Delia aspired to live as a disciple of Baba in his 'ashram' for the rest of her life, but Baba was wiser and, in retrospect, she knows how spiritually unprepared she was for the stringent, physical demands of such a life. Within a few months she and her equally disconsolate co-disciples were shipped back to England by the Master who had changed his mind.

"Jack didn't understand Baba's way of working. He wanted to break us down, to test us. 'Do you really believe in me? Do you want to follow me?' I never minded that. Actually I found it quite exhilarating. But others - there was one woman who had sold her school - for them it was much harder."

According to Jack, *'Minta, who had also made this pilgrimage, returned permanently disillusioned in herself.'* "The whole family was looking for something" concluded Pat. "Delia was looking for something. My mother was looking for something and turned to psychoanalysis. Perhaps all of them were looking for the father they had never really had."

"It's impossible to describe what Baba was like," continued Delia. "He explained to us that all the great avatars shared the same aspect of divinity. He said, 'The book that I wish people to read is the book of the heart which holds the key to the mystery of life.' He said that for the first hundred years after he had given up his earthly body he would be able to be present with us. Sometimes, when a group of friends are together we know he is in the room with us.

"In the 1960's, when I was living at 240 Kew Road, a group of young people came on my horizon. They were nearly all of them taking drugs, LSD and so forth. One of them was Pete Townshend of The Who. He came several times to see me, and eventually he built a centre for us. He made a film called *The Delia Film* in which he appears and talks about Baba. He's a very remarkable man. For myself, I've been with Baba now for almost sixty years."

"What happened yesterday? Nothing," said Baba. "What will happen tomorrow? Nothing. All that happens now — the eternal NOW from the beginningless beginning to the endless end."

The Lewisohns pursued a much more pragmatic approach to life. There was a clear division between those who followed the family dream of a life in the theatre and those who faced the family reality of the shoe business, both in manufacture and exploitation. Of the latter the most successful was Caesar, who shortened his surname to Lewis and married Millicent, a beautiful girl of Dutch origin. He first went into business with a brother-in-law, later working for himself. He would eventually run a large factory, the architect for which was his son Basil, known professionally as Peter Winton-Lewis, and a chain of shops. After Caesar's death in 1968, his daughter Marion took over the running of the factory. Originally Ferdy worked in one of Caesar's shops in Southall. More studious than his brothers and good at figures, he eventually joined the Civil Service.

"At the age of fifteen Harold," records his daughter, Nora, "was asked by his father what he wanted to do for a living. 'Be a salesman,' came the reply. 'It's a very hard life, very tough,' retorted Bernhard from bitter experience, 'but if you can survive calling on Mr. F. you'll be O.K.' Picking up a sample shoe he continued, 'Put this in your pocket so that you have it ready to show him, and before you go be sure to learn our code by heart. The letters of A. B. LEWISOHN represent the first ten numbers.'

Off he went on the morrow full of hope, and presented himself by name at Mr F's shop and asked to see him. 'We don't want no b—— shoes,' boomed a voice from the back room, 'Get out!' With his tail between his legs he left the shop, but the assistant whistled after him to return.

On re-entering he saw Mr.F. in the front of the shop. 'That's no way to sell shoes!'

'I didn't think you wanted any today, sir,' he replied timidly.

Softening slightly, Mr F. switched his tack. 'You sing, don't yer?'

'Yes.'

'Come in t'back parlour. I play the concertina.'

No sooner had they entered than Mr F. called to his assistant, 'Lewisohn wants a bottle of whisky' which was the cue he had been given by his father for putting down four shillings and sixpence on the table. The bottle having been brought, music was made and Harold picked up his first order, thus setting the seal on his future."

Norman, Leon and Stanley were all at some time connected with the shoe business, and each worked at some point as a travelling salesman. "Norman, my father," recalls Peggy, "was the kindest sweetest soul, but as a travelling salesman he was a square peg in a round hole. He should have been an accountant or something like that, but should never have gone on the road. He just wasn't a go-getter."

"He was unquestionably a kind man," her twin brother John continued, "but he suffered from a defect of personality which made him say things which weren't true, either to put off the situation until tomorrow when he knew it wouldn't be any better anyway, or to make himself seem bigger than he actually was. He was in the wrong occupation with the wrong kind of wife."

"Eventually he got a job as manager of Brown Brothers, part of the Hounsditch Warehouse company," concluded Peggy. "He was much happier there."

Leon Lewisohn died on his son Philip's fifteenth birthday, just four months after Lydia died (August 11th 1939). "Early on he had been in management and quite successfully," recalled Philip, "for we had a good standard of living in those days. But he had a very chequered life, dogged by ill health. At one point he went to America and plans were made for us all to emigrate, but this fell through. He had made contact with the American branch of the family who, I rather fancy, didn't want to know us because they had too much money!

"My father was a larger than life character. He brought a lot of songs back from America and performed them for his family and friends. If he had been able to make his living that way he would have been a happy man."

"I remember Uncle Leon," added John, "when he had a stall on Aylesbury market, selling statuettes. He was a great salesman, with the gift of the gab. It was an education." In his latter years he was a travelling salesman, as was his brother Stanley, who also shared his passion for entertaining. "He was a very jolly man," recalled his son Teddy, "and a great entertainer, especially as a female impersonator." Apparently his best impersonation was a hilarious portrayal of Lydia. **With a veil twisted under his chin and a feather boa he was really clever and was his mother to the life.**

"Sadly my parents split up when I was very young," continued Teddy, "and my father moved away to Manchester. My mother, who had been a singer, followed in my father's footsteps and herself became a commercial traveller. She and Grandma Lewisohn became close and so she remained a member of the family." It was to Manchester too that on her marriage the eldest Lewisohn, Helena, had gone in 1908. At first she devoted her time to teaching but got the occasional professional engagement at large private houses. During the First World War she had a concert party of pretty girls dressed as pierrots who entertained in hospitals. She also gave pantomimes with her pupils in aid of the Red Cross. She continued teaching, and when radio started she was to have frequent engagements.

Victor had lied about his age to get into the army and had joined the Pioneer Corps during the Great War. Although he got to the front he wasn't allowed to fight because of his German antecedents. Upon completing his time with the Academy and with Tree he joined the Old Vic Company during Ben Greet's time and here had established one of the most fruitful friendships of his career, with Sybil Thorndike. **When Mama and I used to go to the Old Vic to see Victor, Sybil Thorndike would always come to speak to us. She adored my mother.**

After his spell in the army, Victor joined a touring Shakespeare company. Exactly which one is not now clear, whether it was Greet's Pastoral Players or Sir Frank Benson's company or one of the numerous others, it was here he got his great grounding in Shakespeare. Such a company would perform to the order of, for example, *The Merchant of Venice*, Monday evening; Tuesday evening, *Hamlet*;

Wednesday matinee *As You Like It* with *A Midsummers Night's Dream* in the evening; *The Tempest*, Thursday; Friday, *The Merry Wives of Windsor*; Saturday matinee, *Julius Caesar* and, for good measure, *King Lear* on a Saturday night to round off the week. Victor not only learned his own roles but, like any other actor worth his salt in those days, all the other roles he could possibly play as well so he built up a repertoire of availability.

It was in 1923 that he made his first significant appearance in the West End, when Sybil Thorndike invited him to appear with her company at the New Theatre in Shelley's *The Cenci*. Of the performance on November 13th 1922, Sydney W. Carroll wrote in The Times, "Miss Sybil Thorndike has by reason of this performance been declared 'the greatest tragic actress in England' ... The scene in the court where Beatrice has to address the wretched Marzio, who has under the rack revealed the secret of her complicity in the crime, was firmly, eloquently, and nobly given. It had a dignity, a restraint, and impressiveness that were irreproachable, and her final speeches were delivered with extraordinary purity and tenderness ... The Marzio of Mr Victor Lewisohn was vigorously harrowing and tragic."

The following year Victor played Caius Lucius in *Cymbeline* with the same company at the New and in March 1924 for the first of a total of three seasons he played de Poulegny and the Executioner in Shaw's *Saint Joan*, with Sybil Thorndike gaining immortality in the theatre in the title role. Shaw insisted that Victor repeat these roles in the January 1925 revival and the March 1926 revival particularly for the Executioner where his stature and manner on the stage were so powerful.

Also in 1924 he appeared in one matinee performance of *Heraclius* in which The Times commented he gave the most notable performance. "The actors' voices, owing doubtless to the empty condition of the Theatre - and normally the Holborn Empire is admirable for sound - were so muffled that often I could not distinguish a word. Yet Mr Lewisohn and Miss Beatrice Smith made themselves heard easily enough."

The following year he made several appearances at Q, one of which was, notably, in the ill-fated *The Czarina*. In all the attendant disappointment on that occasion how heartbroken must Lydia Lewisohn have been, finally seeing Victor and Beatie together in a West End production. Victor was to find a successful transfer from Q when he appeared in *Ask Beccles*. The local press reported, "One of the best performances is that of Victor Lewisohn, who, as the inspector, is so real that one can almost see the record of criminals caught by him. He is right inside the character."

Victor had continued to teach to supplement his income. He had married in 1921 and had two small boys, Neville and Bruce. When Beatie and Jack had transferred their energies to Q, he had stayed on for a while at the London Academy at 59

Finchley Road. One student who came to him in 1926 was the actress who would eventually re-open the Q Theatre in 1931 as the eponymous heroine of *The Trial of Mary Dugan*. "My mother was a famous violinist, Elsie Southgate," recalled Daphne Odin-Pearse. "She went on a concert tour of America and, at the age of fourteen, I had to leave school and go to live with my grandfather. I had dreamed of being an actress since I was eight and had seen Fay Compton in a play. My grandfather, who was a composer and a professor of music, knew this and saw Victor Lewisohn's advertisement in the newspaper. He took me to audition for him, and I became his pupil.

"He was a god. A deeply sensitive man, tall and good looking. He taught me everything I knew of the theatre. Voice production, diction, acting. Every lesson began with vocal exercises, breathing, vowel sounds, hitting consonants. With his Dramatic Society I appeared in Ernst Toller's *Masses and Man*. He told me his sister had said very complimentary things about my performance. He had promised me he would try to get me work at Q. I went professional in 1929, and appeared at Q under Mrs Whitty four months later. Then in September 1929, I was in the second try-out of *The Man In The Dock* by Jack de Leon and Jack Celestin. Victor Lewisohn was the Prosecuting Counsel and I was his clerk! That was such a thrill, to be on the stage with him in a professional production.

"For years I went on having my private lessons with him. He had illnesses and my lessons would be cancelled, then I went back to him. I got my bronze and silver medals with him. He lived for a while in a house in Edgware. The eldest boy, only a toddler at the time, used to come in with the clock to show Victor I'd gone well over my time."

"I can't remember a time when we weren't aware he was in the theatre," recalls Neville. "I can remember being told we would have to go into a boarding nursery school. I was just five. He was going on tour and my mother was going with him."

"It was common for us to go backstage," added Bruce. "I saw him very often on the stage but that was never Daddy to me, he was always the character."

"Although I am older than Bruce, I can't remember seeing him act. That is a great sadness to me. I *can* remember going backstage. I don't go to the theatre very often because I want to be doing it. I love performing. I have a snapshot memory of him playing a Mexican bandit because, in the course of it, he had to have a cup of tea and, while he was talking, he had to keep putting sugar in it, twenty four spoons full of sugar, and he loathed sugar."

On September 10th 1928, Victor opened in Leslie Coddard and Cecil Weir's *Earthbound*, in which Peggy Ashcroft appeared. Dame Peggy had little recollection of this play, but remembered Victor's next appearance at Q, as does Sir John Gielgud. "I'm afraid I never met Victor Lewisohn," Sir John wrote recently, "but I did see him as Borkman at Q. Mrs Patrick Campbell acted her scenes with him (and only those scenes) quite brilliantly, and spoke to me most warmly of his talent." "Mrs Campbell's temperament," wrote James Agate, "is that of a player who seeks and demands to find in a similar temperament a soil in which her own art may expand. She found that in Mr Victor Lewisohn, who is that unmistakable thing, an actor. With Mr Lewisohn, as with Mrs Campbell, the expression of an emotion appears to be born at the same time as the emotion itself; the player gives out both together and it seems that they can never be separated. Mr Lewisohn can hold an emotion as a pianist sustains a note - one of Mrs Campbell's supremest gifts - and it was this common faculty which enabled them to merge the great scenes of the second and fourth acts into perfect wholes."

Victor was to enter theatre mythology three years later by way of another Ibsen play. Nancy Price, who had played Mrs Borkman with him at Q, was presenting *The Master Builder* at the Duchess Theatre in 1931, as part of her People's National Theatre programme. Franklin Dyall was to play Halvard Solness and Lydia Sherwood Hilde Wangel. The day before opening night both leading players announced they were too ill to perform. Miss Price contacted Victor and Agatha Kentish to ask if they would learn the roles and appear the following night. Anyone who knows the play will realize the immensity of the undertaking that each of them took on when they agreed.

"I feel I can remember him coming home and saying he had to do this," recalled Neville, "and my mother saying. 'That's all right. I don't mind staying up with you. We can do it all tonight.' And I can remember them starting straight away. I can remember him pacing up and down the room while she was there with the book, prompting him."

"He always paced up and down when he learned his words." added Bruce. "He wore a very clear diagonal mark on the carpet, from corner to corner."

"I also remember he went to the chemist for something to keep him awake; he was so tired at the end of the all-night session. What they gave him I don't know ..."

"... whatever it was he didn't take it. The chemist said it would make him feel rotten afterwards. One of the actresses advised him not to take it as the after-effects were shocking. 'Have a tumbler of champagne,' she said, 'it's *the* thing for keeping you awake.' He did that and he sailed through. Mother, of course, was in the audience, biting her nails and wondering whether he would remember all the lines."

"Mr Lewisohn succeeded brilliantly," recorded Agate, "because he is an Ibsen actor, which means an actor capable of suggesting immensities of mind at work even behind a seeming-perfunctory: 'And do you say that Hilde?' Colossal works call for colossal interpretation, and your good Ibsen actor, such as Mr Lewisohn, makes you feel that if there is a dullard in the theatre it is neither Ibsen, Solness, nor the actor portraying him. Miss Kentish did very well too, and there was a faultless performance of Mrs Solness by Miss Mary Merrall."

Franklin Dyall returned within the week with Beatrix Thomson as Hilde. Agate wrote a less ecstatic notice.

Whether it was something he instilled in his pupils, like her teacher, Daphne Odin-Pearse was called upon to prove her mettle. "I was at home and it was 10.15 at night and I was eating an apple and thinking of going to bed. The phone rang. Would I go at once to the Royalty Theatre, Dean Street, where they were playing *Francis Thompson*. Mary Glynne had been taken ill and her understudy was on. No-one had realised until they got into Act Two that there was no-one to cover the understudy's role! I grabbed my make-up case, got a taxi, got to the theatre, got into costume, the beautiful golden wig, with the script in front of me on the dressing-table as I made up. I was on within an hour of the phone call. Ernest Milton nearly fainted. The door opened and this complete stranger burst on! It was the part of the prostitute and I gave it all I'd got, *and* I was word perfect! I played it until Mary Glynne was well again. When I got home that night, my mother said, 'Where have you been, dear?' And I said, as nonchalantly as I could, 'I've just been on at the Royalty Theatre ...!'

"Eventually I played Phebe in *As You Like It* at Q. Victor was Jaques, that was the first time I *really* played with him. In the following play, *A Prince From Pimlico*, there were three leads, Victor, Ian Fleming and myself. Victor was the villain, Ian the hero and I was caught in the middle. Victor had to try to seduce me. I was supposed to hate him and push him off. But I adored him so much, I forgot for a moment and flung my arms around him!

"Some time later I understudied Fay Compton in a play. Of course it was she who inspired me to be an actress. She was to prove rather a frightening lady. Then I was in a Priestley play in the West End and Sybil Thorndike was in another theatre in a Priestley play. When I told her I was Victor Lewisohn's pupil she was wonderful to me. She thought the world of him."

"My main memory of my father acting is in Shakespeare," recalled Bruce. "He knew pretty well the whole of Shakespeare's plays off by heart. I especially remember his Shylock. I can remember a lot of his mannerisms in that. I can remember him as Mark Antony doing the 'Friends, Romans, countrymen' speech. He had the loveliest voice."

"The almost hackneyed oration by Mark Antony was so sincerely delivered that it seemed quite new," recorded the Brentford & Chiswick Times. "Contrary to the usual procedure, the famous lines of the speech was almost drowned by the clamour of the crowd, and the sarcasm of the repeated reference to Cassius or Brutus as an 'honourable man' emphasised by Victor Lewisohn, gave a new freshness to the speech." The same critic also wrote, "The success or failure of *The Merchant of Venice* hinges upon its Shylock. Given a good Jew the play is practically made. Victor Lewisohn was magnificent in this exacting part. Any student of elocution could do worse than pay a visit to the Q and mark his beautiful voice production, his poise, and his subtle pauses and inflections of speech. He was superb."

Apart from Bruce there was another small boy in the audience who would remember this performance for the rest of his life. "I remember being fired at the age of about eight," recalled the distinguished director Peter Brook, "by *The Merchant of Venice* at Q - it's almost my earliest memory of the theatre."

Of Victor's performance in Chekhov's *The Three Sisters*, the Brentford & Chiswick Times reported, "As the doctor, Victor Lewisohn gives one of the cleverest and most convincing studies he has presented at the Q." It was to be his swansong.

"What I have always understood," commented Neville, "is that my father got a kind of mild shell-shock during the war. On several occasions he totally lost his memory and wandered off. One time he wandered off and came to in Petersfield."

"Another time," continued Bruce, "he walked into a police station in Brighton and said, 'Can you help me, I don't know who I am.'"

And then he was brought to my home. I went through this each time. They phoned me up to say they'd found him walking in Richmond Park.

Margaret Lockwood, who acted with him in the summer of 1934, recalled, "He seemed to me a very unhappy man."

"We had made a move to Ruislip," continued Neville. "He'd saddled himself with buying a house and no work came."

"After this he was diagnosed as being depressive. Nowadays they know that a large part of this depression is caused by a chemical imbalance and they can deal with it by drugs. In those days they knew nothing about that. Diagnoses were based on Freudian theory and so forth."

"One day in November, 1934," concluded Neville, "I was on my way home from school. I saw my mother waiting for me. Gently she told me that my father was dead, that he had taken his own life."

There were various reasons why Beatie had not acted since early in 1927, but the loss of her beloved brother, with whom she had shared childhood dreams of a life in the theatre, gave her a final resolve. If he were no longer acting, then neither would she. The dream had died with Victor.

PART THREE

1935 - 1956

CHAPTER ONE - Q BEGINNERS

WELCOME TO THE Q THEATRE! The commissionaire, dignified, with his head held high, in his smart tailed uniform, greets you as he opens the door of your car. The five pairs of light wood doors are open. To the left is the box-office window, facing you are four pairs of swing doors with engraved glass panels. One of three page-boys, neat in his uniform with white gloves on his shoulders, swings a door open for you. Down three steps to the black polished floor of the foyer, spacious but not cold. Six oval columns with brackets hanging, trailing fuschias. To your left a long polished bar with windows behind it overlooking the office corridor, and a welcome smiling lady. Miss Ellacott can help you to a presentation box of chocolates or at the matinee prepare a dainty afternoon tea. Notice her beautiful finger-nails! As you can see, the bar is a continuation of the box-office. Concealed at either end are doors to the offices. Just down the steps to your left is another box-office window at your service!

Until the middle thirties the theatre remained much the same as it had done since it had opened in 1924. Between 1933 and 1935 the theatre's frontage and offices were re-designed, largely by Charles Reading, to the luxurious style described above, with the support of the landlords, Fuller, Smith and Turner. Previously the theatre entrance had been some forty or fifty paces from the main road.
Apart from the lack of foyer space, the winter blasts penetrated directly into the auditorium and our audiences sat in overcoats with chattering teeth. Although this rebuilding operation continued intermittently until late in 1935 the theatre remained open throughout. The main entrance was moved forward and the old car park covered in to provide a small front foyer and a large lounge and bar.
Opposite the bar is a long, comfortable art-deco couch below high windows. The walls are stippled in a light shade. Side lights are set inside glass panels engraved with the likenesses of Shakespeare, Sheridan, Shaw and Coward (now to be found in the Theatre Museum, Covent Garden.) Overhead lighting is set in the ceiling, diffused by frosted glass. Two more pairs of swing doors open into the inner foyer. Another of the page-boys obliges us. Is that the one I saw lounging on the radiator outside my office one lunchtime and asked to pop across the road with a message for me? He had turned his head, folded his arms, and said, "I'm at lunch." But he's on duty now, cheerful and polite. As you can see, the old box office has become a telephone kiosk with a public

letter box which is cleared by the Post Office regularly. Are we the first theatre to have such a facility? To the left is a raised dais which one day soon will have two pianos on it; to your right is another settee and the swing doors into the pit, and the back wall bench which seats about fifteen patrons at sixpence each. But, for the time being, let's continue down the centre passage with its glass displays of photographs and programmes from Q's past and posters of things to come. There are a couple of settees on the right, and to the left a small door into the club room.

An L-shaped couch fits in the corner and there is another against the other wall. It was difficult to get the large corner couch into the room when it arrived. I was sure it could be done, the men said it couldn't. Our carpenter offered his own opinion. They all argued but it did go in, after manoeuvering, as you can see! Now the carpenter always says, "Don't worry - she'll do it!" We feel it's like Heal's in Tottenham Court Road whenever we come in, with the parquet floor, the rugs, the round art-deco tables and chairs. To the right, opposite the door, is the bar overseen by Bella, a sparkling girl with dark eyes and a lovely smile. If you offer her a drink she will turn her back politely to sip it!

Up three steps to the left are several tables on a lino floor and a snack counter with high stools, served by a man in a chef's hat - could we be the first London theatre to serve meals too? There are flowers everywhere on the tables with their striped tablecloths. Almost hidden by the snack-counter is the other club room door. It leads into my office. On the door there is a light signal which indicates either "Engaged" or "Come in!" I have a push button which opens the door when I want to know what's going on!

Further down the central corridor on the left is a very small public bar and the gentlemen's cloakroom. A fire door leads outside and up three steps to the scene docks and the new studio with its white walls and corrugated iron roof, well warmed, with gold chairs round the room. The small garden has mint and other tiny plants. The large scene dock with several bays for storing sets (in time we will often make scenery for West End productions as well) and the property room are here also. At the end of the passage is the ladies powder room, and to the right several steps to the pass door which opens on to the stage. Two pairs of swing doors lead into the stalls, about five hundred seats, well raked, in alternating shades of burnt orange and yellow plush. You can't at the moment see the orange velvet stage curtain with its old gold Q because of our new safety curtain, painted by Charles Reading, a cartoon-like impression of the river and Kew Bridge and the Q fireman. Suspended above the auditorium are several splendid wooden chandeliers. The emergency door is

open at the moment so we can air the theatre before this evening's performance. Why not admire for a moment our view into the Star and Garter's
charming garden?

By now the theatre is re-established as a fully professional operation. The new
beginning when amateurs and semi-professionals had mingled with the stars on
Q's stage had initially been great fun with their camaraderie and sense of purpose,
but the theatre's identity had been compromised. If there was still to be excitement
for Jack in running Q, there had to be a return to the risk element of new plays and
new authors. There would be no return to the almost manic seasons of the late
twenties however. 1933 and 1934 saw the presentation of twenty one new plays
respectively. The next two years saw eleven and ten, with more ambitious
programmes again in 1937 and 1938 of twenty one and twenty respectively. (1936
included a period of thirty four consecutive weeks which included only one new
play.)

Among the new playwrights from this period were two who would contribute
significantly to the British theatre for several decades to come. September 11th
1933 saw the production of *First Episode* at Q.

*It was almost a good play. Set in a University city, it dealt realistically and
convincingly with the first love affair of a sensitive undergraduate. The authors
knew their people and their background, and at least one of them could write
stage dialogue, easy to speak and with a real sense of character and comedy; the
authors' names were Philip Heimann and Terence Rattigan. The play was
amusing enough to secure a transfer and a long run. The Daniel Mayer Co.
presented it at the Comedy Theatre with a cast including Barbara Hoffe, Meriel
Forbes, William Fox and Jack Allen.*

*Early in 1937 came the first play of a young man, son of the Earl of Douglas and
Home, who was not only in later years to establish himself as one of our small
group of serious dramatists, but as a man with the courage of his convictions.
William Douglas-Home brought to me his idealistic first play* Great Possessions,
*and despite its deficiencies it secured a short run at the Duke of York's where it
opened on March 8th 1937, with the Q cast.*

"I had occasion to bless the name of Jack de Leon several years before I met him,"
recalled Constance Cox. "In 1939 The Daily Mirror ran a competition called 'Youth
Takes A Bow', with awards for the best play; the best poem; the best short story; the
best cartoon, etc., to be submitted by young people. Jack was the judge of the
playwriting section, and he chose my play as the best, winning for me the prize of
£10, the first money I ever earned in the theatre. Moreover Jack wrote, '... the play
is outstanding, and if the author perseveres, she will surely go on to write plays
which will be successfully and profitably produced.'

"His prediction was correct. Three years later I wrote *David Garrick* for Donald
Wolfit which was toured and then went into the West End. I followed this with a

number of other plays, memorably one, *The Picture of Dorian Gray* which Jack himself produced at Q. Later I wrote many adaptations of the classics for television, and I am still happily writing for the stage and radio.

"Jack was great, honourable and lovable. I shall always remember him."

Several performers who would become household names made either their debuts or significant early appearances at Q during this time. Margaret Lockwood had been performing since the age of ten in what she has described as 'cabarets and tea dances'. She had graduated from the Royal Academy of Dramatic Art by the time she was spotted by Herby de Leon who wasted no time in bringing her to Jack's attention.

Herby spotted Margaret, young, fresh, eager and penniless. He persuaded me to give this talented beginner a leading part in House on Fire. *A leading part was something to ask and expect both from me and her. But her talent was manifest after her first scene and Sydney Carroll, astute man of the theatre and journalist, captured and demoted her to a 'bit' in his next production* Family Affairs *at the Ambassadors.*

She returned to Q for one week in 1937 and was caught up in the film industry's search for expressionless prettiness and a photogenic face, and scuttled out of her birthright. Instead she attained first billing as the ideal and idol of the News of the World and the Daily Mirror readers, and considers it undignified to return to the home of her first appearance.

Perhaps her 'black spot' (her ever present beauty mark) is the symbol of a frustrated career and the visible mark of her popularity, but there are vague signs of dissatisfaction, the first step in another direction charged with neglected and dormant possibilities. The Money God, having emptied a profusion of bags into her outstretched hands, has nothing more to offer that the Chancellor of the Exchequer cannot grab; with little persuasion he will make way for One more satisfying and more permanent.

The reasons for this uncharacteristically sour assessment are unclear. There was an abiding snobbishness among the theatre set with regard to the superiority of theatre over the inferior cinema as though the latter was an imitation of the former and not a separate art. Jack appears to have fallen prey to this philosophy, along with many leading theatre people of the day. The cinema was a quick way to get cash; the theatre was a temple. The fact that his earnings from the cinematic exploitation of his work subsidised Jack through the thirties is conveniently forgotten. Margaret Lockwood was never a leading light in the theatre but she became a great star in the cinema because she was very good at her job and people wanted to see her, voting in their hundreds of thousands by paying to see her in the cinema. *Bank Holiday, The Lady Vanishes, The Man in Grey* and *The Wicked Lady* among others have brought her an immortality vouchsafed to few.

In 1954, her daughter Julia Lockwood appeared in the title role of *The Adventures of Goldilocks* at Q. Cast as Papa Bear, at the beginning of an acting career which would be set aside for directing in the cinema, was the future Academy Award winning director John Schlesinger. "The one thing I can recall," he wrote recently, "is that to our great surprise, Margaret Lockwood, Julia's famous mother, took a great deal of interest in the production and ministered to us all - bringing round sandwiches and coffee!"

When she had appeared in *House on Fire* the local press had remarked on Margaret Lockwood's "fresh simplicity." Victor Lewisohn, who was also in the cast, was apparently "his polished self." Victor was also cast in the next play *Triumph*, which marked an early appearance of John Clements, eventually one of the theatre knights. Also in *Triumph*, and three weeks previously in *The Flame* (as was also Victor) was the charming actress Elspeth March.

"I was heavily involved with Clement McCallin," recalled Miss March. "Eventually we were engaged, then he went to Stratford and met someone else, and I went to Birmingham and met Jimmy (Stewart, a.k.a. Stewart Granger). I remember nothing about the rest of the cast of *The Flame* because I only had eyes for Clem. I was playing a Russian Countess, the villainess, and Clem was cast as the hero. In those days, before I went to Birmingham, acting was just a lark. I was very young and I didn't take it at all seriously. At one point I had to announce my name, 'I am Olga Rachinova.' One of the actors dared me to blow a raspberry in the middle of 'Rachinova', which I did. Clem's face was a picture! I've always been able to keep a straight face, but I can't control my diaphragm. So violently did it shake that it knocked the revolver out of Clem's hand!

"In *Triumph* I played an exotic princess. I dressed with Ambrosine Philpotts and we took ages browning ourselves up in the dressing-room. She was my lady-in-waiting. It came to my entrance one night and I strode on, hoping I looked magnificent, drawing my long train behind me. Suddenly I came to a dead stop. Ambrosine had fainted on my train! Fortunately she was still in the wings so I had to back up, kick her off and then go on with the scene. She was always dieting. She'd been carried back to the dressing-room and when I got back I had to cut her out of the rubber girdle she was wearing. Having cut her out of it and given her some sustenance, she couldn't get back into the costume!"

Three notable British actors of future years made early appearances at Q at this time. Michael Wilding played Fedotik in *The Three Sisters* on August 20th 1934. Bernard Miles appeared as Schutzmacher in *The Doctor's Dilemma* the following November 26th and Trevor Howard was the Captain Absolute in a production of *The Rivals* on February 11th 1935. Making one of her earliest appearances, as 'A waitress' in *Search* on May 7th 1934, was an actress who would spend most of her career playing waitresses, maids and nosy neighbours in countless British films, before finding her greatest opportunity in her late seventies as the definitive Miss

Marple on television. "We were all delighted to be asked to come and play at Q," recalled Joan Hickson. "One thinks of it as such a happy place. So many friends and, who knows, the play might be transferred to the West End, as so many were." One such play would be one of her greatest successes, *See How They Run*.

On February 25th 1935, a legend was born at Q when a young actress made her stage debut.

A young and lovely girl, dark, vital and ambitious, was introduced to me by David Horne. Although I have no recollection of our first meeting, Vivien Leigh must have impressed me with her delicate beauty and earnestness, for she appeared as Giusta in The Green Sash *the same month. For the second time in a few months Sydney Carroll came and carried off a potential star. Vivien Leigh's first London success followed immediately.* The Mask of Virtue *at the Ambassadors was the second step in her meteoric rise.*

Indicative of how our expectations of an evening at the theatre have changed was the Brentford & Chiswick Times' review of *The Green Sash*. The critic deplored the shortness of the play. "West End audiences would hardly pay to see a play which begins after 8.15 and finishes before 10.30!" he wrote. Of Vivien Leigh he recorded that she was "charming". Charm was certainly hers-a-plenty, beauty too but her talent, at the time was slight. Because of film we can see the energy and effort in her transformation from the gauche, second-rate ingenue of the 1935 Gracie Fields film *Look Up and Laugh* to the assured and accomplished Academy Award winning star of *Gone With The Wind* only four years later, a tribute to ambition, determination and sheer hard work.

CHAPTER TWO - HOUSE ON FIRE

THE TITLE of Margaret Lockwood's debut play may, six months later, have seemed prophetic. As the curtain fell on the Saturday matinee performance of *Pygmalion*, Dennis Roberts, in his Doolittle costume, discovered a fire backstage. First he called for Rita, his wife, then for Jack and finally for a fireman.

This brought me rushing round to find the prompt side flats already in flames. Dennis released the fire curtain and I smashed the 'Sprinkler Glass' and set the stream of water in motion. Rita ran round in circles, but eventually pierced the nearest chemical extinguisher, toppling over herself in the process, and directing the powerful stream on to her husband. Undaunted Dennis collected Rita and the extinguisher and succeeded in quelling the smallest of the flames. But already the fire had spread, the stage was a blazing, crackling inferno. The theatre fireman, panting and struggling with the weighty hose, appeared from nowhere: "I've called the brigade. We can't stop this without the brigade." Someone shouted, "You can't without water." Someone else turned on the water; the fireman tottered and the gushing water drenched the O.P. flats, as yet untouched by flame. Someone swung the hose round and the sizzling and crackling intensified as the water burst on the devouring fire.

Suddenly the stage was lit only by the roaring flames. The electric mains had been switched off. The fire brigade calmly, efficiently and silently had taken over. The arrival of the fire engines had aroused our neighbours. They came from the Star and Garter, the coffee stall, the tobacconist confectioners and gaped gleefully and in horror.

I was being forcibly dragged from the stage by Beatie, wet, dirty, exhausted and in despair. The Saturday night house was sold out. Even if the stage roof survived the ordeal of fire, how could Pygmalion *be performed without scenery on a smouldering stage?*

In less than an hour it was out. With beams charred in the flies twenty foot high, half the scenery a mass of debris, the stage and front of the auditorium flooded and Dennis Roberts a more authentic dustman in appearance than he had ever intended, what was the alternative to abandoning the performance?

"The alternative," breathed Doolittle, "is all hands on deck. I'll look after the back, you clear up the front." We did, and it was done. The audience watched the final effort and heartened us on. Dennis and Rita had saved the situation. The curtain rose less than half an hour late.

In all, twenty eight of George Bernard Shaw's plays were presented at Q, several of them more than once. *Candida, The Devil's Disciple, Getting Married* and *Man and Superman* were each produced three times and *Arms and the Man* four. In May 1939, *Jitta's Atonement*, Shaw's only play never to have been performed for a run on a West End stage, was presented at Q.

This intense drama, stark and humourless, was a surprising undertaking for the wittiest cynic of the century. G.B.S. stood with me at the bar drinking tea during his matinee visit, but my only memory is of his dry comment that he had no recollection of ever having written the play!

We usually sold out during Shaw seasons. I did once speak to Shaw myself. I telephoned to ask his permission to do *Candida*. Immediately he asked who would be the lady. I said it would be Joyce Bland, to which he agreed. He came to a matinee and asked at the box-office for a ticket. The girl did not recognise him and was selling him a ticket as I passed. He was kindly to everyone, but he never expected complimentary tickets.

Casting was my special responsibility. In the fifties Kenneth Tynan was to write that the casting at Q was sometimes better than the plays! New plays were recommended by our clever and amusing play reader, Florence Roberts, in badly typed play reports with masses of red underlining and writing all over them. She used to turn up wearing layers of exotic clothes and feather boas, each inherited from different theatrical people and each still smelling of their different perfumes!

In the late nineteen thirties she was fat, flabby and flamboyant. She waddled from star dressing-room to star dressing-room; from first night to first night, concocting articles on ladies' attire and stars 'At Home'. She chatted and typed. Her jottings on people at and in the theatre filled columns in the Daily Mirror, the Daily Sketch, Theatre World and The Illustrated Sporting and Dramatic. There were few West End plays produced in the twenties and thirties that did not come under her critical review. But her critical faculties were adjusted not to the serious theatre, but to popular taste.

This in itself was and remained her qualification for the anonymous work she undertook for nearly twenty years. Before I met Florrie she was already official reader for an important West End management. To extend the scope of her new job she asked me to test her. I did; at a mere pittance per play. She submitted flowery, confused and lengthy disreputably typed synopses of her 'trial' script, but the summing up and judgment proved in every case a real enough reflection of audiences' reaction in performance. Subsequently Mrs Roberts was the only play reader permanently attached to Q.

The plays were finally read by Jack and usually discussed with the author; then a director would be chosen. I was told the ideal artist for each part. We made up lists of suggestions, narrowing them down to two or three possibles. I approached them in order of preference. I took particular trouble with the small parts. Many of our plays would transfer immediately to the West End, so the entire cast had to be West End standard. I think I went to every first night at Q and whenever there were new artists, however poor the show and small their part, I used to make it my business to watch them, so that I could remember them for future reference. As we could not afford understudies sometimes a small-part person prepared to be switched to a larger part, and an assistant stage manager would play a small role. If we did a revival, I had usually seen the play already and took charge of the casting. We always kept records of parts already played elsewhere in the United Kingdom by artists who had worked at Q or whom I had interviewed. One day, an hour before the Saturday matinee of *Call It A Day*, the stage manager phoned. She didn't know what to do. Florence Vie, who was playing the cook, had not answered the door when she called at her flat. "I looked through the letter box and she was on the floor. I've called an ambulance, and the police. She's been taken to hospital. What shall I do?" I said, "Come here at once."

Quickly I checked my records and found there were two who had played the role: Blanche Fothergill, who was then at Kettering, and Muriel George, who was scheduled to appear that evening at the Haymarket. I phoned both and said, "Get in a taxi and come along. I'll pay for the taxi." Muriel George arrived first and did the matinee; Blanche Fothergill played the evening show! Only once did we ever have to have a part read.

I enjoyed my casting. I had interviews with practically everyone who contacted me. When we presented *The Women* by Clare Boothe Luce, which had over twenty characters, I interviewed over sixty artists. They sat waiting in the front foyer. I used to walk from the door of my office through a back corridor to the box-office and see them through the window. There they were, as I passed back through the foyer to my office, titivating and lipsticking, silk legs smoothing, expecting to be seen by a sophisticated theatre woman, assuming, probably, that I was the office girl! I had checked their cards before their interviews, which were usually brief. I seldom actually auditioned, although we did hear about one hundred children for *Alice In Wonderland* and many others for *Goodbye Mr Chips*.

Among the remaining Q artefacts several of Beatie's casting cards still exist. One records an interview held in 1948. Under 'Remarks' Beatie had listed: 'Character/ Juvenile; Cockney and Irish; Small parts and small salary; try him in a bit part.' Thus, in advance, Beatie had defined the actor's career. Sam Kydd would spend his life playing small Cockney parts in countless films.

Joan White made her first appearance at Q in Jean Percival's *The Restless Room* on September 2nd 1935, in which she played a woman who having been frozen in a glacier for many years is thawed out bodily but remains icy in spirit! "Jack de Leon asked me to come down to Q to see him," she recalled. "There he was in his office, as he always was, with his feet up on the desk. 'Of course we can't pay you much,' he said." This was an oft repeated line. Thrift was vital in all of London's little theatres. Lilian Baylis at the Old Vic is known to have prayed, "Dear Lord, send me good actors, cheap!" The leader of the People's National

Theatre was known, behind her back, as Nancy Half Price. The managers of Q were no different. Robert Eddison recalled an incident some years later when he was talking to Beatie in her office. "The young man who worked in the accounts department came in and said that a certain actress was on the phone. 'Oh, yes, Beatie said. 'It'll be about her salary' - and then, without drawing breath, she continued, 'She'll ask twelve, she's worth ten, offer her six, she'll take seven.'"

Joan White next played in *Children - To Bless You!* at Q, then reported for the filming of *As You Like It* in which she was cast as Phebe. Laurence Olivier was Orlando and Elizabeth Bergner was Rosalind. Miss Bergner was displeased that there was another actress in the cast with ash-blonde hair and Joan was asked to dye hers black. By the time filming was over Jack had managed to set up a West End theatre for the play. "All hell was let loose when he saw my hair! I was supposed to be blonde. At the end of the run Jack said he had decided to send the play on tour. 'Of course, you will have to take a cut in salary, and, of course, it's not going to make any money.' And so I said, 'Well if it's not going to make any money and we have to take a cut in salary, why tour it?' He must have agreed because the tour was called off!"

On April 12th 1937, Jack tried out an unusual play, *Black Limelight* by Gordon Sherry, at Q. It had previously been done in New York with no success and when the Daniel Mayer Company transferred it to the St James's Theatre ten days later the Punch critic said the play was rubbish. The other critics agreed that it was implausible, but that it was made into a real thriller by the excellence of the acting. ***Margaret Rawlings, dark, dynamic, with smouldering fire, hypnotised her audience from her first entrance.***

"Jack de Leon was a wonderful director and producer," reciprocated Margaret Rawlings. "He shed happiness on us all, and enjoyment. Of course, we all enjoyed our work, especially I did with such a wonderful part. The originality of the play lay in the author's wish that the same actress should play the leading male character's wife and mother of his children while also playing his 'shop girl' mistress. The scene in which the girlfriend appeared, according to the programme, was set in a bungalow and took place in the wife's imagination! The name of the actress playing the mistress was not printed. The Daniel Mayer Company wanted a different actress to play the second part but Jack helped me persuade them that I should do both.

"It entailed a very quick change - hair and voice and bathing suit - almost the first bikini. It is incredible to me how, but it worked. There were actually people who didn't recognise me! It couldn't be done now. The camera has taken over the audience's imagination.

"Jack rose above all difficulties with languid grace and no anxiety, the best temperament for a producer-director with all his responsibilities. He had a way of stretching himself on a narrow wooden bench in the rehearsal room and reclining in a way that made one believe that he was on a soft bed and supported by luxurious cushions!" It would play at the St. James's for four hundred and fourteen performances.

Dennis Roberts recalled, "Rita and I practically lived at the Q Theatre. Jack, as usual, both feet on the desk, puffing away at a cigarette and Beatie also, as usual, on the telephone, making funny faces as she chattered about the business of the moment. It was a very friendly atmosphere for we were all on the happiest terms. If we weren't in the theatre with them all we were often in their home playing the grand piano for Jack loved to sing and Beatie and Jean liked to fool around. We would back horses together, go to the dogs and generally enjoy ourselves."

Between doing the casting I did the catering with the chef for the club. One day I got down to my office before nine in the morning and remembered I had not given the order for fish, so I asked our telephonist to get me through to the fishmonger first. Then I asked her to get the numbers of various artists. The fishmonger's number happened to be engaged and I didn't, at first, discover, as I ordered the fish, that I was speaking to a famous actress and not the shop! Rehearsals were always in progress during the day and these were often started in the foyer. Sometimes four productions were being prepared simultaneously, all at different stages. There might be a reading in the clubroom or foyer of a play to open in a fortnight; a dress rehearsal on the stage at Q for a play opening that night; a run through of next week's show at the Steam Packet pub on Strand on the Green; and a reading of a new play in a West End theatre bar.

We had a reputation for our stage managers trained on our apprentice scheme. Keen workers were often supervised by me. They had to learn to find and borrow props without expense, in exchange for advertisement or complimentary tickets, or to help the property mistress to do so. They had to learn how to handle the cast and staff with tact and firmness, to mark scripts clearly, to supervise the furniture and the lighting cues, the sound effects, to check and double check everything, and to make absolutely certain there was no smoking backstage - the council inspectors might turn up at any time to inspect the stage.

One student had chosen the stage name of Ruth Milroy. Lady Bethune, as she is today, recalled, "We paid a sum of money (probably very little) to be trained at Q. What a wonderful experience it was for a nineteen-year-old. Everything seemed so happy-go-lucky and undogmatic. The training really consisted of watching rehearsals of plays, standing in and reading parts for absent actors (what a thrill) and occasionally being given a small part - an even greater thrill! My personal vivid memories are of watching Arthur Sinclair, Maire O'Neill and Sara Allgood in *Juno and the Paycock* and *The Plough and the Stars*, and realizing I was in touch with theatre history, witnessing their superb comic and tragic performances. Arthur

Sinclair and Maire O'Neill were married but they were not on speaking terms even insisting on having dressing-rooms as far apart as possible. I was told they only spoke to each other through their solicitors. Yet on stage there seemed perfect harmony between them.

"Arthur Sinclair was never happier than when he held court in the clubroom where we sat around and had snacks. He didn't mind whom he spoke to as long as he had an audience, and sometimes that audience was only *me*. Oh! if only I had written down some of those fabulous stories. We were weak with laughter listening as memories poured from him in that wonderful Irish brogue.

"He played a wickedly humorous assistant detective to Austin Trevor in one play. I remember him filling a suitcase with stage weights so that Austin Trevor could hardly lift it. He was certainly not amused. It was a tremendous thrill for me when Jack de Leon came and praised me for my performance in *The Likes of Her*. They were happy and exciting days."

The Q had risen from its derelict state in 1931 to become in 1937 the most successful and perhaps the most publicised theatre in the world. How had this happened?

Perhaps the two most vital individual causes for this phenomenal success were the two most outside the control of Beatie and myself; the virtual non-existence of competition in the field of try-out theatre and the number of excessively short-lived plays produced in the West End during 1937. The former resulted in an avalanche of new plays coming our way and the latter in a record of eight transfers out of the twenty six new plays presented. Both factors combined to influence artists of star calibre to appear and to establish Q first nights as theatrical events which West End managements forewent at the risk of missing a potential winner.

First nights at Q were very animated. Nearly all the stalls patrons wore evening dress and the critics attended. When we went up West for a first night Jack used to give Jean and me similar sprays of carnations and we would set off in a hired car. I remember one West End occasion when Queen Mary was to attend, Jack came home to change with a magnificent bouquet he had collected from Fortnum's to present to her. We dressed, drove off and reached the Chiswick roundabout before I realized that I still had my bedroom slippers on! Thank goodness we had allowed plenty of time and were able to turn back to enable me to change.

At Q the critics had their regular seat allocation and we used to look at the ticket stubs to make sure they had arrived. Hannan Swaffer, with his swirling cloak and its vivid lining, was a particularly colourful critic in the early days. W.A. Darlington of the Daily Telegraph and James Agate of The Sunday Times both took their tasks especially seriously but had excellent senses of humour. Although we did sometimes entertain in the office during the interval

or after the performance, we never discussed the play. Nor did they. When it was a long play, sometimes they would use our telephone to ring through their notices. We were tempted, but *did not eavesdrop.*
We wrote to British Rail, telling them that many patrons were inconvenienced if a play ran until eleven o'clock. We succeeded in having a later train put on! I've always thought any improvement is worth working for. I believe in aiming high and taking a chance.
At supper at the Savoy Hotel after a West End first night I remember being terrified because I was seated beside Agate. I knew he was a great intellectual and a wit. However, he was kind and easy to talk to. He had the gift of making everyone feel important and interesting.
In the early years James Agate was perhaps the only important dramatic critic who rarely came to Q. Whatever his reason, his attitude certainly changed in the 1930's. Eventually, of course he asked me to try out his second, and I believe, final excursion into writing for the stage.
I Accuse was a loosely constructed drama based on the Dreyfus affair, in many scenes and with an unnecessary number of small and undeveloped characters it nevertheless had considerable dramatic tension and scenes of power and emotion. It was presented at Q on October 25th, 1937. D. A. Clarke-Smith and William Devlin gave outstandingly fine performances as Esterhazy and Zola respectively, but my clearest memory of the rehearsals is the revelation of Jimmy's unexpected humility and eagerness to listen to criticism.
His many acts of friendship after this production until his sudden death in 1947 are the clearest indication of how much this production meant to him. Never did he really believe that there were any commercial possibilities in the play, nor, despite his disappointment at its failure to transfer to the West End, did he ever place any responsibility on me or anyone concerned in the production; on the contrary, he was delighted at the reception and the general tone of the press notices. His characters had come to life; they had created an impact on capacity audiences and he was satisfied.
Maybe he remembered the humiliation of being booed at the Vaudeville Theatre many years before, when he braved the stage after his first first night, and by contrast these audiences were vastly flattering.
At Christmas time we sometimes had two productions - a children's matinee and a thriller at night. On Christmas Eve we would have a huge party. Up to a hundred people would be there - artists who had been with us during the past year, staff old and new, as well as the companies playing on Boxing Day.
The 1938 Christmas production was *Alice in Wonderland.* The title role was played by Joyce Redman. The critic of The Times commented, "Alice has stepped out of the book." The previous two Christmases the star of the seasonal show was Phyllis Neilson-Terry, Dennis's sister. She appeared with Donald Wolfit in *The*

Scarlet Pimpernel in December 1936, the following year playing the title role in *Sweet Nell of Old Drury.*

My daughter Jean and her cousin Anthony sat enthralled at the dress rehearsal sharing a box of Nestlé's chocolates. Dennis Roberts, Rita and I were sitting at the back for sound levels.

Phyllis Neilson-Terry, a bewigged and stately Nell Gwyn, gazing out through the window of her Pall Mall residence, declaimed her joy at "the heavens above and the earth beneath"; came a crash and the heavy pelmet board fell bang on her upturned head. Phyllis swung on her heels, holding fast to the curtains with one outstretched hand; her eyes glazed and her taut form, like a marionette's folded up on the stage, dragging curtains and pelmet with her.

She went out like a light, and fortunately could not hear the unsympathetic burst of hysterical laughter from the intruders out front.

It was like a Keystone Comedy! We were wicked to laugh.

Jack was responsible, during the late thirties, for introducing two plays by the leading Czech dramatist, Karel Capek, to West End audiences. The first of these was *Power and Glory* which, without a try-out, he presented at the Savoy Theatre, April 18th 1938.

It was truly a play of power and glory. Oscar Homolka played two contrasting characters with tremendous resource, but even this tour de force and a first rate press failed to attract audiences. War and Hitler were too much in people's minds for them to seek entertainment in the company of Hitler's counterpart and the foreshadowing of Czechoslovakia's tragedy.

He followed it up with a production of Capek's *The Mother* which opened at Q on February 13th 1939, directed by Miles Malleson who had, with Paul Selver, adapted the play.

Its star was Louise Hampton who had frequently played at Q. At the end of the play she had to walk down a flight of stairs and shoot her son with a double-barrelled shot gun. By this time Louise was frail, but determined. While the stage-management huddled with cotton-wool in their ears, Louise would come tottering downstairs. The gun was too heavy for her to lift, so she fired firmly at the floor. In the end she burnt a hole in the carpet!

The Mother *remains vividly in my memory as a play of importance, powerful, moving and original in conception, illuminated by the spiritual insight and idealism of a cultured mind.*

It succeeded in breaking the Q box-office receipts record, and it transferred to the Garrick Theatre, opening on March 22nd. Unfortunately **The Mother** *proved another* **Power and Glory.** *Both plays had been written by the foremost living Czech dramatist; both had the quality of greatness; both had a message of vital import to Mankind. Mankind ignored the message and theatre audiences ignored the play. Ernest Raymond's* **The Berg** *was my first lesson;* **Power and**

Glory *and* **The Mother** *my second and third. I still refuse to accept the obvious* **conclusion.**
Appearing in the cast of both the Capek plays was another descendant of the distinguished Terry family, Anthony Hawtrey, great nephew of Dame Ellen, and son of Sir Charles Hawtrey. For some time he had nursed the idea of running another theatre in conjunction with Q. Early in 1938 the Embassy Theatre at Swiss Cottage which had been run by Ronald Adam came up for sale. The Embassy's fortunes had declined as Q's had gone into the ascendant and Adam found himself in much the same position as had Jack and Delia seven years earlier, with no takers beating his door down. Tony Hawtrey and Jack put in a bid. Embassy (Swiss Cottage) Ltd. was set up with Jack and Beatie as sole directors, and with Tony and Marjory Hawtrey as sole shareholders. Tony was to be director of productions and Marjory was to fulfil the role Beatie pursued at Q. The policy was clear cut. All plays produced at Q would play a second week at the Embassy. The casting and organisation were to be carried on at Q. Q Productions Ltd. was to receive approximately half the actual costs of the preparation of each production from Embassy (Swiss Cottage) Ltd. The saving in the running costs of both theatres varied between twenty five and fifty pounds a week.
The theatre opened almost fourteen years to the day since Q was born, on December 24th 1938. The redecoration had been undertaken by Herman Herrey, a brilliant young German architect who had fled Hitler's persecution. Together with Beatie he had drawn up exciting new plans for the rebuilding of Q.
The important and revolutionary new feature of the theatre was its self-containment. It was elastic in its seating capacity, varying, by the removal or setting up of glass screens, from 600 to 1,200 seats. Both stalls and circle were designed in rising tiers. Restaurant, club rooms, lounges and bars half circled around the fan shaped auditorium. The stage design incorporated a movable semi-circular apron, a full revolve and sliders, a movable cyclorama, a paint frame, a lighting bridge with the entire equipment electrically colour-controlled, a remote control switch-board located at the back of the stalls, two floors of dressing-rooms, with bathrooms on each floor. In fact it was to be the theatre of my dreams. The entire building operation would be carried out while Q remained open, except for the last six weeks prior to the opening of the new Q. The old auditorium was not to be involved in the operation. This would later be converted into a news theatre.
By June the plans were being discussed with the Middlesex County Council. By August the final plans were ready for submission.

Then came September 1939...

CHAPTER THREE - THEATRE OF WAR

"COMING TO Q was my first real theatrical experience," recalled Shaun Sutton, for many years Head of BBC Television Drama. "I had been at the Embassy School of Acting, and as a student had walked on or played small parts in Sunday try-out productions, or plays at the Embassy Theatre, always for free. This was in 1938 and 1939, and there were a lot of angry anti-Nazi plays with titles like *Do We Not Bleed?* or *Achtung - Take Heed!* or *Mein Kampf, My Crimes*. As I was tall and blonde I spent a lot of time in Nazi uniform, being generally unpleasant to the rest of the cast. I remember in one play I had to beat up Kenneth Connor, surely an unequal contest.

"Now I was to be a professional. I was to be stage-manager of the Q Theatre. I was eighteen, and quite oblivious of the dangers and difficulties ahead. I had a sort of lunatic confidence that I certainly haven't got today. On being offered thirty shillings (£1.50) a week as a salary, I had the temerity to ask for two pounds, and got it. I think this is the only time in my theatrical life that I have asked for more money.

"I was now faced with the task of stage-managing twenty six plays a year - each production playing a week at Q, and a week at our sister theatre, the Embassy. The responsibilities of a stage manager at such theatres before the war would horrify his counterpart today. The plays rehearsed a maximum of two weeks, during which time the stage manager would also have an evening performance and three matinees a week of the preceding play. Each week there was the task of getting the play across London to the Embassy. At Q, the stage-manager was also expected to be a scene-hand, a collector of properties, a taker-up of safety-curtains and, in every other play, an actor.

"In my first interview with Beatie de Leon, she explained that the stage-manager always played the policeman. When I asked 'What policeman?' she said, 'Any policeman in any of the plays.' I enjoyed these recurring constables. Sometimes they were just looming helmets outside a window, but quite often they were good-sized parts - even, on rare occasions, *funny* policemen which no doubt, I outrageously overplayed, learning for the first time the intoxicating joy of laughter. My first play, she added, was very difficult. It had four sets - a fully equipped pub, a luxury flat, a tenement hotel and the London docks. I was also to be a radio announcer (in French) and, of course, play the policeman.

"This was my first policeman, and a rather special one. I had to arrest a dockside tough, played by the ex-heavyweight champion of Britain, Bombardier Billy Wells, the original banger-of-the-gong at the start of all Rank pictures. Billy was huge and gentle. He and I shared a dressing-room which meant I was mostly in the passage. He had few lines but he had the greatest difficulty in remembering them, or getting them in the right order. When I wished him 'Good luck' on the first night,

he answered, 'An' good luck to you, boy. I hope I don't forget me bleeding sayings.'
"However, all that was to come. First I was to present myself at Q late on Saturday night, and see the first of the four sets up and ready for lighting. I expected to find a gang of smiling stage hands under their benevolent stage-carpenter, waiting to greet me jovially. Instead I found a completely empty stage, no stage hands and no scenery.

"This was scarcely a situation the new stage-manager could tolerate. In a commanding voice I bellowed, 'Carpenter!' I was answered by a sort of animal growl from the fly-rail above the stage. I looked up and saw what appeared to be a gorilla draped over the rail. This, I realized, must be the carpenter. He was a squat, short, hairy man whose name was, incredibly, Leon Brahms. 'Come along, come along,' I said unwisely. 'This won't do.' Brahms's reply was basic. He came down the rail from the fly-gallery in one long step, turned, and advanced unsteadily towards me with swinging fists. I had time to notice that he was not only very strong-looking, but also very drunk. A placatory note seemed prudent. I retreated towards the open dock doors remarking, 'Now, now, we don't want any trouble, do we?'

"Brahms did. He rushed at me, and I side-stepped. Brahms hurtled past me, through the dock doors, and over a three-foot drop on to the concrete outside. When I reached him, he was unconscious, but breathing well.

"I was aghast. My first night in the theatre and I had caused the carpenter to be unconscious. Stage-managers were two-a-penny, but stage-carpenters ... I need not have worried. The next morning the manager, a Scot called Pringle Roberts, came round and shook me warmly by the hand. 'Hear you knocked Brahms out,' he said. 'Good start. Keep it up.'"

Pringle had relieved both myself and Beatie of a great mass of routine matters that we had until that time undertaken ourselves. Such a weight lifted from my shoulders alone made possible the fabulous amount of work I managed to get through in the late thirties; not alone, for Beatie worked and continued to work at her desk - backing against my own - with unfailing humour, perseverance and understanding.

"Jack and Beatie de Leon maintained an astonishingly high standard at Q," continued Shaun Sutton. "The plays were excellently cast and well directed. Many of them transferred. It didn't seem like work at all; it was the best possible introduction to the profession, for all the best actors and actresses of the day came to Q."

One future star made her first appearance at Q in 1939. Like Elspeth March, five years previously, she was blinded by love. "My time at Q was short and very sweet but my memory of detail is very blurred," recalled Phyllis Calvert. "I had just met Peter Murray Hill and had fallen in love, so hence the lack of interest in things around me. I was in a rather second-rate play called *Punch Without Judy* with Peter and Henry Kendall. My agent rang to say that Noël Coward would be coming to see the play as he was looking for the cast of two plays he would be producing in the Autumn. None of the cast believed he would turn up, but he did. He offered me parts in both plays which turned out to be *Present Laughter* and *This Happy Breed*. I always felt Q was my spring-board to the West End and have always had grateful thanks for Jack and Beatie. Incidentally, the Noël Coward plays were originally scheduled to open in Blackpool, on September 4th 1939 ....!"

On Saturday August 7th, Jack, Beatie and Jean set off on their annual holiday. *We spent the most peaceful, carefree fortnight I can remember, sailing the Norfolk Broads in a hired wherry, landing daily only to take on supplies and re-fuel, remote from telephones. The hours were spent in lazing in the sunshine, reading innocuous novels or playing Ludo or Snakes and Ladders. The days and nights passed happily and uneventfully; we had no immediate cares and hardly gave a thought to the problems of Q.*

We arrived back in time for the first performance of This Tender Age, *a new play by Tom Macaulay. We found that the minds of our audiences, of the whole country, of all Europe, were obsessed with the single terrible thought - War. The theatre's receipts virtually collapsed, yet we continued to rehearse our next production.*

The next Sunday, September 3rd, Mr Chamberlain's voice tragically announced what to many of us seemed the doom of civilisation. The sirens wailed and we waited for death to rain upon us from the skies.

"On September 1st, all theatres closed," continued Shaun Sutton. "Typically I was stage-managing a violently anti-war play at the Embassy at the time, and its final performance was given to twelve rather embarrassed people." (The play was a revised version of *The Fanatics* by Miles Malleson, the original version of which had been presented at Q in the first weeks of Mrs Whitty's tenancy.) "Jack did not dismiss his staff. He knew it would not be long before the theatres opened again, and within three weeks he was proved right. My first war work consisted of taking out all the bulbs from the canopy above the entrance to the theatre, dipping them in dark blue paint, and putting them back again."

We spent our time painting fanlights black, hanging heavy black curtains or pasting black paper over the great expanse of glass about the theatre.

As the days passed it became clear that the complete absence of some form of relaxation could not be continued indefinitely. We expected the War of Silence to break forth into one of poison gas and high explosive at any moment, but the tenseness and morbid anticipation could not continue unrelieved by purposeful occupation or release from the monotony of just sitting, gossiping and waiting. Theatres and other places of entertainment were asked to "carry on". Beatie and I immediately set to work. Improvisation was the order of the day. As in the early days of the 1930's, I took on responsibility for the stage, and she for the front of house.

My daughter Jean had just left school, and although she had grown up in the hectic, topsy-turvy atmosphere of the theatre it was never our intention that she should become permanently involved. But with the disappearance of the box-office staff she was roped in as emergency assistant.

Thousands of circulars announcing our re-opening were prepared and dispatched within hours. The Q again opened its doors on the afternoon of Saturday 23rd with Rattigan's French Without Tears. *Although the box-office receipts were somewhat less than our then established average they were considerably higher than we had anticipated.*

"Later that year," continued Shaun Sutton, "we did the most exciting production at the Embassy, and later at His Majesty's, a modern dress version of *Julius Caesar*, an idea sharply relevant to the current dictatorships in Europe. It starred Eric Portman, Godfrey Tearle, Clifford Evans and Tony Hawtrey. I note with interest from my programme that 'Other parts were played by Ian Carmichael and Hugh Griffith.' The sets were boldly designed. A huge central scenic structure revolved through 360 degrees, giving many different planes and aspects (nothing exceptional today, but very new then.) The backgrounds were projected by two slide projectors on to an eighty foot, semi-circular cyclorama."

The central magnificent staircase was designed by Herman Herrey. It occupied the vast stage of His Majesty's like a flowering oasis in the desert; an heroic, imaginative effort, doomed, even with Godfrey Tearle as Brutus, to failure.

Taking Shaun Sutton's place in the Q stage-management complement was Mark Moore. "I soon learned that the boss, Beatrice de Leon, was one of whom I as a youngster needed to stand in awe," he recalled. "Her rule was absolute and she deferred to no-one except, perhaps, to her husband. My first play was *Rain*, the adaptation of Somerset Maugham's short story 'Sadie Thompson'. *Rain* is a challenge for the stage-management. The stage directions require that the rain should be seen and heard throughout two of the three acts. At Q this was not easy as there was no space underneath the stage for drainage. The theatre made up for some of its lack of normal facilities by being the only theatre, I believe, in the London area to have a double revolving stage. Two turntables were mounted side by side taking up the whole width of the stage but requiring only half the depth. The theory was that you could mount even three sets if necessary, each taking up one third of the circular space on each turntable.

"But that did not help us in *Rain*. We were warned of the awful consequences of water getting into the substage electrical system. A wooden trough was constructed and a tarpaulin draped inside it; we hired a hand-pump and hose which was insinuated through the dock doors out to the tarmac area between the main theatre building and the dressing-rooms. A strong-armed ASM was detailed to keep pumping throughout Acts 1 and 3. It worked.

"I never set out to be an actor; my interest was in making things work, by creating unseen the magic that is seen by the audience. But always from time to time members of the stage-management are called upon to help the economy of the production by playing some unimportant part, and so it was for me at Q. In *Rain* I had the part of a native boy with perhaps just one speaking line. There was also a similar part for a native girl which was played by a delightful young lady straight from drama school, whose name but not whose figure I have long since forgotten. When it came to the allocation of dressing-rooms for us small fry, there was only the one little room left. This caused a certain amount of consternation because our parts require both of us to have dark make-up all over. The young lady was persuaded that she could trust me, and at this distance in time I can swear without fear of contradiction that her trust was not misplaced, and the honour of Q was unsullied.

"One thing led to another and a week or two later I was back again as stage-manager for a production of Noël Coward's *Design for Living*. This has a small part, just one scene, for a newspaper reporter. In expert hands it can be a comedy gem. I had to play it opposite the eminent actor Hubert Gregg and his despair increased by the minute as he tried to rehearse it with me. The trouble was that, small though the part was, it was the first time I had ever been put on the stage with a real part to play; I was terrified and just did not know how. Ever since then I have had the greatest admiration for actors and I made sure subsequently that no producer ever roped me in without an absolute understanding of my limitations. But for the time being, there was a war on, and by early December I was learning new disciplines in the army."

A new ASM arrived as Mark Moore was leaving. "I was very shy, a very protected boy," recalled Michael Northen. "For years I had seen the Q advertisement in The Stage and longed to work there. Finally it was arranged. Beatie introduced me to Sara Lewis the stage-manager saying, 'This is the woman who is going to look after you.' She was a tough Northern woman and summed me up in a flash. For my first job she instructed me to telephone the actors with their calls for the next week. 'There is a telephone kiosk in the foyer.' I was promptly sick. She understood and began to dial the first number herself. Then she handed me the receiver. I never looked back. She took me in hand and taught me everything there was to know about stage-management. She was later instrumental in setting up the Swan Theatre, Worcester.

"We were all very frightened of Beatie! You couldn't get round her in any way. You quaked if your bus arrived late. Her office door was always ajar so she could pounce on latecomers. I have to say, however, that she taught me discipline this way.

"During those early days of the war we were desperate to keep the theatre open. We all worked like beavers. We had one object, and that was to get the curtain up each week. Later when I became stage-manager myself and was running the show I had to operate the switchboard. I would take out the house-lights, then I had to dash round backstage to open the curtain, then dash back again to put on the stage lights. Then Beatie would say, 'Who's going to do the ice-creams?' If there was no-one free at the interval I would bring in the curtain, rush round backstage and bring in the house-lights, get my tray and rush out front to sell my ices, checking my watch every minute or so, ready to ring the bell, take out the house-lights, open the curtains and so on. I wore myself to a frazzle."

Sir Peter Saunders recalled, "Everybody loved Q. And everyone mucked in to help the de Leons. My first memory of this extraordinary set-up was when I was backstage before a play was opening and I heard Beatie saying to quite a well-known actress, 'You're not on during the last ten minutes of the first act and you don't come back until half way through the second so you won't mind helping us out in the coffee bar during the interval?' And of course she didn't. Q was like that."

"Jack was an expert at stage-lighting," added Shaun Sutton, "and he was generous with his time, teaching me all I was ever to know about theatrical lighting. Nowadays, of course, it would all be done by a lighting-director, but in my days, the director did all the lighting."

My standard of lighting had been set by Milton Rosmer and all subsequent directors were silently judged by his colourful and somewhat artificial approach. Jack soon proved that he had an instinctive flair for the art of lighting, something he had recently been able to prove on the production of Capek's *The Mother.*

My devotion to the play inspired an experimental approach to the lighting. The production was designed around a scheme of lighting whereby the 'living' characters moved only in the cold light of a hideously astray world, and the 'dead' only in the warm glow of the Invisible Spirit.

For the first and only time I was offered a fee to reconstruct my Q lighting scheme when the play was subsequently presented at the Garrick Theatre. I soon discovered that the antiquated switchboard could not cope with the great number of independently controlled spots necessary to reproduce the effect. A temporary board was installed and a battery of supplementary spots. With short meal breaks the electrical staff worked all Monday, throughout most of Monday night and Tuesday until they mastered the intricate light movement in time for the Tuesday evening dress-rehearsal and the Thursday opening.

Fifteen years later a Canadian actor/director took over the direction of the play *Angels In Love* for Jack at the Savoy Theatre. "At that time it was customary in England, except for the Tennants company, for directors to light the play themselves," recalled Bernard Braden. "Not so in New York. When we came to the lighting rehearsal I found, to my horror, that there was no lighting director. I didn't know whether to pretend or tell the truth. I decided to tell the truth, so Jack took over the lighting. I remember being fascinated by the way he did it, starting in the dark and going through the lighting cues, talking to me in the meantime and to the head electrician. Then, when his eyes had had enough, he would order lights off and start again from the beginning. He would only take twenty minutes at a time. It was an education to watch."

One of the great lighting-directors of the British theatre is Michael Northen. "Jack's great quality in lighting was economy. There weren't a lot of lights, but he was able to get the maximum out of a minimum of equipment. I always admired this and I have followed this principle throughout my career.

"Jack liked working at night when there was no-one else in the theatre. We used to sit there quite quietly and Harry Pegg used to move the scenery. There was no telephone ringing, no interruptions. And he used to play a lot, experiment. There was an ever elusive shadow on the cyclorama, caused by no-one knew what, which he was always trying to get rid of but never could.

"My main memory of Jack is of him sitting in the club room after a rehearsal. He would loll, with his legs going out for miles! Or he'd be in his office with his feet up on the desk ..."

We had gathered around us an almost completely new staff of young enthusiasts, too young or unfit for immediate war service. They acted as carpenters, scene-shifters, property-masters and stage-managers, and we all flung off our jackets and worked together again as in the early thirties. Tanya Moiseiwitch, daughter of the celebrated pianist, arrived to design and paint the setting for Temporary Residence, *the first wartime try-out production anywhere. We worked together again, but with a difference. There was no return to the amateur or semi-amateur 1931 beginnings. The highest standard we had ourselves established was the standard we sought and succeeded in maintaining.*

One day I was told a boy wanted to see me. From the top of an open bus he had seen Tanya Moiseiwitch at work in the open area beside the theatre. We had no appointment but I invited him in.

"Total boredom and a longing for something green sent me off on a bus to Kew Gardens to see the Pagoda," recalled Derek van den Bogaerde. "But I never got there in the end. Stopping for a moment at Kew Bridge, the bus provided a grandstand view of what appeared to be a builder's yard. Doors and windows, some scattered fireplaces, piles of junk and a girl painting a cut-out tree which was leaning against the wall of the yard. Beside the muddle of wood and canvas was a small squat building. Across the facade, in shabby letters, the words 'Q THEATRE'.

"I ran down the steps, jumped off as the bus started again, and went towards a half open door into the yard. The painting girl looked up rather crossly. She was covered in blobs of green distemper and wore an old pair of navy blue trousers and a man's shirt. She was startled and hot.

"'What do you want here? This is private, you know.'

"'It is a theatre, isn't it?'

"She looked crosser than ever. 'You'd better clear off ... or else.'

"'I was wondering about a job ... that's all.'

"'Well, don't bother me with your wondering, I'm busy and the office is in there.' She indicated a door which said Fire Exit and went back to her tree.

"A dark, untidy corridor, with a fire extinguisher and a glass-fronted door with 'Office' painted on it. It was half open and there were voices. Just as I was about to knock, it opened and a small, hurrying little woman came out eating a cheese roll. She looked up at me mildly.

"'Yes?' She finished chewing, her eyes bright and interested, the half finished roll in her hand. I said I wondered if there was a job going. I'd seen the yard from the top of a bus and ... She cut me short with a wave of the cheese roll: 'Not auditioning today, dear ... next week is all cast and we don't see anyone without an appointment ... come again.' She started to turn away back into the office, when I said: 'I meant painting, scenery and things. I'm an artist not an actor.'

"This stopped her. She took another bite of her roll and asked me where I came from. I said from nowhere particular but had trained at the Poly and worked in Sussex and at the Uckfield Playhouse. I made it sound like the Liverpool Rep.

"'What happened to the Uckfield Rep then?' she asked with a shrewd smile. 'They fire you?'

"'No. They got commandeered for evacuees.'

"'And you did the sets, is that it?'

"I nodded. I didn't say I'd done one only. She finished her roll, licked her fingers and turned back into the office. 'You'd better come in and see my husband,' she said."

The young man mucked in with everyone else, beginning by helping Tanya with the sets for the Herbert and Eleanor Farjeon musical, *The Two Bouquets*. "It's a sod," she said, "three big sets. One's the entire bloody Twickenham Regatta." As time went on he gradually graduated towards the stage area, occasionally prompting the play when everyone else was on stage, or ringing up the curtain when the stage-manager had a complicated light change and hadn't time to dash from one side of the stage to the other.

On January 15th 1940, the actor who should have played the photographer's assistant in *When We Are Married* was taken ill. Beatie cornered Bogaerde. "You know the lines, dear, don't you? There are only a couple anyway, and if you don't know them you've plenty of time to read them up before this evening. Hop off and see if his suit will fit you: if it doesn't wear your own and carry his hat. Off you go. We're up in a couple of hours."

"Breathlessly I reported this news to my director, a red-haired young man in a wrap-round camel hair coat called Basil Dearden, who was assiduously modelling himself, with considerable success, on Basil Dean, a director noted for his brilliance, sarcasm, acidity and apparent abhorrence of actors.

"'Christ Almighty!' he said. 'Now I know there's a war on: they've started to ration the Talent!' And to my eager face he quietly said, 'Well, don't stand there, piss off and see if the blasted things fit', starting a deep friendship which only ended with his death more than thirty years later."

When We Are Married took him, "with two thin lines, a few physical miles nearer to the West End." Eventually, of course, he would simplify his name to Dirk Bogarde.

He also played a telegraph boy in one play. As he left the stage, surreptitiously he put out his hand behind him for a tip. It was his own business. It got a laugh and impressed me. I remember thinking "That boy is good." From then on I gave him parts - small roles, whenever there was an opportunity.

After playing in another Priestley play *Cornelius*, Bogarde felt he had found a role he was comfortable with. "I said to Beatie: 'It was a *marvellous* week for me. I really feel now that I'm a proper actor.' Beatie shot me a distant flicker of a smile. 'Do you dear?' she said. 'That's nice.'"

Shortly afterwards, Sarah Churchill appeared in a series of plays at Q, most notably in Sutton Vane's *Outward Bound*. It was quite a feather in Q's cap to have the Prime Minister's daughter working there.

Audiences cheered her performance as they cheered her father. She gave a delicately sensitive performance in the part of Ann. Mrs (later Lady) Churchill was among our matinee audience. We had tea in the interval and talked about Sarah, but not of the war.

She was a beautiful and gracious girl, quiet, gentle and sensitive. She was generous and thoughtful and would bring me precious lemons and eggs when she came to see us in war time. She made no fuss about the tiny dressing-rooms, just went on attending to her performance. She was absolutely exquisite in *Mary Rose*, with her lovely Titian hair. I was very upset when she died and the press showed her looking so different. I remember her looking like a madonna. The day *Outward Bound* transferred to the New Theatre the first German bomb fell on London. It was September 1940.

Londoners were urgently called upon through radio and press to evacuate and spread themselves throughout the country. Day by day, night by night the second great exodus proceeded; and the sirens wailed their plaintive frightening note. Twenty or thirty heroically foolhardy supporters of the Q found themselves nightly surrounded by a great expanse of empty seats. Beatie and I stood there, night after night, chatting to the twenty or thirty patrons and moving them forward into the first two or three rows of the stalls. Pringle Roberts, during this his last week in the theatre, kept up our spirits with his gay unconcern.

Exactly one year after the abandonment of a Q dress rehearsal and opening night, another dress rehearsal was disbanded.

George Relph arrived with his wife, Mercia Swinburne, on Sunday September 8th for the final rehearsal of Avery Hopwood's farce Fair and Warmer. *For the second time within twelve months Q closed its doors in conditions of despair.*

Within a matter of weeks a fire bomb plunged through the stage roof of the Embassy, putting it out of action for the next five years.

CHAPTER FOUR - RISING ABOVE IT

For a few days Beatie and I worked at Q in an effort to clear up the muddle. The few remaining members of our staff went their several ways. My three London productions, Leslie Julian Jones' revue **Come Out of Your Shell,** *the Avery Hopwood farce* **High Temperature** *and* **Outward Bound** *were simultaneously withdrawn amid sad farewells. London was in the front line, and London's theatres were plunged into gloom. For the first time in Q's history telephones and electricity supply were disconnected. There was nothing to be done; nothing to do. I offered through ENSA to provide entertainment for the forces. The answer: as soon as my services could be of use I would be called upon.*

Inactivity being anathema to Jack he settled down to adapt *The Silent Witness* into a novel. Then 'Biff' Killick suggested chancing a revival of *High Temperature* at the Comedy Theatre. It was a time to take chances and Jack leapt at it.

In a sense it was heroic fun. I recruited a sporting company at £5 a week, plus shares of profits all round. There was no audience and no profits, but I had returned to the terrible game and was soon hankering to re-open Q. There was pathos in its closed doors and in its dusty, cold and darkened auditorium. An empty derelict theatre is indeed a place fit only for ghosts to haunt.

Hope presented itself in the shape of the actor Sebastian Shaw who had a Kenneth Horne play he wanted to do. Leslie Julian Jones also let Jack know he was working on a revue to follow *Come Out of Your Shell.*

It was no easy matter in those days to make decisions - in fact it never has been for me. Maybe that is why my decisions have always been made impulsively and without thought of consequences.

Having once made the decision I inveigled my wife back to Q and once again we set to work under the most uncertain and primitive conditions, to prepare for re-opening. Beatie concentrated on collecting together a few enthusiasts including young Michael Northen who, with Mrs Maynard back in the club room again, removed the cobwebs and washed away the dust and the dirt. Miraculously a brilliant cast, at a loose end, agreed to brave the bombing and the possibility of empty houses to get the theatre going once again. With a depleted and scratch staff we somehow managed to surmount every obstacle, working for the first rehearsal week in a freezing theatre, by candlelight and without telephones.

Q re-opened on its seventeenth anniversary with *A Lass and a Lackey* with performances daily at 2.30 pm and Saturdays at 2 pm and 4.10 pm. The next production, the revue, was to be a major milestone in the story of Q.

Henry Kendall had first worked at the theatre in the original try-out of the ill-starred *The Czarina.* He cursed his ill luck at the time that, due to a contractual obligation, he was unable to transfer with the play to the Lyric, but found cause to review his initial reaction. Twelve and a half years would elapse before he returned to Q, this time to direct as well as star in Cyril Campion's *This Money Business* in December 1937. This was the first of several engagements at the theatre.

"I must say a word about Jack de Leon," he wrote in his memoirs, "for he was one of the most remarkable men I have ever met. Dark, extremely handsome, with great charm of manner and an ice-clear brain, he had a marvellous theatre sense. He could analyse, and would sometimes take to pieces, an author's play and put it together again in a couple of hours. I have known him do this on the day of the dress-rehearsal to the discomfiture of the (director), the cast - and the author. But Jack was nearly always right. He knew *exactly* what was wrong with a play, but as pressure of work always kept him away from the early rehearsals this skill was often exercised very late, and finally we did manage to break him of his habit and persuaded him to sit in on a rehearsal a week before the opening - which gave the wretched author ample time in which to re-write his play!"

Jack hoped to interest him in appearing in the revue *Rise Above It*. "For me the most interesting and exciting thing about this show was the opportunity to work with Hermione Baddeley for the first time. Believe me, it was quite an experience! 'Totie' Baddeley (was) a great comedienne, and utterly unpredictable; one never knew what she would say or do next. In *Rise Above It* she would spontaneously introduce new bits of business, and time and again I was obliged to stand with my back to the audience shaking with laughter, hoping for some cue from her to get back to the script.

"There was one sketch in which I played a Chelsea artist and she was the model. It was timed to run six minutes, but by the end of the first week the laughs and Totie's improvisations had extended it to sixteen! She was a genius with props. In this same sketch she performed a dreadful strip-tease, unrolling herself out of a revolting black velvet gown to reveal an equally horrible Edwardian-type corset and a pair of grey flannel drawers. All the time she kept up a running commentary about her various lovers. 'But he's a mere boy,' I had to say to her at one point. Back came her reply, spoken with an awful leer, 'There's nothing *mere* about a boy!'"

Also in the cast were Edward Cooper, Carole Lynne, Virginia Winter (Leslie Julian Jones' wife), Georgina Cookson, Frith Banbury, Peter Cotes, and a twenty year old actress with an elfin prettiness and a surprisingly sensuous voice, Joan Greenwood. Completing the cast was Wilfrid Hyde-White. Under his original stage name of simply Hyde White, he had first appeared at Q in *Virginia's Husband*, June 28th 1926, when the reporter from the Richmond & Twickenham Times noted that he gave "a very clever study of a silly ass."

Wilfrid Hyde-White was such a bad actor. He was one of Herby de Leon's clients. We used him several times but usually when we couldn't get anyone else. But then he went into *Rise Above It* and played himself. He was such a silly fool and he got away with it. And he's been playing himself ever since.

The scripting of *Rise Above It* was the responsibility of Alan Melville, for many years the creator of the wittiest situations and scripts both in revue and eventually in television. His career began in the BBC variety department and he was in the Royal Air Force by this time, taking what leave he could to watch his material being rehearsed.

For one week the brilliant group of players romped through the twenty five items in the programme to comparatively empty houses. But we all knew that here was a revue in embryo which at the propitious moment would find its West End stage. Hedley Briggs, who undertook the initial direction, was insignificant in appearance, effeminate in manner and neurotic in behaviour. He worked in brilliant flashes, always with taste and cynical wit. Leslie Julian Jones' lyrics had life and topicality; occasionally vulgar innuendoes were exaggerated by Totie Baddeley to the vast amusement of everyone but myself and the Lord Chamberlain.

After the Q week we weeded out the dud items, and Leslie set to work to fill the gaps. Within two or three weeks I had arranged a few provincial dates. During this second series of rehearsals Hedley Briggs lost interest and eventually disappeared. Leslie and I took over the final rehearsals and I staged the show at the Arts Theatre, Cambridge, on February 25th 1941. One week at the Royal Court, Liverpool, followed and, finally, a week at the Opera House, Manchester. Playing an intimate entertainment of this kind in the vast Opera House was difficult and senseless, but to arrive on the night of Manchester's first and most violent air-raid was disaster. But we all still believed in the show's future.

"All the company used to go back to London for weekends when they could," recalled Hermione Baddeley in her autobiography. "Edward Cooper, our leading man, loved to plop into a large leather armchair at his favourite little club. Unfortunately, one weekend he had too many relaxing drinks and fell down the stairs at this club and injured himself quite badly. He had to withdraw from the show and in fact never really recovered.

"The loss of our leading man ... was a great blow - *Rise Above It* was so obviously going to be a hit when it came to London. That weekend I went up to London and arranged to call on Jack de Leon to talk about a replacement. There had been a terrible air-raid the night before and I was picking my way through the broken glass and debris that littered Charing Cross Road when I was hailed by someone walking towards me. It was a BBC producer friend of mine called Brian Michie. With him he had a lady he introduced as Miss Gingold and the two of them suggested I join them for a drink.

"We found a nearby pub, settled ourselves at a table and of course all started to talk about ourselves." Eventually she remembered she had seen Hermione Gingold before, in a show called *The Gate Revue*. Sir Alfred Beit had taken Douglas Byng, the celebrated entertainer and female impersonator, and Miss Baddeley to see it. Apparently Sir Alfred had thought Gingold had been copying

Baddeley's act. "It was true this lady wore the same kind of crazy make-up that I did and used a similar tone of voice. But in other ways she was the exact opposite to me. In fact, Douglas Byng nudged me and whispered: 'I think it's me she's trying to be like.'

"And now this lady and I sat together with Brian Michie at a pub table. I asked her what she was doing and she pulled a face (she had a most unusual face). She too was doing a revue that had run into problems. I told her about *Rise Above It* and we sipped our drinks reflectively. So, Miss Gingold's revue was going to have starred Walter Crisham. I'd worked with Wally and he was a lovely dancer; and there was this lady who was undoubtedly very funny. It might work, I thought to myself. The idea floated round in the air and then we started to talk about the possibility of all joining up ... I telephoned Jack de Leon and he came over and joined us; negotiations went ahead at once."

"Of all forms of theatrical entertainment," continued Henry Kendall, "revue is the most bitchy. The material is bitchy, the artists are bitchy, and strangely enough, the average revue audience is bitchy. And here was I starring with two acknowledged 'Queens of Revue' and faced also with the task of (director). It was a situation calling for every possible ounce of tact and diplomacy, although to begin with the two Hermiones got on like the proverbial house on fire.

"Then came the vexed question of 'billing' - who should take precedence, Baddeley or Gingold - or should I say Gingold or Baddeley? It was the responsibility of the management to make the decision, and a very difficult one it was, calling for one of Jack de Leon's characteristic pieces of theatrical judgment. His solution was quite simple: we had two sets of bills and placards, one set with Baddeley first, and the other with Gingold, and these were used on alternate weeks throughout the run, which satisfied both ladies.

"(Directing) this slightly explosive mixture of artists was no easy task, but somehow I managed it, and after a preliminary week at Brighton we opened in town ... Only one glorious bust-up had enlivened the proceedings, when after the matinee at Brighton one of my leading ladies called the other 'a bloody amateur', but in the main the inevitable bickerings were kept under control, and I'm quite sure they went unsuspected by the audience."

The two Hermiones had never before appeared in the same show and the atmosphere was electrically charged with serpent smiles. Hero de Rance had taken over the leadership of a joyful trio of two pianos and drums, struggling like a Hero all through rehearsals until one of the two Hermiones, angered by an accidental change of tempo, would throw her props across the floodlights as cue for the Hero's tears and for my intervention to soothe the rising tempers.

I shall never forget the hours spent with slips of paper, each containing the name of an item and the artists involved. On the floor in the little office at the Comedy, Leslie and I would manipulate these slips to find a practical and at the same time a 'theatrical' running order. The successful sequence would invariably be proved unsuccessful by one of the Hermiones. "No time for the change between five and seven" or "Hermione B has four appearances in seven items, while Hermione G has only three." Back to manoeuvres on the floor upstairs, or the game is transferred to Kew Road; but next morning Totie decides she'd rather have a serious monologue to replace item ten, and the substituted slip makes all previous running orders abortive.

At last the first night is on us. It is the most exciting theatrical event since the outbreak of war. Once again I hear and rejoice in laughter and cheers. Next morning the press notices hail **Rise Above It** *as the best intimate revue produced on the London stage for years. James Agate compares it with his favourite of all time,* **Buzz Buzz.**

Henry Kendall had one particular song in the show which caused consternation in the Lord Chamberlain's office. On the typescript page it had seemed perfectly innocuous when it was presented with the licence application. "I'm afraid there must have been something about the way I put it over," added Kendall. "As they recorded of Marie Lloyd, 'It wasn't what she said, but the way she said it!' The song was called 'It's Lovely Anywhere' and I dressed myself up as an elderly aunt at her niece's wedding, and I sang this entirely innocent little lyric: 'It's lovely in the morning, just as soon as you awake,/And round about eleven o'clock, it makes a pleasant break;/They say too much is bad for you, but that is a mistake,/It's lovely anywhere ...etc.' The pay-off was that 'it' was a cup of tea, but I'm afraid someone must have tipped-off the Lord Chamberlain's office that Henry Kendall was doing an outrageous song at the Comedy, because when a representative came along he found the audience (mostly servicemen on leave) rolling about in their seats almost as if I were singing about something quite different ... and the order came for that number to be deleted."

In fact a representative from the Lord Chamberlain's office appeared at the theatre every week to keep an eye on Hermione Baddeley. Several risqué lines had been deemed unfit for West End audiences. On occasion these lines would creep back. Jack wrote numerous placating letters to the effect that Miss Baddeley was such a sensitive artiste and that sometimes she forgot her lines and reverted to the ones she used originally. Of course, the truth was that the lines were outrageously funny and she couldn't resist putting them back in.

It wasn't only the Lord Chamberlain who had to keep an eye on Miss Baddeley. "Hermione Baddeley and I weren't overly fond of each other," recalled Hermione Gingold in her memoirs. "I found her very unprofessional: she'd alter lines and business without warning, which made it impossible to play a sketch to get the maximum effect and balance. She'd upstage, tread on laughs, and insert unfunny gags designed to amuse the cast more than the audience. Often in the middle of a sketch, she'd hiss under her breath, 'What's my next line?' Well, I had enough trouble remembering my own lines; why should I remember hers, too? ... Considering (we) only appeared in three shows together, it's strange our names have so often been linked. I suppose it's because there is a great similarity in our Christian names. I've never understood it, but I have been told the clash of our personalities on stage created some sort of special magic. Nothing more than sheer hatred spilling across the footlights."

Gingold's favourite sketch involved she and Baddeley as two elderly dowagers trying on a succession of even more ridiculous hats while they gossiped together. "If this war goes on much longer, we shall all be living on grass," went the dialogue. "But I don't like grass," said the other. "It will grow on you," came the reply.

"I had a divine song," continued Miss Gingold, "called 'I like a little ballet with my lunch' - about a culture vulture who would rather forego her three-course lunch to spend her one and sixpence on feeding her spirit with poetry in motion. Her plea was:

Just a piece of cake that's seedy,
and a faun that's après midi .....

"A rat who appeared at one matinee created quite a scene. He or she came up from the bowels of the orchestra pit, walked around the orchestra pit rail, looked at the show for a few minutes, and then made a slow exit. Meanwhile ... Hero de Rance turned out to be no hero - for glancing up from her piano, she found herself eye to eye with the rat, gave a piercing scream, and tried to climb out of the orchestra pit. She got one leg over the rail but her remaining leg wouldn't follow, whereupon she fainted clean away. The audience thought it was all part of the show and the box office told me that people rang up and before buying tickets, asked whether the rat would be appearing."

Jack and I went almost every night to hear the laughter. In the war people needed to laugh. It was so successful that servicemen on leave often went again and again. After six months a second edition was produced with new material. Several of my brothers put money in it and they were well rewarded. Earlier, when we had presented *High Temperature* at the Duke of York's, we had a huge laughter thermometer installed outside. We sometimes used to go and look at it, as it registered the roars of the audience. The police asked us to remove it because crowds were causing congestion on the pavement!

We lived beneath volcanic skies, but such is the optimism among theatre folk that we gave no thought to the danger of irruption and Rise Above It ran its successful course. The receipts soared with the introduction of the second edition and a third and fourth might well have followed but the Hermiones, much to Leslie's and my annoyance, committed themselves to appear in Sky High for Tom Arnold and only realized their disloyalty when it was too late. Rise Above It was not only a successful revue, but its title represented the state of mind of a great majority of sorely harassed Londoners, and its ever changing service population on leave.

The last performance on April 12th 1942 was not only to me, but to most of the audience, a somewhat sad occasion. We had gathered to bid farewell to a rare source of gaiety and laughter.
Hero de Rance was still charming audiences with her entr'acte playing well into the seventies, and is remembered for the way she would smile at the audience as she played, acknowledging both stranger and friend in the auditorium. Playwright Norman Ginsbury had less happy recollections of an actress who would similarly greet her acquaintances as she made her first entrance in the title role of his play *Viceroy Sarah*. Recreating this role the actress in question, Dame Irene Vanbrugh, appeared in a revival of the play at Q on April 12th 1941. Also in the cast was Barbara Lott who scored a great success as Ronnie Corbett's formidable mother in the television comedy series *Sorry*.
"I remember sitting in the club room at Q before a matinee," she recalled, "all of us so anxious that everyone was safe after a really bad air-raid the night before. I also remember a production of *The Guardsman* with Avice Landon and asking her why I was not getting a laugh on a certain line. She said, 'You can't see what Ada Reeve is doing with the roses behind you.' Happy days! I adored playing at the Q, the productions were so good and all done in a week!"
"I remember Q as being a very glamorous theatre," recalled Maxine Audley, also a Q player during the war years. "I had played in a barn in Maidenhead; at least Q had a stage-door! In S.N. Behrman's *No Time For Comedy* and Lillian Hellman's *The Little Foxes* I played the black maid! In those days there weren't any black actresses. I didn't mind blacking up. At that stage in my career I would have played *anything*."
A young actor just beginning to make his mark in films brought Jack a new play in the summer of 1941, offering to direct and play in it if it could be tried out at Q. This would not be his Q debut. He had appeared in *The Man Who Has Nothing* in May 1937. James Mason had had everything for one member of the de Leon clan. *Jean, aged thirteen and a half, fell in love with James, but James, dark, attractive and determined, had other plans. Jean may once have sat on his knee as a reward for her daily vigil in the theatre on her way back from St Paul's, but Pamela Kellino sat beside him and guided him, then as after, through the years to Hollywood and film stardom; surrounded him with an aura of cats and fabulous pronouncements. In 1937 he knew where he was going and what he wanted.*
In 1941 he got what he wanted when Jack presented A. J. Cronin's *Jupiter Laughs* first at Q and then at the New Theatre on October 29th 1941. Sadly it did not catch fire. To try to save it Mason himself paid for several display advertisements in the London evening papers but to no avail. Two years later he appeared in the film *The Man In Grey*, giving some of the earliest indications that he would become Britain's most accomplished film actor.

One day Ronald Kerr asked me to see a boy whom he had directed in *Ah Wilderness* at the Intimate Theatre. His name was Richard Attenborough. He made his debut at Q in Aimee Stuart's *London W1*. Dickie was keen and exceptionally talented. Also in the cast, and making her Q debut, was an actress who had been at RADA with him, Sheila Sim. Later they were married and sent us a piece of wedding cake.

"Apart from Shaftesbury Avenue," recalled Sir Richard, "to act at the Q really meant that your career was serious. The de Leons loved theatre as much as any couple we have ever known, and they were immensely kind to both of us. The Q and Beatie and Jack meant a tremendous amount in our lives. There were theatres dotted amongst the big cities and on the peripheries of London (fringe was a word unknown) - but there was only one Q."

The Q passed through these years of uncertainty and the perpetual menace of fire and explosive without even a broken pane of glass. The by then ramshackle, council-condemned building stood up miraculously to the periodic blasts around Kew Bridge. The rising Thames caused more damage than the falling TNT. At the worst period of bombing after a short closure - audiences were sparse and heroic, sitting through air-raid warnings, spontaneously ducking for protection as a bomb whizzed down. We and the audience survived without even a fainting casualty.

In those days James Agate came occasionally to matinees. If the first act bored him beyond endurance he would sit in the club room waiting for his car, drinking and talking. One of these occasions (I had just finished reading his Ego 5) I accused him of deception in calling his 'Diaries of Doings and Theatre Gossip' autobiographies. This conversation was the most self-revealing I ever had with Jimmie.

"You want to know why, well I'll tell you, then you'll shut up and give me a large whisky." He told me in words I can't remember, but by the end he was red in the nose and wet with perspiration. "No sex, because I can't expose my weaknesses to the world. No religion, for I know nothing of God. No philosophy, eternity or death, because I won't think of death ... I sweat in terror when I think of death. Annihilation of Me is unthinkable. Me without my body is unthinkable ... You can get me a large whisky." I did and never again did I mention religion or death to Jimmie.

Early in 1942 he heard Alexis Kligerman playing in the foyer at Q. "Is that alive, or out of a tin?" he asked. "That's Alexis. Come and listen." We sat in the corridor out of sight of the piano. Alexis was, I believe, playing a Chopin study. After a few minutes Jimmie whispered, "I'd like to meet him" I introduced them. Shortly after Alexis left Q. Jimmie Agate had taken him under his wing, though later he would return.

On one occasion Agate arrived just as the curtain was about to fall on the first act. He saw the second and was so excited about the play I offered to persuade the cast to re-perform the first act for his special benefit at the end of the show. The cast did not need any persuading and Agate and I sat in solitary state as they re-played Act One as they had never played it before. The play was **Dark Potential.**
After the first night I knew that Sonia Dresdel, already acclaimed for her performance as Hedda Gabler at the Mercury should, and could, be a star of the first magnitude. The play was transferred to the Comedy Theatre on the strength of Agate's prophecy of success. He advised: "Change the title and rely on Sonia. Call it **This Was A Woman.***" We did. This was the beginning of a long, bewildering, exhausting association with an adorable actress whose greatness was too frequently put to the test in mediocre plays. For my share of responsibility for this I stand convicted.*

"It was 1943 when I was invalided out of the Navy," recalled Sir Ronald Millar. "I had been sea-sick from the start. 'So was Nelson,' they said. Quite. But he had Lady Hamilton. Penniless but stagestruck and with a mother who was a fine actress 'with connections', I made my way out to the Q Theatre with an introduction to Jack and Beatie de Leon. Young men in civvies were scarce in wartime and before you could say, 'Overture and Beginners' I found myself playing leads in plays old and new.

"Sometimes Beatie would ring up on a Tuesday and say, 'Can you do Danny in *Night Must Fall* for me?' The part is huge. 'When?' 'Monday, dear. We've got the Prompt Copy.'" The Prompt Copy is that copy of the script which had been presided over by the stage-manager in the original production and in which all the actors' moves had been recorded. In many cases it was the only copy of the play as presented in existence.

"'We've got the Prompt Copy' was a Beatie special. There's a story - almost certainly apocryphal - that she once rang a certain actor and enquired, 'Can you do Hamlet for me next week? We've got the Prompt Copy.'

"Beatie was indomitable. She treated me like a son and I loved her dearly. Salaries were modest and the canteen wasn't Claridges but somehow, despite wartime rationing, food materialised. Every now and then Beatie would say, 'Come to lunch Sunday, dear. Got a lovely bit of lamb.' Where and how she got the coupons for the lovely bit of lamb one didn't enquire, but it was a godsend.

"As was the Q itself. I must have played in and directed dozens of plays there, learning the rudiments of professional theatre as I went along. One production in particular I remember vividly - *Love In A Mist* by Kenneth Horne in which the charlady was played by an unknown comedienne called Irene Handl. She convulsed the audience nightly and, at one memorable matinee, the cast as well, which of course was disgraceful and brought the performance to a temporary halt. I stepped forward and said, 'I'm sorry ladies and gentlemen but it's impossible to act with Miss Handl.' The audience roared its approval, and one more star was born at Q.

"When I wasn't acting or directing I had begun to write a play. I mentioned it casually to Jack one day. He asked to read it, suggested a few amendments and said, 'Right, we'll do it.' I was over the moon. He and Beatie got together a fine cast - Eric Portman, Hartley Power, Sheila Sim and a host of fine character actors. The Sunday after we had opened I was thunderstuck to read a long article in the Sunday Times by James Agate praising the piece. *Zero Hour* transferred to the West End and changed my life. It might never have seen the light of day but for the de Leons and their readiness to take a risk."

"I ASM'd *Zero Hour*," recalled Richard Pasco. "I also had a tiny scene at the beginning of the second act as a young soldier on guard at the house where the action took place. I had to say to Sheila Sim through the window. 'Everything alright, Miss, all OK and hunky-dory!?' To this day Ronnie Millar knows who it is when his phone rings and a voice says, 'Everything hunky-dory, Ronnie?'

"My father had paid the premium and I joined the theatre as a student apprentice stage-manager under the gentle guidance of Maggie and Jill (Margaret Dunlop and Jill Bullough) also Elizabeth Agombar the expert scenic-designer and Jack the master-carpenter. How did they turn out those incredible sets - some spectacles like *Anna Karenina* - in a week in wartime London?

"I remember the smells of the little theatre - the coffee brewing in May's bar (May de Looper - a mother figure to us ASMs), Ernest A Mitchell's cigar (the avuncular treasurer who gave me my thirty shillings a week salary in the front-of-house office, a pound of which I gave to my mother, managing myself on ten shillings for fares and food and *savings!*) Then the eternal smell of size on the gas-ring in Jack's outside workshop and Elizabeth's paints and, of course, grease-paint in the six little box dressing rooms.

"There was a pompous male stage-manager who worked us into the ground and when I asked if I could go and get ready for my walk-on part, his retort was, 'Of course you can't get made-up when there's work to do on the set.' We were made to get our priorities right!

"There was a club performance on Sunday evenings, so with the 'get-out' and 'get-in' on Monday mornings we often worked a seven day week, and I don't remember asking for or wanting time off. Stripping the set on Sunday nights and getting in the props and furniture from the Old Times Furnishing Company van on Monday mornings was a very hard-working and exciting time; heavy furniture had to be carted from the front of the theatre, across the vestibule and into the auditorium and over the front of the stage. And then the lighting! Jack de Leon taught me the basics of stage lighting and was a kind, though strict, guide into many sides of the theatre.

Sarah Churchill frequently played at Q. Here she is with MichaelGodfrey in
House on the Sand

Jack welcomes her parents, Sir Winston and Lady Churchill, to Q

Elizabeth Agombar's
designs often drew so
much applause that the
action of the play was
held up for several
minutes. This is her
set for *Caesar's Wife*
from June 1948

Jack de Leon - impresario

Two more Q beginners. Dirk Bogarde and Joan Collins, early in their careers (B.F.I. stills)

Two West End successes. (Top) Jack hosts the party celebrating Allyn McLerie's take over of the starring role in *To Dorothy A Son*. (Left to right) Richard Attenborough, Miss McLerie, Shelia Sim and Roger McDougall, author of the play. (Bottom) Jessie Royce-Landis, Leslie Henson and Betty Paul in *And So To Bed*

"We would often rehearse on the stage of the Comedy Theatre or in the spacious bar of the Saville Theatre. I collected boxes of wigs from Nathanwigs and made my way back to Q heavily laden. The air-raids were on from time to time and journeys were sometimes hazardous, especially returning home at night.

"I remember triumphantly making my first professional appearance in *She Stoops To Conquer* as Diggory, carrying a lighted candelabra and my period wig very firmly stuck on back-to-front! The fringe across my eyebrows was a sight to behold and the company 'corpsed' uncontrollably.

"I was always keen to keep MY STAGE clean and well swept and the coffee and tea-cups and glasses well washed and presentable at all times. Brenda Bruce, a very young ingenue in 1943, calls me 'Pot Boy' to this day!

"I remain eternally grateful for that start - to my father who made it financially possible; to Beatie and Jack for taking me on and to the dozens of good people who worked with me, for me and on me to mould and shape and turn me eventually into an actor with an appreciation and knowledge of the technical support all actors need."

Zero Hour opened at the Lyric Theatre on June 14th 1944. During the summers of 1943 and 1944 Jack extended his activities to the Savoy Theatre, Kettering, where he presented plays on a weekly basis. Originally he probably wanted to use the theatre for the transfer of Q productions as in the Embassy days but only a handful of plays transferred there. The majority were produced specifically at the Savoy by Q directors using actors who had often worked for Jack and Beatie.

Among the many leading actors to play at Q during the war years were Jessie Matthews, Yvonne Mitchell, Margaretta Scott, Kenneth Connor, Robert Beatty, Sidney Tafler, Joy Shelton, Lydia Sherwood, Renée Asherson, David Tomlinson, Patrick MacNee, Jack Watling, Helen Cherry, Ursula Howells, Patrick Cargill, Margaret Johnstone, Moira Lister and June Whitfield.

On June 6th 1944, a British force landed in Normandy. On June 13th the first V1 fell from the skies to shatter the black silence of London. The effect on Q and the West End theatres generally was instantaneous and devastating. The already sparse audiences evaporated.

Simultaneously with this sudden and violent change in conditions and outlook I began suffering extreme pains which at certain moments daily became almost unbearable. In an attempt to avoid an operation I subjected myself to a series of twice-weekly injections; but my condition became worse. I was left with no alternative but to undergo an operation. I entered University College Hospital five minutes before a V1 exploded within a few yards of the private wing and only two days after the withdrawal of Zero Hour *on the first Saturday night of its ill-fated run.*

Apart from *Rise Above It* and *Thy Name is Woman*, there had been another successful transfer of a Q original, a taut four-character psychological thriller by

J. Lee Thompson originally entitled *To Fit The Crime*. Agate once again offered an alternative title. As *Murder Without Crime* it had a substantial run at the Comedy Theatre. (Thompson would eventually work as a director in films, his most notable of which was *The Guns of Navarone*.) Another thriller was presented at Q a week after *Zero Hour*'s West End opening. Originally it had been entitled *Playing With Fire*.

This play which I had only read and not seen was to prove my most profitable West End production since my advent into the theatre and would remain so until the early fifties. During my absence, Beatie had miraculously succeeded in keeping Q open with a series of small cast, one set revivals. A group of friendly players stood by her and constituted the nearest approach to a professional repertory company ever to be retained by us at Q.

The playwright Edward Percy had re-titled *Playing With Fire* as *The Shop in Sly Street*. Then a solicitor's letter turned up on behalf of a gentleman who kept a shop in Sly Street in London's East End. With its final identity, *The Shop at Sly Corner*, the play opened at the St Martin's under Henry Kendall's direction to poor notices and a lukewarm public reaction. V.E. Day on May 8th 1945 re-awakened the public to pursuits of pleasure and business picked up. The play would run for two years. "Keneth Kent (had) the part of his life as an old antique dealer who is also a 'fence'," recalled Kendall. "In addition ... a fine cast included that wonderful old-timer Ada Reeve, who gave an outrageous but very funny performance as Mrs Catt, the daily help ('my feet are swoll' was her catchword); John Carol, brilliant as the black-mailing shop assistant who gets strangled for his pains; Cathleen Nesbitt, Victoria Hopper, and an unknown young actor playing the detective - Derek Guyler." John Witty, who was also in the cast, remembered performing during the bombing. "In typical British fashion, we carried on acting while the explosions flourished around us - with one exception, Keneth Kent. Whenever he heard a bomb he dived under the table, which made it very difficult for the rest of the cast who had to bend down to floor level to continue the dialogue!"

Henry Kendall was also to direct a farce at Q which had previously tried out at the Peterborough Rep under the title *Moon Madness*. Three years after he had offered his services to ENSA, Jack was invited to organise entertainment for the troops in this country. He chose to stage Philip King's new farce. At the end of the tour of camps the play was presented as the 1944 Christmas attraction at Q. As *See How They Run* it opened on January 4th 1945 replacing *This Was a Woman* at the Comedy Theatre where it would run for eighteen months. With George Gee, Beryl Mason, John Deverell and Ronald Simpson, was Joan Hickson as the maid, and an actress, new to comedy, who had been acting at Q since 1942.

"I recall the Q Theatre with affection and gratitude," volunteered Joan Sanderson. "I played in a great many productions there including one called *We Are the People* which afterwards toured for a while. It was this play which led to my being cast in *See How They Run*. I had just returned from North Africa and Italy where I had been touring with ENSA and expected to be out of work for some time. But Jack remembered me from *We Are The People* and before long I found myself in my first West End play. Looking back I realize that that was the start of my career in comedy which I have grown to love more and more. I feel great gratitude to Jack de Leon for that."

The lights of London were ablaze again. Q's box-office receipts were continuously maintained at a level sufficient with other sources of revenue to cover the considerably increased running costs. Three successful West End productions, **The Shop at Sly Corner** *and* **The Sacred Flame**, *playing matinees, both at the* **St Martin's Theatre** *and* **See How They Run** *at the Comedy, were providing considerable profits. Yet I was obsessed with a sense of futility and a restless urge to motivate my continuance in the theatre with a moral justification which more than ever seemed lacking.*

CHAPTER FIVE - THE LIGHT OF SETTING SUNS

"I WAS NOT VERY BRIGHT at school," commented Jean. "I was of average intelligence. Nevertheless, I think St Paul's was a good school - apart from the awful smell of the brewery when there was a West wind blowing! It was purgatory for me to have to do sports, however my parents were told that I must undertake all exercise and all sports so, as you can imagine, I was not popular with my contemporaries who were forced to have me in their teams.

"Although I gained my School Certificate I didn't do well enough to get into University. Besides we were a very close family and I don't think I would have wanted to have left home with war starting.

"One day a week I travelled to Stepney. St Paul's School had a welfare centre there in Duckett Street. Each school year had a Stepney representative and in my final year it fell to me. I continued my Stepney visits throughout the bombing. My main job was distributing orange juice and cod liver oil.

"Soon after war broke out I worked in a local school assisting the teacher with a class of about forty children. In those days they were taking children from the age of three to free mothers for war-work. After about a term the teacher had to have a major operation and, aged seventeen, I was left with forty children in my charge, many of whom couldn't even tie their own shoelaces!

"I was there for about a year, right through the Dunkirk period. Then I was called up. I was a committed pacifist. I think it was a bit showily heroic of me to take a stand as, because of my leg, I could probably have got an exemption, but I wanted to go before the tribunal and claim classification as a conscientious objector. I was naturally filled with trepidation when the day came. As I recall there were three or four on the bench. One of them looked up, an elderly lady in a wide-brimmed hat. I said to my mother, 'My God, it's Miss Strudwick.' The head of St Paul's School was naturally patriotism personified. We were both horrified to see her. I realized how important it was to have someone to speak for me and Mother immediately telephoned my father at his office. I suspect most people think my father would put the theatre before everything but it was his family that came first. He dropped everything and came with all haste. Daddy was above conscription age but I have always felt that were he to have been placed in the same position he would have taken the same steps. When he arrived he found me less anxious than I might have been as Mother had overheard Miss Strudwick say to the chairman, 'She was one of my girls; she is a good girl.'

"I told the tribunal I was prepared to do community work. A great friend of mine who worked for Peace News had become a fire-fighter. I wish to stress that pacifists are not cowards - it took great courage to go into the fire-service. Because I had taken a course in shorthand and typing I was ordered to take a job in a hospital and became a very junior junior at the Royal Hospital, Richmond. I remember for ten minutes every morning we had to function with our gas-masks on, answering the telephones and handling enquiries and so on!

"On Saturday mornings and some evenings I helped out at Q in the box-office. This was something I thoroughly enjoyed - answering the telephone, booking tickets and, when there was an extra large set to build, helping out with a paint brush! Eventually the box-office manager, Alan Barker, was called up and I was allowed to leave the hospital to take over the management of the box-office.

"All my spare time - oh, please don't think I didn't find time for boy friends, I certainly did - but most of my spare time was spent in singing lessons. From an early age I used to sing about the house, selections from *The Desert Song* and so forth. Granny Lewisohn was always fond of music - we all were - and suggested I ought to be trained as a singer. I auditioned at the London College of Music in Kensington but chose not to go there full time. Eventually I was sent to Elena Gerhardt, the celebrated lieder singer, in Hampstead. My voice was not sufficiently strong for opera but I enjoyed a short success singing several informal concerts in London including the Chenil Gallery, hospitals, clubs, forces' clubs and the Castle Hotel Richmond.

"What other time I had, one evening a week, was spent at the local University Extension in Richmond where I studied, among other subjects, International Affairs. Partly, perhaps, as a result of this I became a member of Federal Union."

"Federal Union's aims were "to secure support in Great Britain and elsewhere for a Federation of Free Peoples under a common government elected by and responsible for their common affairs, with national self-government for national affairs," also "to ensure that any federation so formed shall be regarded as the first step towards ultimate world government ... to secure peace, economic security for all, and the civil rights of the individual."

"I suspect it's because I am Jewish that the phrase 'le monde c'est mon pays' means so much, because one is a citizen of the world, rather than of one particular country," suggests Jean. "I helped run the International Forces Rendezvous which met once a fortnight at the old Cadena Cafe in Richmond. It was there I met people like Manny Shinwell and Richard Acland, the founder of Common Wealth. Many politicians came down completely free of charge to talk.

"Cousin Anthony says that my father was interested in Federal Union because he was a pantheist. It is true that he was a pantheist, but it was also because he was a great humanist and believed in harmonising the peoples of the world. He was an idealist and that was what made his life so hard. My father thought a little like Walt Whitman whom he greatly admired. In 'Song of Myself' Whitman wrote:

Do I contradict myself?
Very well then, I contradict myself.
(I am large, I contain multitudes.)
And that was true of my father, he contained multitudes. He was a cosmic person. Of course, at times, he was concerned with the vicissitudes and trivia and anxieties of everyday life which were particularly wearing because he was a particularly sensitive person. He had a very keen intellect, but he was also very emotional; many's the time I've seen him weep, seen his lip tremble. He had never lost his sense of wonder. He loved little children, loved exchanging stories with them. I think because he was so very much aware of how harmonious and wonderful life could be, he was particularly distressed by the conflicts and animosities and the trivial back-biting of everyday life.

"He wrote in my childhood autograph book, *Be good, sweet maid, and let who can be clever. Do noble deeds not dream then all day long.* The doing of the good deed and the sense of humanity that is there in Walt Whitman were what I would say were central to his character. Blake influenced him a great deal in his suggestion that everything that exists is holy. My father was not a Christian in that he believed in the literal resurrection, but he was a Christian in believing in the spirit within one. I know Wordsworth perhaps isn't a pantheist but if you read 'Tintern Abbey'

And I have felt
A presence that disturbs me with the joy
Of elevated thoughts; a sense sublime
Of something far more deeply interfused,
Whose dwelling is the light of setting suns,
And the round ocean and the living air
And the blue sky, and in the mind of man;
A motion and a spirit that impels
All thinking things, all objects of all thought,
And rolls through all things.

and Shelley talks of 'all things one within the universal sun' These ideas of the god innate are also pantheistic. I think it was no accident that one of the first books I remember Daddy giving me was of the teachings of Spinoza. 'Christ In You', which was one of the last books he studied, stressed the value of silence and listening to the still small voice. From Eliot's 'Four Quartets' that line: 'At the still point of the turning world.' That was one of the qualities, at times, that my father had. When he looked at the rose, loving the flower, I think he was in touch with the still point of the turning world or what Yeats described, 'The universe is in the blade of grass.' If you have the mystic vision which Daddy may not have developed but which he certainly had, you get beyond duality as in Blake's 'Tyger, Tyger': 'Did He who made the Lamb make thee?' Daddy believed there was something beyond duality, that that was simply a way of human speaking. If we didn't have a word for 'day' we wouldn't have a word for 'night', yet get far enough above the earth's surface and you can see day and night at the same time. That is there with Blake and it is there in Goethe. In *Faust* he says that God allows the Devil because the Devil is doing necessary work, and all action is the choice of a greater or a lesser evil. Mephistopheles says, 'I am a part of that force which forever wills evil and forever produces good.'"

"Jack was a man of engaging enthusiasms," commented Anthony Lewison, "but one at a time. He would love to express the all-consuming idea with which he was presently occupied and, each weekend, I would look forward to hearing his latest development of it. After completing his play about Francis Thompson, he widened his horizon and incessantly groped for spiritual understanding. He tried to distinguish its path and thought he could see it being carried from one great prophet to another, each adding to its intensity. So he scanned book after book, extracting what he saw as the essence of each man of genius. The Book of Isaiah, Plato, the Gospels were all probed in turn and at the end of about a year he had also squeezed extracts from Marcus Aurelius, Leonardo, Luther and Spinoza. It was a delicate operation to find a convincing connection between these great thinkers, but he struggled with the self-imposed task, spreading his thoughts over many exercise books. Gradually his interest in this process waned and he moved on to a study of pantheism.

"As his mentor he started with Spinoza. He worked avidly at his philosophical writings and did his best to explain them to me. He was a great teacher. Alongside Spinoza he concentrated on the poems of Shelley. He spent much time with me describing the inter-connection and inter-dependence of everything. Shelley led him to Donne and then on to Blake. He took and gave much delight in reading their poems to his listeners on a Sunday afternoon, as he rested his long length on a floor cushion.

"During the dark nights of the war he began to imagine writing a mythical account of the creation of the cosmos and its whole evolution. Jack was never daunted by the immensity of a task and disregarded the almost certainty of failure. Although he became deeply depressed by failure in the outside world, I never saw him disturbed from giving up one of these literary endeavours. He simply moved on to the next enthusiasm.

"An example of his attempt at the impossible was his struggle with Goethe's *Faust*. This he considered one of the greatest works and, since it was written in dramatic form, he found it an irresistible temptation to try and stage it. He realized it was no play and that it dealt with concepts far beyond the practicality of production. Nevertheless, undaunted and unopposed he doctored it, concentrated it from its inordinate length, and, probably for the first time in the English theatre, squeezed its essence into theatrical form. He even directed it himself, filling the little stage at Q to overflowing. It was indeed a *tour de force*. But even Jack stopped at the end of Part One!"

"I remember the day," continued Jean, "when Daddy, working on his *Faust*, came up with the following passage: 'Sublime Spirit! You gave me everything for which I longed. It was not in vain that you appeared to me in the flame. You gave me glorious Nature for my kingdom; and the power to perceive and enjoy my kingdom. You have allowed me to gaze deeply into her heart; (and not merely with cold superficial glances.) You have brought the full range of living things before me, and taught me to know my brothers in the silent woods, in the air and in the water. And when the storm rages and the hillside thunders with great pines uprooted and bearing down their neighbours then - oh, sublime Spirit of the Earth, you lead me to the safety of some cave and there reveal me to myself. And the deep secret wonders of my being are laid bare. (Then the clear moon rises from the walls of rock and the moist bushes, hazy images of the past rise and float around me. They temper the stern delight of contemplation. Now I know that man can never attain perfection.)' That summed up Daddy's view of nature. Of course, it was Goethe's view but the fact that my father worked for more than a year on it shows how much he felt an affinity with this view."

Jack's production of his own adaptation of *Faust* opened at Q on April 30th, 1948. Joseph O'Conor, who was cast in the title role recalled, "My memories are clear in some areas, dim in others. I remember Jack directing, very well, his hand gestures moving always forward as if to grasp the ungraspable, his directions always subtle, always courteous, never dictatorial. He moved with an air of Byzantine glamour, made palpable by a most exotic after-shave or whatever, the recipe for which I imagined must have been dug up in Petra and made up by some arcane perfumier of Jack's acquaintance."

"Joseph O'Conor," wrote Barry Morse, "is a lovely, lovely actor with a great sort of personal nobility which equipped him to play Faust. Whether by the same token you could say I had a sort of personal malevolence which equipped me to play Mephistopheles I don't know, but Jack felt, and I did too, that the whole spirit of Mephistopheles, both philosophically and theatrically, would best be delivered by a sort of baffled, comedic fury, that despite all his resources and all of his ingenuities, he is constantly being defeated. I remember one of the things I did was to play him with a limp as though, somehow or other, his cloven hoof was bothering him a bit."

"I remember standing with Barry Morse," continued O'Conor, "on a mere two feet deep rostrum while twenty six students flailed besom brooms around on Walpurgisnacht. (The brooms were cut after the first night) There were two hundred and forty five lighting cues, on two lighting boards, all operated by a red-haired girl in thick glasses, past whom we had to push to make a debonair entrance! Hard work, but enjoyable, even at the time."

"I have a great deal of pride in having been involved in that production," concluded Barry Morse. "I think Jack realized from the outset that it was not likely to find its way into the usual commercial theatre. One has to remember that at this time there was no major subsidised theatre like the National or the RSC. There was nowhere for this kind of work to go. That made it an even more courageous venture, his attempt to produce something of such quality knowing it could not be anything but a commercial failure. In the context of the theatre in England at that time it should be seen as a very very worthwhile and extremely courageous undertaking."

"It had seemed quite out of character to many," continued Anthony, "that one of Jack's favourite forms of relaxation was to be found at race meetings! There was all the mystic side, his intellect. Set against that his love of gambling, his passion for the horses and the dogs!"

"Everybody wears many masks! You should have seen Daddy on holiday. He was a lovely holiday person, very untidy and tousled. Right into my thirties my parents took me on holiday with them. Even if money was scarce it was all somehow found for holidays."

'We'd take the money from the box-office and go abroad!'

"Holidays were central to our family life," added Jean. "He was just as much true to himself on holiday as he was in the theatre, for he could enjoy nature and art. That was just as much the real Daddy as was Jack de Leon the impresario."

We flew away for holidays abroad for the first time in 1945. I remember we flew KLM. When I told the assistant in the travel bureau we were nervous, he said gently, "First, tighten your stays, rest a while in a comfy chair and then smoke a cigarette." I took his advice, and continued to do so for several years. The flight to Zurich over snow-capped mountains, above silver clouds, was like a trip through heaven. When we arrived in that clean sunny city and ate *omelettes surprises* **to round off a square meal such as we had not enjoyed for five long years, it seemed another world.**

We spent some of our happiest hours in Italy. In Milan, late at night, with our friend Pierre Rouve we walked in the well-lit warm arcades and drank coffee at midnight and in the morning admired the doors of the great cathedral and went round the city in a *carroze.* **Nevertheless I also recall the barefoot urchins begging in the streets.**

We stayed in Florence at the Grand Hotel on the Arno. It is a world of beauty, the very heart of the renaissance. The Arno runs gently and even the voices of the people are soft.

A memory of Rome is of a friendly elderly Jew taking us in his car to one of the seven hills to a quiet monastery in the early evening, and *lazing* **as we saw the lights of Rome start to shimmer in the clear air. In that clear air at night we heard** *Aïda.* **We had spaghetti somewhere. Nearby an elderly gentleman nearly exploded trying not to laugh at our attempts to deal with it. We made friends. The editor of an Argentine newspaper, he visited us in our hotel in**

Florence later with masses of flowers for Jean, and took her out.

Assisi was peaceful and lovely and the Giotto paintings in the Franciscan church and the monastery where the gentle saint lived I still remember. It is best to visit this city of steps before your legs are old.

In Montreux, from the balcony of our Hotel du Lac, I saw the most sublime sunset I have ever known. More than forty years later I still remember that glorious evening. I remember Jack, sitting alone on our balcony, with his back to me. I went out. I thought, I must look at this until it fades, I must be still and never, never forget. Jean was there too and joined with us in silent adoration. Money spent on a holiday is never wasted for these memories are our true riches. Only what we have within can we take with us always.

ON SEEING BRUNELLESCHI'S CRUCIFIX AGAIN

With what agony of tears and love did you, oh
Brunelleschi,
Create from wood this still immortal Man of pain?
Did you know that now 'neath darkening sky,
Alone I'd sit and watch the sunset glow
Illuminate that face sublime? And did you know
That I would watch the shadows cross the downstretched
form,
And see his face alone, alight, alive, with trembling
eyes
And trembling lips that yearn to whisper words
Revealing all that Man need hear and know?
And did you know that I would sit and gaze,
And gaze until through mist the wondrous form
Would sway and live and breathe and breathe?
Intent my ears, intent my eyes, my heart,
Until I hear the whispered words, "For You".

On August 30th 1946 Jack and Beatie celebrated their Silver Wedding anniversary. It was a busy year but we booked a suite of rooms at the Imperial Hotel, Torquay, and with Jean went off for a few days break. We weren't making a big fuss about the occasion but in the morning Jack gave me a special gold pen which he knew I wanted. With it was a slip of paper on which he had written, "To the most complete and dearest wife in the world, with my love ..."

CHAPTER SIX - RED LETTER DAYS

IN THE SUMMER of 1945 a shy young man walked into Jack's office and asked to be allowed to direct a play at Q. His entire experience consisted of one previous production.

I cannot now say why his enthusiasm and ideas impressed me. Maybe he came at a time when I was most receptive to atmosphere, and his sensitivity registered. Within a few minutes we arranged that he should direct a revival of Rudolf Besier's The Barretts of Wimpole Street. *The promise of his future success was apparent in this, Peter Brook's first and only Q production. His subsequent rise to prominence in the English theatre was swifter than even he could have expected. The Barretts opened on July 3rd, 1945. Within two years Peter Brook had made his impact on press and public and mysteriously entered the realms of operatic production at Covent Garden.*

As had already been noted, Brook, who would become the most exciting and innovative director of his generation, has claimed as one of the earliest and most inspiring of his childhood experiences of theatre the production at Q of *The Merchant of Venice* in which Victor Lewisohn portrayed Shylock. "My memory of working with you at Q," he wrote to Beatie, "is a warm and pleasant one, everything went so well." In the canon of his work Besier's slight but charming piece is scarcely among his more prominent credits. However, for those hungry to learn, Q offered opportunity to those who needed a stage and actors to exercise their craft. In December 1954 when the Christmas confection of *The House In The Wood, Being The Adventures of Goldilocks and The Three Bears and The Big Bad Wolf,* written especially for Julia Lockwood by Jack in collaboration with Felicity Douglas, (featuring, as has been noted, the future Academy Award winning film director John Schlesinger as the senior of the three bears) was playing matinees, the evening alternative was a production of Emlyn Williams' ghost play *A Murder Has Been Arranged* directed by Tony Richardson. Some months later William Gaskill would direct a new play, *The Hawthorne Tree* by Margaret Gibbs.

In those days of austerity immediately after the war Jack and Beatie relied heavily on a solid core of directors. The most frequently employed was the actor Geoffrey Wardwell.

He was a delightful, gentle person, an attractive forty-five who could play down to thirty and up to infinity. He was a great favourite of old mother Maynard in the canteen and was a Q matinee idol. He had his own dressing-room - number six - and once, when he was out of London, our little dressing-rooms were repainted. I thought this would be a lovely surprise but he was horrified. He said he liked every inch of the old paint.

I only knew him once lose his temper. The company adored him and so they promptly went to his dressing-room where he had dramatically retired. They opened the door and found him reading The Times upside down!

Nevertheless in the post-war years Q's roster of directors would include the likes of: Dennis Arundell, Desmond Davis, Basil Dearden and his brother Peter Dearing, Graham Evans, Leslie French, Wyndham Goldie, Hubert Gregg, Frank Hauser, Charles Hawtrey, Irene Hentschel, Warren Jenkins, Stephen Joseph, Joan Kemp-Welch, Jack Minster, Robert Morley, Laurence Naismith, Ellen Pollock, Pierre Rouve, Wendy Toye and Herbert Wise among many others.

For some directors and some actors, Q offered the possibility of a short stop fill-in during lean career patches. It was not a major aspiration of any actor to spend two weeks rehearsing and playing at Q, but an engagement there paid the rent and there was always the possibility that an engagement in a *new* play might lead to several months work in the West End. For some actors Q would prove a very lucky place.

In 1946 Laurence Olivier produced Garson Kanin's *Born Yesterday* at the Garrick Theatre. It was the play which had made a star of Judy Holliday on Broadway and it would do the same for Yolande Donlan in London. A young actor was interviewed for the juvenile lead. Olivier asked him if he could speak with an American accent.

"I'd dreaded that question," he recalled, "hoping that the part could be portrayed as an Englishman, so I shook my head. 'But you've been to America?' he said. I muttered something fatuous about having also been to Scotland, but I still couldn't speak Gaelic. 'That's not quite the same thing, boy.' Desperately as I needed the job, I could never abide phoney accents, and, rather self-consciously, quoted the Bard: 'To thine own self be true ...' Laurence smiled quizzically, saying, 'Well, I appreciate your not wasting my time. I shall remember you.' Regarding this as another version of the usual fob-off, 'Don't call us, we'll call you,' I went out into the cold Charing Cross Road feeling deflated. Several months were to pass before I found out how wrong I'd been in this assumption."

Anthony Bushell, Olivier's right-hand man, who had been present at the interview, takes up the story in the book 'The Film Hamlet' in which he was describing the casting of that film "... Osric, that sinister Beau Brummel of the Danish Court, fell pat into place. Casting our stage production of *Born Yesterday*, in the autumn of 1946, Laurence and I had seen a clutch of young actors for the juvenile lead, among them a striking looking character, Peter Cushing, who stuck in our minds by a frank refusal even to attempt an American accent. Weeks later, watching another actor at the Q, I was struck by a performance of the Frenchman in *While the Sun Shines*, so true in style and accent that I looked for a French name on the programme. It was Mr Cushing, and he speaks no French. Here evidently was an actor, and his test for 'Osric' disposed of the last of our problems on the male side ..."

Rattigan's play was the eighth of nine appearances by Peter Cushing at Q, but it was sufficient to change the course of his career. His appearance in the Academy Award winning Best Film of the Year 1948 was followed by many others under Laurence Olivier's banner, including the celebrated Australian tour by the Old Vic in 1948 and subsequent seasons at the New and St James's theatres. "So you can imagine," concluded Mr Cushing, "how grateful I was to have been in 'the right place at the right time', and why there will always be a warm place in my heart for the dear old Q."

Such is the theatre that a firm refusal to use a phoney accent could help advance the career of one actor, the deployment of one could lead to the same result. Donald Sinden recalled, "I worked at Q in six productions between August 1951 and October 1952. In those days I was paid £10 for playing one week and nothing for rehearsal which worked out at £5 per week. If I could do two consecutive plays, I could get £20 for three weeks work thus averaging £6.13s.4d. per week! After the first week of my second engagement at Q, Beatie asked me to stay on 'for the play after next'. Down would go the average. 'Is there nothing in next week's play?' 'Only a very small part of an Italian in *Two Dozen Red Roses* - I can only pay £6.' 'I'll do it!' (It was better than nothing.) I 'invented' an accent and a make-up and got the required laughs.

"Months later I was sent to see Jack de Leon for a part in his West End production of *Red Letter Day*. 'What a pity,' he said. 'We cast the juvenile this morning - so sorry.' I was just leaving the office when he called me back. 'Just a minute, didn't you play an Italian at Q for Beatie?' 'Yes,' I replied. 'Well, there's a Brazilian in this play, will you do it?' I used the same accent and the same make-up.

"*Red Letter Day*, in its all too short run, was seen by film director Charles Frend who asked me to do a test for his next film ... If I had not played an Italian for £6 at Q, I could never have landed the leading part in *The Cruel Sea*, and a subsequent seven year contract. Thank you Beatie..."

Q had seen one or two of its own red letter days. The projected Christmas production for December 1947 was an adaptation of *Alice Through The Looking Glass*. The casting of the title role was something of a problem until that old stalwart, Nancy Price, who was set to direct the piece happened to see a lovely young girl with waist-length Titian coloured hair gazing into a shop window. It transpired that she was an actress. Thus it was that Adrienne Corri embarked on her career. She was such a success in the role that her photograph appeared in various newspapers. This brought to the attention of Principal Kenneth Barnes that Miss Corri, still a student at RADA, was working without permission and almost cost her her place at the Academy.

Clement Attlee was a friend of Nancy Price and he came down to a matinee. He joined us for tea in the office and Mrs Maynard made some of her fresh little buns. He sat in the yellow-upholstered comfy chair and suddenly Treacle, the

theatre cat, leapt on to his lap and settled there. Mr Attlee obviously loved cats and would not let us remove the intruder. He had enjoyed the play and was kind and courteous to us all. Treacle, incidentally, was quite at home on the stage, and sometimes appeared at the wrong time - once during a very dramatic scene in *Henry IV, Part One*, much to the chagrin of the leading actor.

In April 1949, when Sarah Churchill was playing in *The House on the Sand* at Q, we had a phone call from the House of Commons to say Winston Churchill and his wife were coming to the matinee. The message was that he was on his way and he had not had a meal. We dashed next door to the Star and Garter where the food was good and asked the friendly manager quickly to prepare something to eat. He provided large trays and starched white napkins with a buffet including fresh salmon, salad and rolls and a bottle of whisky and syphon, and this was brought into our office.

Churchill was so charming and so courteous when he arrived. He took my hand as though he were going to kiss it, but shook it instead. There was an almost ethereal quality about him, quite different from what I had expected. He sat at Jack's desk opposite mine and Jack sat by our lovely corner stove in the art-deco chair. Jean remembers Churchill after the performance kissing his wife goodbye at the pass-door. She was going back-stage and he was returning to the House of Commons. Although I was not of Churchill's political party, meeting him was a highlight in my life. Oh, and by the way, he didn't touch any of the food, but the bottle was nearly emptied ...

The seat at Jack's desk was virtually permanently vacant at this time. There had been a period when many of Q's successes had transferred to the Comedy Theatre. Jack was allocated an office there which he maintained until the theatre changed hands. After an interim office he took what his secretary Margaret Shepherd refers to as 'that poky little office in New Row.' The first 'Jack de Leon production' as such was Aldous Huxley's *The Gioconda Smile*, adapted by the author from his own short story. It was the first post war production which was not a Q transfer and had a distinguished cast including Clive Brook, Pamela Brown, Mary Merrall and Brenda Bruce.

Although Jack considered Huxley one of the most articulate and talented writers, he was not above doctoring his play. When he first received the script he decided he wanted several alterations. Huxley was, at the time, at his home in the mountains of California, some distance from a telephone. It was arranged for Huxley to be at a telephone at a given time and the two talked for half an hour at a cost of about one pound per minute. Secretaries at both ends took down the entire conversation. Less than a week later the revised script arrived by airmail.

Aldous Huxley was a gentle person with deep blue eyes and a soft voice. Jean recalls squashing into a car beside him on the first night of the play. His eyesight was poor and she told him about the London we were passing through.

We dined at the Savoy. Huxley said to me, "Sit here," indicating the chair beside him. I was very shy but he was such a kindly persons he soon put me at my ease.

Some Jack de Leon productions were successes, others failed. Jack could pick losers as well as anybody else. Even Florence Roberts was not infallible. She advised Jack to turn down *Seagulls Over Sorrento* which was ultimately a major West End hit.

"What I remember most about Q is the warmth with which the de Leons treated a spotty-faced, junior reporter from a suburban bi-weekly who had pretensions of grandeur," writes Jim Biddulph, now running his own news service from Hong Kong. "Jack was very kind and asked me to assess those mountains of scripts he used to get. Self-importantly, I would bustle back, having rejected a couple and recommending the rest as the stuff of which theatre was made, or something. One of the rejects I remember. I said it was totally unstageable (with the wisdom of a, whatever it was, twenty four year old?) and an insult to the intelligence. Jack grabbed that, said, 'Sounds interesting'. and put on *Down Came a Blackbird* at the Savoy!"

"There was a clause in the contract for plays done at Q," commented Margaret Shepherd, "that if a play was taken up by another management and transferred to the West End within a reasonable time after the try-out, then Q would receive one per cent of the box-office receipts. *Reluctant Heroes* which had been tried out at Q under the original title of *Those Were The Days* in April 1947, was put on in the West End three months after the expiry of this option. One per cent of that would have been delicious."

A few hours at Q each week sufficed to deal with my correspondence. An occasional appearance at a rehearsal and Mondays spent on lighting and in critical appraisal of dress rehearsals kept me in sufficiently close touch with my wife's virtual control of Q's destiny. Beatie's determination and sense of humour, her unfailing sense of the ridiculous more than anything were what kept Q going.

"The only deviations from this routine," added Margaret Shepherd, "were when there was nothing much happening in the West End and he would get into mischief and put something on at Q himself. The most notable of these occasions were *The Picture of Dorian Gray*, a very interesting production with Barry Morse, and *Faust*, of course. He was extremely creative and needed the occasional time of mischief at Q.

"Originally I had worked for Beatie as much as for Jack, but then Monty arrived and became Beatie's right-hand man. Jack and Beatie - you could say they were as mean as hell, but they were doing it *entirely* for the *theatre*, never for themselves. They weren't making money on the backs of other people. And people would work their guts out for them. Jack was much easier to work for. Often we would get angry with Beatie because we thought she was being unreasonable, but she was just single-minded. Forty years later, Beatie just had to make a telephone call and people leapt to attention."

Monty (Bruce Montgomery) had lived at Ealing and visited Q several times before the war. After the war he had been working in a clock factory when he saw a job at Q advertised in the local paper. He was originally engaged as the book-keeper and to answer the telephone. Each week he would read The Stage newspaper and had a good memory as to where and in what actors were working. Beatie found this knowledge useful and gradually he became involved with helping with the casting. "Beatie would get in touch with the agents of the stars," he recalled. "I would deal with the lesser ones. 'We can only offer you four pounds...' I would ring up and say. "Working for Beatie ... She was the kind of person you'd gladly murder one minute, then she'd turn round and smile at you and you'd say, 'Maybe she's not so bad ...' But she could be the most irritating person alive! I would storm out of the office in a flaming temper, then she would say or do something stupid. How can you be annoyed with anyone like that? She had a very good brain and when she wanted to she could charm the birds out of the trees, especially bank managers. She had a unique talent for charming *them*!"

Another loyal, steadfast member of the staff at Q, like Monty and Margaret Shepherd still a friend decades later, arrived at Q as a premium student on the stage-management course in January 1949. "To begin with you worked for nothing and after you'd been there three months you were paid £3 a week," recalled Euphan Scott. "Several of the premium students at that time were there just for fun, blowing their demobilisation grants - although £150 was quite a lot of money in those days. There were about six of us on stage-management and a very good stage director, Jill, was in charge, so we didn't have to work as hard as we would have done in rep. We weren't on every show. It *was* fun - I don't know when I've laughed so much.

"Jack was up in town most of the time. The Gioconda Smile was then running in the West End. He would turn up at Q for the first night every Tuesday, but it was Beatie who really ran the theatre. She was strict and her standards were high. We kept a time book in which we conscientiously noted anything that went wrong during the show. The book was left outside her office every night and if there were too many lapses, she wanted to know why.

"First rehearsals were usually at the Steam Packet pub. On Wednesday we would move on to the stage, rehearsing in the set of the play running that week. Monday was the day for our set-up. After unloading the furniture from the pantechnicon, we would dress the set with curtains, pictures and carpets and then the stage would be lit ready for the dress rehearsal to begin at about six o'clock. This would usually end by midnight so that the actors could get their last buses home. Often the electrician would stay after the rehearsal to re-light and to struggle with the notorious 'shadows on the cyc'.

"After finishing my stage management course, I became more interested in lighting and eventually took over the 'electrics'. I remember one production vividly. Hugh Cruttwell was directing - he later became Principal of RADA - and we worked through the night on the lighting. There comes a point where you've done all you *can* do and really it's better just to give up, go home and wait for new inspiration in the morning. Hugh kept saying we must re-set a certain 'flood', which was on the floor lighting the 'cyc'. I shifted it here and shifted it there. We shifted it so much that one of the leads inside must have rubbed bare. Hugh picked it up and got a terrible shock, 1000 watts worth, and couldn't get his hands off it. When he did, he sank into a chair. I was appalled - a dead director on my hands at two o'clock in the morning! Thankfully, he revived and I managed to get a taxi to take him home."

"It was terrifying," Hugh Cruttwell recalled. "My whole body shuddered violently before I could let go of the thing. When I told Beatie about it the next morning she replied in her usual delightfully chirpy fashion, with that bewitching smile: 'Oh well, darling, these things happen don't they? Never mind, it can't have done you any harm, you've got a lovely healthy complexion - I've never seen you looking better.'"

"Among the actors I remember during my time at Q," continued Euphan, "was the American film actor, Douglass Montgomery, who played in *The Devil's Disciple*. He amazed us by arriving with his own secretary and valet and they all packed into the dressing-room which was about the size of two armchairs. But he was very amiable and sent each of the crew a first night telegram.

"There were acting students too; their premium was £50 and they played all the small parts. We were inclined to laugh at them and say how hopeless they were. One of them was Brewster Mason. Another was Joss Ackland; we thought he was a terrible actor!"

"Rehearsals at Q," recalled that terrible actor, "were made more complicated by the management cutting down the expenses by giving us cue scripts, so that instead of having the entire play, you only had your own individual lines and the few words that preceded them. The actors had to sit in rehearsal with their eyes glued to their script until someone came up with their cue. This would lead to complications and it was very near the end of a week's run of an Agatha Christie play that a sweet old actress came up to me and said, 'Sorry to trouble you, dear, but do tell me - who killed me?'

"It was after *Appointment With Death* that I swore never to play in an Agatha Christie again. One of my lines had been, 'No, no, a thousand times, no', and another, 'She is dead, but she won't lie down!' The first night was fraught with disaster. Ferdy Mayne dropped his walking stick at the beginning of the first act and out fell a bottle of poison - far too early. Molly Urquhart who was the murder victim had to be discovered on a rock half way through the second act apparently asleep but, in fact, dead. However, as she had finished all her dialogue by the end of Act One she completely forgot she had to sit conspicuously on stage throughout Act Two. Halfway through the act she walked on stage, sat down in her chair and, with a sigh, slumped down grotesquely into *rigor mortis*."

Christopher Morahan, later to distinguish himself in television, planned to get married to his fiancée Joan at the end of the post London tour of Jack's production of *Angels In Love*. Christopher was company-manager, also playing Little Lord Fauntleroy to Barbara Kelly's Dearest. Joan was stage-manager. However, Beatie arranged for an extra week at Q at the end of the tour. "What about our honeymoon?" asked Christopher and Joan. "You can have it at Q," was her reply. So they married on a Saturday, 'got in' at Q on Sunday, and opened on Monday. "I was very impressed when, on coming to see Beatie for the first time," recalled Sarah Lawson, "I expressed a deep desire to play the pregnant daughter in *Black Chiffon*. 'Alright dear,' she said there and then. 'Here's the script. You start on Monday.' I thought, is it always going to be as easy as this? During rehearsals I asked if the management could provide me with the where-withal to buy a maternity smock as in those days actors had to provide all modern clothes themselves. The answer was, 'No. But we will go halves and you can keep it. It will come in useful later on.'"

"Q was a marvellous place to work," commented Terence Alexander. "One earned more in rep but at Q you got the chance of working with really good people. When I played there in *The Cocktail Party* I was acting with half the West End cast." Mr Alexander was introduced to Q by Peter Dearing who had directed him in the West End. His first Q play was Vernon Sylvaine's *The Anonymous Lover* in which his co-star was the delectable Kay Kendall. "She killed all her laughs by talking through them. Nowadays she is remembered for her comedy but she had previously done only films, no theatre work and didn't understand that she had to pause to allow her laughs. After a couple of performances she asked 'What am I doing wrong?' I organised an extra rehearsal and pointed out all the places she should pause. Afterwards she played the part with great success. She was very sweet and good-natured about the whole thing."

Ellen Pollock first worked at Q in 1937 and had directed and acted there many times. "Jack asked me to direct a new play," she recalled. "After the first rehearsal I rushed into his office in a great state. 'Jack! I can't possibly use the girl you've given me to play the juvenile. She can't project and seems very awkward. *Please* give me someone better or the play is doomed!' How wrong can you be? The girl was Claire Bloom. Some years later Robert Henderson was engaged to direct a new play, *A Witch In Time*, in which I was to play the lead. He introduced me to an unknown dark chap who he had discovered in the north of Scotland. 'I'm sure you'll find him very suited to the part. He'll be playing opposite you, but, of course, *you* will have star-billing!' I remember I had to represent a painting that he falls in love with and for the first twenty minutes I had to sit perfectly still (in a mauve light) in a huge gilt frame! So we didn't really have a great romantic scene. But he was a nice unassuming lad. Oh! didn't I mention his name? It was Sean Connery!"

"I was doing one of the three or four plays I did at Q, being directed by Robert Henderson," Connery recalled. "I was lying on the floor in the darkened dressing-room with the usual nerves of a first-night actor, when Beatie threw open the door to wish me good luck - to discover the light was out. I was running my lines, and she said 'How considerate of you to save the light.' Nothing could have been further from my mind."

Another potential superstar and James Bond appeared at Q shortly before Connery. "I remember Q with great affection," recalled Roger Moore. "I appeared in *The Governess* and *Off The Record*. My opening line in *The Governess* was, 'Hello, mother! What's going forward here?' and forty years later I still don't understand it!"

Making her professional stage debut on March 25th 1951 was one of the latest products of the Rank Charm School. Indeed, after a screen-test in which she was partnered by the aforementioned Terence Alexander, she had made a couple of successful film appearances in *Judgment Deferred* and *I Believe In You*. By this time she was involved in a tempestuous relationship with actor Maxwell Reed who had been her childhood fantasy hero. However as Joan Collins' career was in the ascendant, Reed's was plummeting meteorically. They decided they wanted to act together on stage and agreed to appear in Muriel and Sydney Box's *The Seventh Veil* at Q. This was the stage version of the film in which Ann Todd had played a talented pianist and James Mason a sadistically cruel piano teacher. "(Max) played it so authentically," recalled Miss Collins in her autobiography, "that in one of the scenes where he is terrorizing me, he threw me across the stage with such violence and ferocity that I was black and blue for three days. The sadomasochism obviously appealed because we immediately started rehearsing yet another similar story: A 'young frightened girl, intimidated but mesmerised by an attractive, sadistic older man' - absolutely the basis of *our* relationship. This one was called *Jassy*, freely adapted from the film of the same name with Margaret Lockwood." She was excited to be acting in the theatre and was only frustrated that Q plays ran for one week only. She and Reed were back in November in Thornton Wilder's *The Skin of Our Teeth*. She was cast as Sabina, the Vivien Leigh role, and Reed was the sixty year old Mr Antrobus. "Although it was a small intimate theatre it nevertheless put on excellent productions," Miss Collins continued, "and it was considered a coup to play there ... The reviews for *The Skin of Our Teeth* were excellent and I enjoyed it more than any film I had made so far." (A tantalising possibility presents itself with a glance at the programme. Listed among the smaller part players is one Jacqueline Collins. Could it be Joan's sister putting in a stint on stage before sharpening her claws and becoming the best-selling novelist she is today? "Sorry!" apologises Jackie Collins, "It was not me. I was still at school when my sister did *The Skin of Our Teeth*, although I can vaguely remember being taken to see it by my proud parents.") Joan Collins would play twice more at Q - as a young Byzantine empress who, after making love to her men, sends them away to be executed, thus giving rise to the title, *The Praying Mantis*, which Jack sent on a deservedly short tour, and finally in the Dorothy Maguire role in *Claudia*.

A local theatre-goer, Joan Chapple, recalls that she was so taken by Joan Collins' performance in *Jassy* that she named one of her dogs 'J.C.' thus preempting the day many years later when the actress would have a late success in the film *The Bitch*.

But Q also brought cherished and well-loved performers to its audiences. Appearing with Joan Collins, as Claudia's charismatic mother, was Bessie Love. The American actress had made her screen debut at the age of seventeen in D. W. Griffith's epic motion picture *Intolerance*, later appearing in the first sound film to win an Academy Award for best picture, the MGM musical *Broadway Melody*. She appeared several times at Q, most notably perhaps as the tragic wife, Lola, in William Inge's modern classic, *Come Back Little Sheba*.

Twenty years and one month to the day after her RADA contemporary Aminta de Leon had played the title role in Shaw's *Saint Joan* at Q Rachel Kempson was to be seen there in the same part.

She had heard it rumoured that we were to do the play. She came into the office and said, "If you're casting, consider me as Joan." She was excellent. During rehearsals one day. She heard that we needed a young page and recommended her son for the part. Thus Corin Redgrave was added to the list of those actors who made their professional debuts at Q.

A new play came to us which had a leading role in it I thought would be perfect for Flora Robson. She was a really big star and had not long returned from America where she had repeated her West End success in *Black Chiffon*. I knew she was between plays and so I decided to take a chance. I sent the script round to her in a taxi. A message came back to say that she would prefer not to do the play, but she would be happy to appear in a revival of the play she had always regarded as her greatest West End hit, *Autumn* by Margaret Kennedy. We were delighted and agreed to it. She was a real trouper and mucked in with everyone in the most friendly way. We all loved her at Q.

Jack was having his own West End hits. He had decided to transfer Graham Fraser's *The Prodigal Father* which had tried out at Q on March 21 1950, but with a different title, *The Dish Ran Away* ... The play did not run away with rave reviews, rather the contrary. The cast prepared for the play's withdrawal by the end of the week. However, Jack had a brainwave and sent out invitations to six hundred Members of Parliament to see the show. Two hundred and fifty of them turned up! Each was given a card and asked to state whether he agreed with the critics' assessments.

Ninety-eight per cent of them disagreed, and the newspapers were obliged to print the result. The play then ran for nine months.

Two of his greatest hits were not Q try-outs. The first was a play, the second a revival. The revival was of the 1926 comedy *And So To Bed*. Based on the play by J. B. Fagan, with music by Vivian Ellis, it was a charming free adaptation of the diaries of Samuel Pepys. Leslie Henson starred with Betty Paul and the sophisticated American actress Jessie Royce Landis in support. This was the first presentation of the work as a whole as Jack included scenes omitted from the original production which had proved impossible to stage. At the New Theatre, and subsequently at the Strand, the show would notch up almost three hundred and fifty performances.

The enchanting costume designs for *And So To Bed* were by Elizabeth Agombar who had been with us at Q as our scenic designer throughout the forties. Her sets were so magical that, when the curtain rose, the action was often held up by tumultuous applause. Our sets which were built in our own scene docks had to be first class because they had to be able to transfer to a West End theatre within a matter of days. Elizabeth became a designer for BBC television and remained with them for twenty years.

Wendy Toye directed *And So To Bed* and it was conducted by Mantovani, who was a real charmer. It was in this production that the Australian actor Keith Michell made his West End debut. We are reminded of that lovely show every day as we still have in our hallway the wine-coloured velvet-covered chest in which Pepys was concealed, and peeped out from, in Act Two.

A friend of playwright Roger MacDougall had taken his new farce to Herby de Leon. Herby is reported to have said, "I didn't think it was my brother's cup of tea. He's far too highbrow." However, he recognised his brother's talent in spotting work of worth and his ability to coax from an unpromising piece an eventual success. Four hours after he received the script, Jack had decided to put it on himself. The play dealt with an expectant father, an impecunious young composer, who, whilst waiting at his second wife's bedside for the happy arrival, is embarrassed by the unexpected arrival of his first wife. Jack decided to give the part of the twice married man to Richard Attenborough. Everyone thought he was crazy to do so as Attenborough was best known for his villainous roles in films, such as the vicious young spiv in *Brighton Rock*. But Dickie had played at Q, unnoticed by the general public, in comedy and Jack remembered this other side of his talent. He cast the wacky star of *Born Yesterday*, American comedienne Yolande Donlan as the first wife. The second wife scarcely appeared in the play. Only her arms could be seen as the bed faced away from the audience and the actress was forced to talk upstage. This feat was performed by Attenborough's real-life wife, Sheila Sim. "*To Dorothy, A Son* was a unique theatrical experience," recalls Sir Richard Attenborough. "We opened on tour and, commercially, proved to be the most enormous success So much so, that by the tour's completion we were already in profit. However, all three of us felt that the play was not worthy of the West End, and we closed on tour, much to Jack and Beatie's disappointment. Later - and I am talking about 1950, Stanley French was in danger of losing his Savoy lease by virtue of the failure of two productions in succession. He had seen *To Dorothy, A Son* on tour, and begged us to reconsider our decision and open at his theatre."

By this time Roger MacDougall had done a deal of rewriting. "We rehearsed at night," continued Sir Richard, "as I was by then playing in a film. Elizabeth Agombar's set was rebuilt, the second act was in large measure rewritten, and we opened with hardly any publicity and certainly without the panoply of a West End premiere.

"The curtain went up and the first two or three lines, which had received a reasonably warm reception on tour, were greeted with laughs worthy of the Crazy Gang. The evening built to what can only be described as a roaring tumultuous reception as the final curtain fell.

"Then the three of us took our call, Sheila emerging from behind the bedhead with twins in her arms. Stanley French's lease was saved, and Jack and Beatie had a smash on their hands. We ran for fifteen months."

During its run the play transferred from the Savoy to the Garrick, and eventually Allyn McLerie took over the role of the first wife. Forty years later Miss McLerie found new celebrity as the mother in the above-average American television series, *The Days and Nights of Molly Dodd*. While the play was still running Jack decided to stage the play at Q for the 1951 Christmas presentation, a quite unprecedented event. Derek Bond, Barbara Murray and Pat Sandys made up the Q cast.

"Christmas at Q was chaos," recalled Monty. "The Christmas show would open on Christmas Eve and there would be a party for cast, staff and friends. Beatie and Jean would go up to Fortnums by car round about closing time." "Funnel, our chauffeur would drive us," continues Jean.

Fortnums said, "We close at one. At 12.30 you can have what you want at half price." In those days you could park in Jermyn Street so it was all fun. We loaded up with goodies, iced gateaux and decorations left over at half price. Sometimes they gave us their Christmas trees. Once I was presented with some lovely moss roses. Laden with trees and pies and iced puddings we dashed back to Q.

"It was always a great joke about Beatie and Jean rushing up to Fortnums and getting everything at half price, or even *quarter* price," chips in Margaret Shepherd. "They would arrive back from Fortnums absolutely laden," continues Monty, not a little thrown by the interruptions. "At about three we would get out the ladders. Jean and Beatie would arrive and we'd say, 'They've bought out the store,'" (Jean is mouthing the words as he says them.) "Then everyone was involved in blowing up balloons. The dress rehearsal was going on in the auditorium while all this was taking place." "There was a Christmas tree in the inner foyer where the pianos were," Jean is impatient to say. "Everything was very artistically done. The electrician would deal with the lights ..." "... complaining bitterly because he was trying to light the dress rehearsal," interposes Monty, "and by about six o'clock we would have it finished."

"Mean as we all know they could be" adds Margaret, "they were very generous at Christmas. We used to have lovely Christmas parties."

Everyone knew it was an open invitation. Actors arriving back from their performances all over the country would make Q their first stop. I had something in an envelope for all the staff. They were lovely happy days.

Enjoy it while you may. There are other days around the corner.

CHAPTER SEVEN - THE END BEGINS

DURING THE LATE FORTIES Jack's main preoccupation was Entertainment Tax and its inequities. "He battled for years to have it abolished," recalled Margaret Shepherd. "In this he had to distance himself from Q, as he might have been accused of having a foot in both camps. Binkie Beaumont got away with it with his Tennent Productions and H. M. Tennent Ltd. - he didn't even change the name. One paid Entertainment Tax and the other didn't. Beaumont was the biggest ripper-off of Customs and Excise ever."

Binkie Beaumont is a clever man, a brilliant organiser and perhaps the greatest opportunist in the modern theatre. He commercialised his partly-educational activities by enrolling on a profit-sharing basis, almost the entire galaxy of available star names. He glamourised Wilde, Shaw, Congreve and others in Motley and Cecil Beaton splendour and to a great extent saved the theatre from extinction during the war and early post-war years. He satisfied the financial and artistic aspirations of his ever increasing stable of stars, and by so doing surrounded himself with an aura and earned their loyalty which alone has made possible the perpetuation of his empire. He captured Rattigan and Fry and taking Hastings in his stride conquered America and France. All this by exploiting to the zenith the privilege of Entertainment Tax exemption. Multiply the tiny Q's tax payments by twenty and you have a conservative approximation of the financial advantage accruing to the Tennent tax free ventures during the seven years 1940 to 1946. Half a million pounds is an appreciable sum. Yet it was only the means of the acquisition of the many other advantages which in a dozen years transformed the theatrical industry into a semi-monopoly.

Five theatres had been bombed out of existence and between four and six remaining straight play houses were more or less permanently occupied by one or other of the Tennent companies.

The stars encircling the Tennent sun were, and still remain in the main, unwilling to gravitate to the lesser lights of the West End system and casting difficulties grew and continue to grow to almost insurmountable proportions. What purpose could the Q as a try-out theatre continue to serve if it must rely for its existence on profit royalties from the sale of its most successful try-out productions? And not only profit royalties but on the publicity consequent upon the transfer of productions to the West End. Without this possibility the greatest inducement to author and actor vanishes.

In 1952 he finally freed Q from the stranglehold of Entertainment Tax. This was achieved by his relinquishing his role as Licensee. A non-profit distributing company, Play Live, took over and seat prices were immediately reduced. The administrator of the new company was one Beatrice de Leon, and the first presentation was *For Love Or Money* !

Jack was always keen that the building should be more than simply a theatre. The club-room became a centre for various cultural activities. Exhibitions of paintings were regularly held to encourage local artists. Ellen Pollock's artist husband, James Proudfoot, mounted one such exhibition, a collection of portraits he had made of various theatre luminaries.

During 1945 James Proudfoot asked me to sit for him, and the resultant portrait, much to my disgust, represented me weighed down with my overcoat and the sins of the world and a grotesquely enlarged left ear listening for sounds I could not hear. If that portrait captured my years in my early forties I looked seventy ...
This portrait was one of those mounted in the exhibition. Peter Saunders bought it as a present for Herby with whom he was very friendly. When, late in life, Herby moved to a smaller house, he gave the painting to Beatie and it hangs in the house on Kew Green over the velvet covered chest from *And So To Bed*. Both Beatie and Jean thought it captured nothing of the Jack they knew. Delia, however, insists that it is as he was 'when he was in that mood.'
The Proudfoot exhibition was held in September 1954. The following month saw the creation of what would become something of a local institution. The first Sunday of every month a series of discussions and debates would take place in the club room. Eventually these became known as the Brains Trust and were held at both Richmond Adult College and at the Festival Hall. Over the years many celebrities would appear as panelists, among them Kenneth Tynan, Tom Stoppard, John Mortimer, Bamber Gascoigne, Edward Bond, Michael Billington and Roy Plomley as well as many Q actors. One of the very early panelists was Petula Clark. The future pop star had appeared at Q in two plays, *Sauce For the Goose* and *The Constant Nymph*. In those days she was a reserved, well-mannered girl, very much under the thumb of her manager father. The series was launched by a debate, the motion of which was 'Television is a threat to the Theatre'.
Television was the novelty of the age. It might have been nothing more but for the events of one single day, June 2nd 1953. This was to change the cultural life of the nation in a seemingly irrevocable way. Seeing the potential, manufacturers of television receivers brought down the price of what had been seen as merely a middle-class toy. The opportunity of having a chancel-side view of the greatest event of the decade, the Coronation of Elizabeth II, proved irresistible and there was a boom in the sale of television sets. In these days when a balance has been found and the public are returning to the theatres and cinemas, it is difficult to appreciate how overnight the British public became a slave to television. The majority at the time would have maintained that they only watched the set on special occasions, that it was not going to take over their lives. But its influence was insidious. Why turn out on those cold winter nights to battle one's way to the theatre when one could stay at home by the fire and watch just as good a play?
Even a reduction in the price of seats at Q, brought about by the new regime, could

not combat such an adversary. Ever adventurous, Jack had, at one time, sought to harness the popularity of television in Q's work. On September 3rd 1948 the BBC had televised Kenneth Hyde's *The Rossiters* live from Q.

It was at this juncture that the need for subsidy arose if the British theatre were to survive and Jack was quick to act on Q's behalf. In March 1955 he presented a petition signed by more than a thousand of Q's regular patrons to Brentford and Chiswick Borough Council, asking for a small annual subsidy. "All we are asking for," he told reporters, "is the equivalent of one penny on the rates. The money would not be put in anyone's pocket but used to meet losses. Unless a production plays to nearly full houses at each performance, it is unlikely to pay its way." The request was considered at special meetings over two days. It was turned down.

Bernard Miles' long association with the Mermaid Theatre which he created at Puddle Dock, reflected, at a later date, many of the struggles Jack had experienced at Q. "I am glad to be reminded after all these years of the old Q and Jack and Beatie's heroic tenure of that famous little theatre," wrote Lord Miles. "I think it would be true to say that they fought the good fight in a most unhelpful period of our theatrical history, before the arrival of the Arts Council and their own, all too niggardly, funding. How they hung on there no-one but Josephine and myself could describe. But the Q still lives in the hearts and affections of many old actors and must find an honoured place in any future history of the British Theatre."

"I've always felt," claims Margaret Shepherd, "that if Jack had organised a consortium immediately after the war with Hermann Herrey's plans for the rebuilding of Q it could have gone ahead, and Q might have survived." Herrey's plans, which were published in The Architectural Forum in June 1946, imaginatively combined both playhouse and community centre, incorporating a restaurant, a dance floor with an orchestra, separate club rooms for ladies and gentlemen, a library and a reading room and tea room, apart from staging and workshop facilities which would still seem innovative today. Those pre- and post-war dreams contrasted starkly with the reality of the mid-fifties. The old building had soldiered valiantly on but it was showing its age.

In an attempt to gain a high profile Jack chose to publicise the theatre by means of demonstrating the reason for its justifiably high international reputation. He organised a competition for new playwrights to mark the thirtieth anniversary of Q's opening. The competition was open to all British dramatists whose work had not yet been seen on the professional stage, with prizes of twenty five guineas each for the winners and the guarantee that their plays would be tried out at Q.

"When I first came to England in 1949," recalled John Wiles, "I had spent the few years since demobilisation after war-service, stage-managing for various theatre companies in South Africa, including that of Cyril Wentzel, an actor who had done pretty well for himself in English reps before the war. He had been given his first chance by the de Leons at the Q Theatre, sent along by his brand new agent who didn't know what else to do with him, and there was Beatie. 'No experience, dear? Well, you know we can't afford to pay you anything, but you've got to start somewhere. Now how do you spell you name and can you start right away?' So, long before I'd seen her I'd heard of her, and when, a few years later, I in my turn was persuaded to enter a piece of mine in a play-writing contest being held by Q, I had a pretty good idea where it was going.

"And it came - no, not first, but second! I assume I was bowled over. The de Leons were certainly among the most illustrious names in management. As far as I can remember Beatie took complete charge, introduced me to my director and designer. 'Well, you've written a nice little play and we'll do the best we can for you, but you do realise, don't you, the Q is only a little theatre so we can't afford to pay much ...' Pierre Rouve took it on and gave it a splendid production for which I shall always be grateful, with Michael Gough, John Stratton and Carol Marsh. It took the notices and the late lamented Bryan Bailey picked it up and carried it off to the Edinburgh Festival fringe (purely professional in those days) as a vehicle for Jack Rodney and another spectacular appearance by John Stratton, where it caught the critics again and only escaped by a whisker coming in to the Haymarket the week after the Festival closed. Oh, well. But it played reps and TV and led to other commissions."

Between five and six hundred plays were submitted and they were read by a panel consisting of Kenneth Tynan, Clive Brook, Lady Carisbrooke and Jack. In all, seven of the plays were presented at Q towards the end of the 1954-55 season.

The theatre now operated in seasons with complete closure during the summer months. From 1949 onwards Jack and Beatie had always taken the summer off, but originally they let it out to other managements. One summer Peggy Ramsay, the literary agent, who had acted at Q, took the theatre with a colleague. However, by the mid-fifties it had become an increasingly less attractive proposition. In the press it was announced each year that the theatre was to be closed for partial re-decoration but no-one was really fooled by that. In October 1955 The Times reported that when the theatre had closed in June it seemed unlikely it would ever re-open. Middlesex County Council was demanding a new roof and other rebuilding and there seemed no prospect of finding the finance to put this into operation by 1957. However, Play Live had announced that they were about to arrange a building scheme which would go far beyond the structural requirements and would re-open the following week.

"After a four month closure," reported the critic of The Times on October 11th 1955, "it was, surely, the moment to play an ace; instead *Moonshine* is the kind of hollow, verveless light comedy which cannot but cause the most dedicated first-night goer to wonder whether regular visits to Kew are not something of a fool's errand ... Not even such accomplished actors as Mr Douglas Wilmer, Mr George Coulouris and Miss Jessica Spencer can make cardboard appear other than flat." At such a juncture Jack and Beatie could have done without this kind of publicity.

By this time Euphan Scott, who had been working elsewhere, was back at Q. "The County Council licence required a qualified electrician to be present," she recalled. "They turned me down because I wasn't qualified but gave way in the end. By then they knew that the closure of Q was inevitable."

Jack had made a decision. To run Q the way it had been run for more than thirty one years was no longer feasible. Professional production must come to an end. Apart from anything else, for reasons which will be dealt with later, he no longer had the physical stamina to cope with the constant setbacks. The Fortune Theatre in Drury Lane, which had been available for use by amateur companies for several years, was to withdraw this facility three months later. Q had once upon a time risen from the ashes by means of amateur actors. At least the building would be used for the purpose it was best suited to if he made it available to those who had lost their showplace at the Fortune.

The local press announced that the closing play would be Arnold Ridley's new play, *You, My Guests*. However, two more plays were announced before the inevitable closure. With immense irony the first of these was entitled *The End Begins*; and the second, *Who Cares?* Perhaps the greatest irony of all was that both of these plays were guaranteed by the Arts Council under a scheme for the promotion of new drama. Commented Jack, "Had a guarantee come earlier from the Arts Council, the present position would never have arisen." Kenneth Tynan was at the final performance. He said, "I want to be in at the kill."

Thus ended an era in the history of the British theatre. Film director Bryan Forbes, who had twice acted at Q, has written, "I think it is to be regretted that such theatres have now passed into history, for it was a wonderful staging ground for young actors and was sufficiently close to the West End to encourage managements and agents to make the trek. The loss of such theatres means that there is less and less hope for the stars of tomorrow to have a showcase, for it was a real theatre and not a tiny rostrum set up in a pub."

A short list of some of the young actors who appeared at Q in its last decade gives some indication of that loss. Apart from those already mentioned, Peter Barkworth, Jill Bennett, Patrick McGoohan, Geraldine McEwan, Robert Shaw, Patricia Routledge, Denholm Elliott, Margaret Tyzack, Donald Pleasance, Siobhan McKenna, Leslie Phillips, Irene Worth, Ian Carmichael, Kathleen Byron, Ian Bannen, Miriam Karlin, Bill Travers, Natasha Parry, Geoffrey Palmer, Diane Cilento, Anthony Newley, Sir Michael Hordern and Bryan Forbes' wife Nanette Newman, were among the thousands offered the opportunity to exercise their art when they were finding their feet in the profession. The number of new playwrights to see their work presented can be judged from the complete list of new plays presented at Q which can be found in the Appendices. Today writers have no such facility. Q was a unique institution, and its passing an immeasurable loss.

After the closure on Sunday February 19th 1956 the theatre was used, as had been planned, for some amateur and student shows. The Brains Trusts continued. Fuller, Smith and Turner who, throughout the history of Q had been the most thoughtful of landlords, had changed in their attitude. Once before they had renewed Jack's original lease, but the extension was running out, they had an offer and the sooner the building was demolished the better for them.

"The first week in March, 1958, we started striking the equipment," continued Euphan. "There was a blizzard and an icy wind whistled round the theatre and blew through the gaps in its sides. I had help to get the lamps down. It seemed awful to be tearing down all the equipment we had spent years trying to keep up and keep in good order. Yet, I think in a way, at this point, we wanted to pack up Q and end the struggle of trying to hold it together.

I disconnected the old switchboard from the mains, but disconnecting the board itself was much more difficult and took me nearly three hours - it was like unravelling knitting. The Pirelli Cable Factory had bought it and they had a job getting it out of the theatre. It took all four of their men plus the van driver and mate to shift it on to a trolley. It got knocked about in the process and I sadly watched my poor old switchboard being borne away through the falling sleet, leaving a trail of nuts and bolts behind it."

It was bad enough to see the gold stage curtains taken down but my heart was wrenched most of all when they took down the safety curtain showing the theatre and the old fireman. That was one of the worst moments of my life. I had advertised the sale of Q in the local papers in February 1958. Everything had to be cleared at any price.

On the day we had a continual queue and were offered amazing sums for such things as door-closers. Naturally we removed them all from the doors. We laid out everything including the carpentry tools which were also in great demand. The theatre fittings fetched about £500.

"Beatie had arranged long tables in the foyer and we laid all sorts of things out on them, rather like a jumble sale. Beatie showed the Pirelli party round and asked them if they wanted to buy anything. Before you could say knife, she had sold one of them a clock without any hands and the other an empty tin box. 'I've never met anyone like her before,' one murmured to me.

"Two small boys turned up. One said he had come to buy a washbasin for his uncle; he had a pram to cart it away. I brought the big old drum out of the prop room. After I found a small boy pushing it around. 'I've bought it,' he announced. 'I know it's bigger than me, but I expect I'll be able to manage it soon.'

"I remember Beatie stopping suddenly in between selling somebody a pair of curtains for seven and six and someone else half a dozen glasses for one and three, and saying to me 'We're destroying all our happy memories, you know. That's what I want. Then I shan't mind leaving.'

"When we returned after a cold Easter we found that the two wild cats which had haunted the theatre for the last six months had fallen down the ventilation shaft sometime during the weekend. They had been living on a grating over the auditorium and the mess and stench were terrible. We had to get the police, fire brigade and RSPCA before the poor creatures were rescued. They slipped off like greased lightning and by the afternoon were back in the scene dock.

"In the end we had only forty eight hours notice to organise the get-out and decide what was to go for auction, what was to be stored and what was simply to be abandoned. People came and went, collecting things. It was chaotic. I used to go and rest on the stage, because that had altered least of anything."

On that last day, in silence we loaded Euphan's car with the oddments of value which we wanted to keep, including the Addressograph machine with its mailing-list of nearly 30,000 names.

It finally came to the moment when we had to close the doors for the last time. Euphan and I did it together. We didn't say a word. Both of us had tears in our eyes.

CHAPTER EIGHT - THEY HAVE THEIR EXITS

JACK, HOWEVER, was spared from witnessing the final sad destruction of Q. **In July 1955, Jack and I went to Manchester for the opening night of a tour of Roger MacDougall's *The Delegate*, accompanied by the director, Peter Ashmore, and Vivienne Moynihan, the stage-manager. The next morning, in the hotel lift, Jack complained of indigestion.**

"Earlier that summer," recalled Jean, "I had seen my father mowing the lawn. It was slightly less than the size of a tennis court. He was absolutely worn out after doing it, panting for breath, his face grey. I didn't think much about it at the time." **We travelled back that morning from Manchester to London by train. In the early hours of the next morning at home in Kew Road, he woke with violent chest pains and I called in our G.P. He examined him and said he would come back an hour later to see how he was.**

"Neither of us thought this a satisfactory response," continued Jean. "For the previous six years I had been working three afternoons a week for a Harley Street physician. I decided to telephone him. Dr Salmon came immediately and did an electro-cardiogram. He told me that Daddy was very seriously ill. He phoned for an ambulance and then the London Clinic - he knew we had private health insurance, and he was friendly with the matron there."

It started on a Wednesday. I remember a shot of morphia. I remember a voice, a voice I didn't know, a voice saying, "In this hot weather it sticks." I remember being lifted head down backwards and I remember thinking, "Are the neighbours watching? What are they thinking?" And I remember an ambulance and faces, my wife, my daughter and one of them saying, "Are you coming too?" **In the ambulance going into the clinic in excruciating heat, it was ghastly, terrible, Jack lying unconscious. We had to sit there seeing him not knowing us.**

And from then time ceased. Scenes - thoughts - incoherent - no time - no ego - no individuality - the conscious I, and the subconscious I, and all the subconscious I's that add up to personality started a battle. Interminable. Timeless. I was an onlooker. Later they told me it was five days. Five days dead. **Jean and I were utterly dazed. We stayed with him in the clinic for several weeks, during which there was a severe heatwave. The specialist was marvellous and, through the kindness of the matron we slept, at first, in an empty room opposite which happened to be free. When the room was needed we slept on mattresses on the floor of the waiting room. The cleaners got us up at five. As Jack remained on the danger list our dear friend, the Hon. Philip Samuel, arranged for us to rent a ground floor room in nearby Gloucester Place, in the same building as his own flat. Friends and relatives dragged us out for short**

drives in Regent's Park. Dozens of letters and flowers arrived daily. I kept my vigil by his side.

"Mummy sat stoically by his bed all day and most of the night for at least six weeks. He was completely unconscious at first, but later his consciousness came and went." "When I visited him one day," his sister-in-law Evey de Leon recalled, "he told me he had had a wonderful vision of the Christ coming to him. He had felt a great sense of love. It had changed his whole life."

I remember ranting, ranting about the heat, the inferno of the concrete and the terrors of the room, of the room in which they wanted me to die. Then they moved me. My wife told me later that when I came into this room I smiled and said, "That's better."

In this room came the visitation. The beginning. I say a visitation because I can't find any other word. But visitation doesn't really describe it. There was no visual presence. It was a pouring out of love and compassion from a presence which filled me and went outwards to the walls and inwards surrounding me, lifting me and supporting me. I was choked with humility. I didn't know how to receive it, this warm embrace. The tears in my throat, the mist before my eyes; I don't know if it was night, I don't know if it was day.

"God is love." What could that mean? To me it was something incomprehensible until it came and swept me up and showed me the infinity of its being. It showed that "God is love" is a truth which can only have reality if this love descends, ascends, flows out over you as it happened to me. Indescribable and un-understandable, but sense. They won't believe. They will say it was in my own mind. It was the effect of drugs. It was the beginning of my recovery. Maybe all these things are true, but maybe the truth also includes the truth I knew and cannot dismiss.

Beatie took an evening away from his bedside to attend the West End opening of *The Count of Clérambard* by Marcel Aymé at the Garrick Theatre.

I consider Clérambard *the most important play I have ever presented, and my illness the most vital event of my life.* Clérambard *is a difficult, strange play, but it is fundamentally simple. Seven characters go through different experiences to reach the same path, the path of love and of God.*

My illness has given me a completely fresh view of many things. Lying here, I have been able to think with a detachment I have not known for years. I have gained a new perspective.

The first night at the Garrick was the first of his first-nights Jack had been unable to attend. However he heard everything by means of a private telephone wire which was set up for him. Jean remained with him that evening. "He used to say, 'Sing for me, sing for me' day after day. Though I didn't much feel like it I would do my best. Gounod's 'Ave Maria' and Brahms' Lullaby."

On Thursday night the Night Charge Sister came in to see me. She had been away

154

*on her holiday for nearly three weeks, so of course she only remembered me as
I was after I had been here the first three weeks. We talked for a little while, then
in her forthright smiling way she referred to the first four or five nights when she
was almost continuously in and out of my room. She said, "Good gracious, how
you've improved. In those first days I really thought you were a goner!"
I told this to Barbara the next morning. She was shocked, almost beyond speech.
To think that a Charge Sister could say such a thing to a patient. I told her I had
known and that I was glad to hear it in this amusing way from someone else.
I had hardly said this when the maid, whom I also hadn't seen for some days,
arrived with my lunch. She also started chatting. "Well, well. To think that when
I first saw you in that other room I didn't think I should ever see you again."
So twice within a few hours has come from the outside, confirmation of the sense
of resurrection which has taken possession of me.*

Jack passed the hours by speaking his thoughts into a tape-recorder. Margaret
Shepherd dutifully typed it all out. Thus he was able to keep a record of everything
that had passed through his mind during this time of vivid awareness.

*How does one explain these strange incomprehensible dreams? At the time, last
night's dream was not remotely amusing, but in the waking, quite funny, quite
ridiculous.
It was the first night of a play. I was in the theatre, a small, very small theatre.
A play had just finished. Henry Kendall had played the lead and for some
extraordinary reason was left alone on the stage to make a final speech. Instead
of the normal speech of thanks he told the audience, to my astonishment, that
the play was being done for the financial benefit of some charitable organisation.
He told a long, confused story about the people who would benefit and was on
the point of leading to, presumably, a plea for the audience and critics'
recommendation, when a clergyman walked through the audience, ran up the
steps which, rather strangely, led to the stage, and said, "Isn't it time we
prayed?" My embarrassment was such I didn't know how to deal with the
situation. I was trying to tell Harry that, before the prayer, we must at least play
"God Save The King" so that those of the audience who wished could leave. I
couldn't get at him to say this. The clergyman seemed to be turning over the pages
of a Bible and he was saying, "Chapter three to chapter six, that won't be too
long. Let's start by reading these, chapter three to chapter six."
Then I woke up. The clock outside was striking three. I wasn't amused then. I
was in a bother. I was in trouble. I kept on, half awake, half asleep, still trying
to stop Harry, to get the curtain down and to play "God Save The King". But I
kept on hearing the clergyman's voice saying, "Chapters three to six. Chapters
three to six ..."*

Though many expected it, the curtain hadn't come down for Jack. Eight weeks after
he was rushed into the clinic he was taken back to Kew. "Barbara, his nurse,

accompanied him" recalled Jean. "She was a deeply religious young Scottish woman, and she adored my father. We put him in the large ground floor room at the back overlooking the roses because he wasn't supposed to climb stairs. Mummy slept in the small adjoining room."

"Although one could say that Jack enjoyed and loved his family," his nurse, Barbara Nash recalls, "I don't, somehow, think he could be regarded as the usual cliché 'family man'. His culture and vast interests in what was happening around him made him very observant and humanitarian in his approach to nature and to people. Nothing was too inconsequential for Jack. He enjoyed conversation and was particularly inquisitive regarding other people's interests and hobbies.

"There were some people who visited him whom he loved to speak to, who never seemed to tire him. Others he couldn't stand and he'd tell me to be very officious, even though they hadn't used up their 'allowed' time! Jack called me his A.G.F. (adopted Godfather) and used to address his letters to me in this manner.

"His tremendous love of flowers always seemed to follow him. He loved going for rides in his wheelchair in Kew Gardens, his favourite shawl round his shoulders or over his knees."

Even before his heart-attack we had been planning to sell 200 Kew Road. Indeed, it was when we were in Liverpool that we heard an offer had been made, but we did not clinch the deal until later.

"It was a dreadful wrench for me leaving the house which had been my home for all my conscious life," commented Jean. "It was exactly like the last act of *The Cherry Orchard*."

Jack and Beatie made a 'temporary' move, which ultimately lasted a whole year, to 280 Kew Road where Jack's mother lived. Jean went to stay with Stanley and Evey de Leon in Barons Court. The reason for selling the house was because Jack had a hankering to return to the south coast where he had spent happy years at boarding-school. He wanted to write and felt he could be more productive there, commuting, when necessary to his business interests. After his illness they lived with his mother as her guests, on the capital from the house sale. He was still determined to write as this seemed now the only path open to him. Indeed during this time he completed *Out of the Whirlwind*, a play dealing in part with miracle healing. He chose to write under a new *nom de plume*, Graham Baker. The play would be presented a month after his death at the Intimate Theatre in High Wycombe.

In order to seek out somewhere to live, he and Beatie took a furnished flat for two months in Hove, but an exciting event brought him back to town. Associated Rediffusion, one of the original Independent Television companies, had decided to televise his play *The Silent Witness*. Jack called on one of his talents and adapted it for the screen, shortening it to the required fifty one minutes, and decided to present it under its original title, *The Man In The Dock*. It was televised on Thursday

September 20th 1956 at 9pm. Earlier that day, as a favour to Jean, he recorded a reading of 'Prayer before Birth' by Louis MacNeice. She was to begin teaching the following Friday week at Richmond Institute, and wanted to use the poem. **He read it beautifully and we still have the recording. As it was a fine day, Jack and I drove to the towpath near Richmond Green, and we sat in deck-chairs in the sun. Two days earlier, I recall him coming into our room and embracing me. He said to me, "You are wonderful."**
In the evening a friend, who was due to pick up my mother-in-law from her Christian Science church in Chiswick was late, and she arrived back agitated and harassed just as the live transmission of the play was about to begin.
With Jean they settled down to watch the play. The cast including Cyril Luckham and Derek Bond was performing magnificently when suddenly the screen went blank. A card saying that 'Normal Service will be resumed as soon as possible' was flashed up. There had been some kind of breakdown. The live performance in the studio continued. The times of commercial breaks had to be rigidly enforced over the network so there was no possibility of repeating the action that had been missed. Jack's version of the play had condensed the action to a very sparse framework. Miss a moment and the viewer would lose track of the plot. As the minutes ticked by Jack grew more and more frustrated, knowing that the denouement would make no sense whatsoever. When the sound and picture were restored he saw he had been absolutely correct.
Because the Hove flat was free Delia, who loved the sea, had decided to take it for those few days. Jean had moved into Delia's flat. "I have seldom in my life ever slept completely on my own," records Jean. "On that particular night I was entirely alone for the first time, in Aunt Delia's flat. There was a telephone call about 4am. It was Mummy. She said, quietly, 'Daddy's got indigestion again.' I guessed what she meant, threw my clothes on and rushed along to Granny's. When I got there he was still conscious. Mummy, who is always calm in a crisis, had phoned Dr Salmon."
The last thing Jack said was, "Not again. Oh God, not again."
Dr Salmon arrived just before he died. He led me gently into the sitting-room. If it wasn't for him I could not have gone on. My whole life had gone from me.
Television had killed Q. Ironically it had directly contributed to the death of the theatre's presiding genius.
"When I played in *Thunder Rock* at Q," recalls Barry Morse, "the role of the Viennese doctor, one of the ghosts, who tries to encourage the lighthouse keeper to break from his cynical attitude about the future of the world, was taken by Frederick Valk. Freddie had a wonderfully impressive voice, still imbued with the native notes of his Czechoslovakian origins. As the doctor, he listed all the great human beings in history who had overcome discouragements and setbacks to contribute to the growth of civilisation. Addressing me at one performance he said,

'Consider, Mr Charleston, the great men in human history who have always carried such great hope within their hearts; think of people like Leonardo da Vinci, Ludwig van Beethoven, Jack de Leon ...' of course I had the greatest difficulty in keeping control of myself because it passed without a flicker of recognition from the audience. I suppose they were so transfixed by Freddie's great command that it passed before they were quite aware of it."

Or perhaps there were those in the audience who were quite prepared to accept Jack's place in this scheme of things. "If Jack had not chosen the theatre for his vocation," argued Henry Kendall in his memoirs, "he might have been a great preacher or a rabbi. He was deeply religious, something of a mystic, and a fanatical seeker after Truth. I remember (directing) for him a play called *Man From Heaven*, which concerned reincarnation, and we got into a religious discussion which went on till the early hours of the morning. I am not a particularly religious person, and I was soon out of my depth, but the blazing sincerity of Jack's beliefs almost led me to believe that I was in the presence of a descendant of one of Christ's disciples."

Lest we get too carried away with the idea that Jack was a saint, we must hear from his detractors too. Henry Joachim had been one of Jack's friends since the days of The Towers in Finchley Road at the beginning of the twenties. His brother Freddie became an agent and directed Dirk Bogarde's career for many years. Of Jack he says, "He was very conceited, always dogmatic in his opinions. With him there was never any question as to who was right. No-one else's opinion meant anything to him. He thought of me, not incorrectly, as a person of no importance whatsoever, who knew nothing about the theatre. I don't know if it was an act with him, or if it was natural, but he was enormously conceited. His sham covered up what might have been an uncertainty about himself. People were overshadowed by him."

Henry Joachim, himself, remembers Jack for his great enthusiasm for life. "Much of the great success of his life he owed to his eager acceptance of so many of life's enhancing thoughts and, wherever possible, his ability to translate these thoughts into great waves of action. This creativity is the cause of people remembering him with great affection today after over thirty years of his passing."

Peggy Nicholls, Beatie's niece, remembers Jack as "a slightly remote personage, in a world above my kind of world. I found him aloof. I don't think one was frightened of him, or in awe of him. You would talk to him, he would listen, but you wouldn't automatically run to him." Her cousin, Teddy Lewisohn, has a different recollection. "I *was* in awe of him. He was a man of exceptional charm. If he spoke to me I felt honoured. I was very, very careful not to get into any kind of argument or debate or discussion with him because I was going to be mercilessly defeated." As we have seen, Teddy's cousin Anthony Lewison sought out debate with Jack finding him stimulating and challenging. Their cousin Marion has quite a different view. "I don't agree that he was remote at all. I always found him very

affectionate as an uncle. He was a lovely man." And Jean, of course, has her own thoughts. "He had a sense of the mystery of life."
"Jack had such an obvious and *cheerful* passion for the theatre and such a charming and persuasive way with him, he must have lured many an initially reluctant actor into working for him," recalled Peter Copley. "He seemed to *like* actors, and you were always there, chatting and *smiling*. Jack was (was he not?) always dressed in a dark suit with white shirt and dark tie - like a barrister: he was ready to do any necessary job, not just *run* the theatre. At one long and difficult fit-up I remember him back-stage in his dark suit, but jacket off, full length on the floor of the stage pulling cables through for lights in the wings: he was filthy but happy."
Any man is the sum of many contradictions.

When Jack was in the London Clinic, still very ill but expecting a visitor, I left him quiet for a few moments. I was standing all alone by the lift, feeling desolate, when I felt a hand gently touching my shoulder and a soft voice saying, "Are you alright. Do you need help?" I knew he meant practical help because he knew I was under great strain. The terrible thing is Bill Linnit, of the firm of theatrical producers, died a few weeks before Jack.
"Daddy insisted on going to his funeral. He was impressed by the service. Anthony made all the arrangements for Daddy's funeral and arranged for a similar but non-denominational service ending with the lines from the Revelation of St John which begin, 'And I saw a new heaven and a new earth.'"
Anthony was in the first car with Jean and myself. I was grief-stricken but I noticed him wiping away his tears. He was like a son. We had taken the largest chapel at Golders Green and it was packed. We obtained special permission to go into Kew Gardens one morning before it was open to the public. There was a particular place Jack liked to sit, near the roses, behind the Palm House. We scattered his ashes there. Later we donated a bench in his memory at the very spot.

> *There is no happiness without freedom*
> *There is no freedom except in fulfilment*
> *There is no fulfilment without harmony*
> *There is no harmony save in unity*
> *There is no unity without God*
> *There is no God but the King*
> *There is no King but yourself.*

"I remember after the funeral, Mummy sitting there. 'I must go on living,' she said."
The words of Kipling are hackneyed, but often recur in my mind:
"Stoop and build it up with worn out tools."

PART FOUR

1956 - 1991

CHAPTER ONE - STOOP AND BUILD

"MY PARENTS kept me until I was in my early thirties," recalled Jean.
"Although I worked I didn't earn enough to live on. After Daddy's death I realized
I had to earn my living."
Jean had worked for Dr Salmon three afternoons a week since 1949. She enjoyed
this work as she had great respect for Salmon both professionally and intellectually. There had been other jobs too. At one time she used an employment agency
in Baker Street. Along with several run-of-the-mill temporary positions, she
became the envy of many another secretary when she was sent one day in the early
fifties to St John's Wood. "You are interested in literature and your father is a
writer," announced the agency's manageress. "Raymond Chandler is over from
America and needs a secretary."
"I found him an affable teddy bear with a magnetic, attractive personality and
mischievous eyes, a most captivating boyish smile which concealed a centre of
steel. He could be courteous and 'old world' even in slippers and dressing-gown.
Interested in people of all sorts, a woman lover though not a seducer, he was
changeable in his attitude to people but very kind and generous to his friends. He
was in love with words, as capable of writing his famous crime thrillers as he was
of writing poetry. He dictated long letters with great attention to detail. He was an
exciting person, capable of ruthlessness and anger. I remember telegrams to
members of the Mafia.
"In his thoughts he often returned to his long dead wife, several years his senior,
whom he had nursed through cancer. This ordeal led to his life-long addiction to
alcohol. He was very submissive to his close friend Helga Greene, his agent-
manager, whom he later married.
"I worked for him for several weeks. The next time he was coming to London he
rang me up from California and asked me to work for him at a place in Swan Walk,
Chelsea. The last time I worked for him he was living at the Ritz. Actually we didn't
do much work as he wasn't well at the time. Sometimes I had lunch with him and
once he invited me out to dinner, treating me to fresh salmon. At the Ritz there was
always caviar. I recall the gentle, vividly blue eyed Stephen Spender, whose wife
Natasha was one of Ray's great friends, coming to his room at the Ritz. I left them
together. Even asleep on a couch, Ray's warm personality filled the room. He was
kind enough to come and visit my father after his first heart-attack, when he and
my mother were still living with Granny de Leon."

At one time Jean also had a job in the Department of Haematology at Charing Cross Hospital, typing blood counts. Later she worked in a Family Planning clinic in Pont Street, organising conferences and typing. Both of these occupations she found deadly dull.

Jean had no direction in life. This contrasts with her parents whose determination and single-mindedness kept Q going for more than thirty years, no lack of direction there once the direction had been located. Perhaps Jean was overprotected by her parents because of her disability. Intellectually challenged, spiritually challenged, certainly, but not expected to meet the challenge of everyday life. Several careers had presented themselves as ideas to Jean including poetry-reading and broadcasting. She had half expected one day to follow her parents into theatre-management, but, until now, there had seemed no necessity in pursuing any career.

There seemed a dramatic inevitability in the fact that Jean's life work began exactly one week after her father's death, and that one of her tools was a recording Jack had made the morning before his fatal heart-attack. Thus, neatly, the baton passed from one hand to the next.

Jean had been invited to take a class at Richmond Adult College. She had made a success of it, was asked to take another and was eventually asked to teach Speech and Drama one day a week at the College. It soon became clear that she had the prospects of an interesting career, following in her mother's footsteps, not in theatre-management, but in theatre-education. However, if she wanted to pursue such a career in earnest it became apparent that she should have a paper qualification. Maisie Cobbie, Drama Adviser to the ILEA, introduced her to Greta Colson with whom she began to study for her LRAM (Speech and Drama). Miss Cobbie also suggested she approach the City Literary Institute where she was offered a class in The Art of Conversation. She went along in trepidation, not knowing how she was going to handle it but made an immediate success. The one session grew to three. Then she was asked to teach an Appreciation of Literature course with foreign students. A lunchtime London Theatre course was added. She still continued to work her three afternoons a week for Dr Salmon for the time being.

After Jack's death Jean and I had stayed with Granny de Leon, sharing a room. She was very kind to us but, after some months, she needed the spare room for a housekeeper. Delia came to our rescue. She noticed that we were anxious and agitated, not knowing where to go. Gently she put her hand on my shoulder and comforted me. "Don't worry," she said. "You can both stay with me."

So we moved to Delia's attic flat. She slept on a divan in the front room which overlooked Kew Gardens. Our bedroom at the back was small and the beds close together but we managed. It was here, in such difficult circumstances, that Jean studied for her LRAM.

Beatie coached her in two speeches, one of them Cordelia's last speech to her father, the other from *Black Chiffon* in the role in which Flora Robson had made a great hit. Jean managed to pass the examination within three months. Rather modestly she suggests she was able to accomplish it in such a short space of time because of her having been an adjunct to the Q Theatre for all those years, but Beatie was justly proud of this outstanding achievement.

Beatie had to work too. Although she was not far short, at almost fifty-six, of retirement age, retirement was not something Beatie would ever greet gladly. Had she not needed to work for financial stability, Beatie would have wanted to work nevertheless. Initially, even after Q's closure as a working theatre, she looked for ways to keep the building alive. She and Jack had already planned to use the theatre for a Drama Summer School in the summer of 1957. Indeed Jack had helped plan the publicity. Peter Brook and the actress Adrianne Allen agreed to become patrons and the course was directed by Roy Walker and Pierre Rouve. It was such a success that Beatie determined to try to make it an annual event. By the summer of 1958, however, the Q was no more. An ugly office block would soon rise on the site. Beatie took the Park Lane Theatre. Kenneth Tynan and E. Martin Browne joined the list of patrons, as did the actress Moira Lister who had been the guest of honour at the previous Summer School's public presentation of scenes from Shakespeare, Fry and Giraudoux. She had told a local reporter she had never imagined amateurs could be so competent. "You could see them thinking as they spoke their lines," she commented, "instead of just reciting them as you would expect of amateurs." Chloe Gibson and Jean joined the teaching strength.

Beatie was lonely as she had never been before in her life. Not only was she a widow, learning to live without that other half of her life, but with necessity sending Jean out to work, she was often alone and she hated it. When several of the students at the 1958 Summer School told her how much they would like to continue working with her, she leapt at the chance, organising a ten week course. Thus was born the De Leon Drama School. Initially classes were held in church halls and local studios, sometimes at her home.

My aim was to have a school which would be quite small, say about twenty four students, who would learn mainly through practical work and workshop performances directed by professional directors. Among the directors who worked for me over the years were John Fernald, himself the Principal of RADA for a number of years, Hugh Morrison, Warren Jenkins, Oliver Cotton and John Dryden as well as two actor-directors who lived locally, Paul Shelley and Bob Cartland. There were regular Speech and Movement classes with highly qualified staff such as Robin Winbow and Greta Colson, who founded New College of Speech and Drama. Jean did voice and choral work and taught drama history to first year students. When we did productions our old friend Euphan Scott lit them for us.

Actors are born not made. Their hearts and souls, especially their souls must be in their work, and they need imagination and feeling. Without these qualities they remain mechanical and not true to life.
Technique, however, is helpful, and stage presence can be developed. The purpose of stage-training is to learn basic acting skills and to gain experience before an audience. In the past many actors have made a career without formal training, but very few can enter the profession today without some tuition.
In my drama school, as in all other drama schools, auditions were held to assess each applicant's talent. I was also looking for signs of dedication.
Additionally Beatie took on several classes at Richmond Adult College.
My two evening classes included Mime, Improvisation and Acting. Both classes began with exercise in all types of movement and gesture. Although movement on the stage needs to be larger than life it must appear natural. In Improvisation I tried to help students overcome their inhibitions. I often suggested very dramatic situations such as peasants in a Sicilian village hearing a messenger announce a volcanic eruption; being locked in an attic and smelling fire; trying to get out of prison. After a few weeks students were divided into groups and either given a subject or invited to devise their own work. Team activity is important.
The acting classes also began with exercises including breathing and relaxation or mime. Gestures of all types, especially hand movements, how to enter or exit and how to sit and place the feet, all needed attention. Then we would work on text. At first I chose scenes, working around the members of the group and selected for individual students so they might gain confidence. Later I gave them a chance to stretch their imaginations. Every term we did a full-length play.
One of her evening students in the early seventies was a young barrister. She yearned to be an actress and saw an advertisement for the evening classes in a local newspaper. Her mother was delighted that she would be studying with Beatie de Leon as she had been a Sunday night patron at the Q for many years. When Nancy Price appeared as *Nurse Cavell* Eileen Cruickshank had been a nurse. Her matron had sent her and some of her colleagues to see a performance dressed in their uniforms. "Beatie taught me a great deal about life as well as about theatre," recalled Cynthia Cruickshank. "In my work as a barrister I was able to gain a greater appreciation of people's characters. I was very lucky as a student because I was given many wonderful opportunities. The highlight was the role of Catherine Sloper in *The Heiress*, directed by Beatie."
Shirley Carlyon, the Vice-Principal at Richmond Adult College, suggested to Beatie that she might like to hold the 1960 Summer School on the college premises. In 1962, a new Principal was appointed. Her name was Margery Leslie.

"In 1948 I came to live and work in Chiswick," she recalled, "within walking distance of Q. It was an amazing place. The people who sold you your ticket, the people who showed you to your seat, were all deeply interested in the theatre. I had known other little theatres with an equally pleasant chatty atmosphere, but at Q, as well as this, the productions were of an infinitely greater professional excellence. I suppose, at the time, I vaguely wondered who was responsible for this. I remember being appalled when it closed.

"In 1962 I was appointed to transform what had been an engineering and hairdressing college into an adult community college offering a whole range of subjects. There was a hand-over term in which I would go down regularly to see the retiring Principal, Dominic Bruce. I found the roots of culture well established, though in very stony soil. Drama and Music were well represented by the de Leons, mother and daughter. Dominic Bruce told me that a decision had been taken to provide extra space for a canteen and another classroom. This meant removing the stage. He was particularly concerned about the effect of this on Mrs de Leon's Summer School.

"When finally I met Beatie I asked how much of a problem it was going to be. She said, 'Don't worry, we'll think of something.' Well, she thought, and the next time I saw her was in the Oddfellow's Hall in Parkshot, chatting up Reginald Maudling, the Chancellor of the Exchequer - in his personal, not his professional capacity, alas. It was after the Summer School presentation of *Electra*. His daughter, Caroline, had been awarded the annual De Leon prize."

The prize of ten guineas was awarded by Beatie to the Summer School student who gave what she considered to be the best performance in the end-of-course show, in Jack's memory. One young recipient of the prize would go on to become one of the most enchanting actresses of her generation.

"My first memory of Beatie," recalled Anna Calder-Marshall, "is of her sitting-room. It was the first day of the De Leon Summer Drama School. I was sixteen, my sister fourteen, and there were lots of other children. We all had to recite something. There was a little platform just by the window which overlooked Kew Green. Beatie was sitting on the sofa, a small, smiling bundle of fun, full of encouragement.

"The next ten days were Heaven to me. I couldn't eat, I was so excited. Each day was filled with voice lessons, improvisation, mask, mime. Beatie asked me to do a speech from *Saint Joan*. It opened up a new world for me. I was hungry to act, and Saint Joan just filled my days. The individual sessions I had with Beatie were the highlights of the week. She was so passionate, yet practical. I had read books by Stanislavsky, and here in her sitting-room they were put into practice. When Joan says, 'Give me that writing! Go light your fire', she made me tear the imaginary piece of paper with such force that I really believed it was there. Joan's voices weren't airy-fairy, they were practical.

"This groundwork - imagining what it was like for Joan to be imprisoned, fighting for her faith - learning from Beatie how to project, was going to be an immensely valuable stepping-stone into drama school, and finally the reality of playing Saint Joan at the Birmingham Rep. I can never thank Beatie enough for her enthusiasm and encouragement. When I was awarded the De Leon prize, I knew definitely that acting was for me. Playing Saint Joan on a tiny platform in front of an audience was thrilling. I remember my body tingling all over as if it was full of electricity. I had always felt I was too emotional and here I was being given the chance to channel it into something positive.

"My friendship with Beatie didn't end there. Jean, who was a fine voice-coach on the course, was going away and I was asked to stay a week with Beatie to keep her company in the evenings. I became a sort of secretary - not a very good one. I've always been hopeless at paper work, but it was a wonderfully crazy time. Beatie's office work spilled into her bedroom. There was correspondence everywhere - in clothes drawers even - and because it was so higgledy-piggledy, I felt even more at home. In the evenings she would give me delicious suppers and a thimbleful of alcohol to make me feel grown up and ever so daring. She would recall the days of the Q theatre, with fond memories of her husband, and of the young Dirk Bogarde.

"She advised me to work backstage, which I did the following year at the Richmond Theatre. I broke more cups than any other ASM in the history of the theatre, but had the chance, in the lunch hour, to practise my audition pieces on the darkened stage. Then I would go and try them out on Beatie. She advised me to play Viola in *Twelfth Night*.
When I said the line. 'I left no ring with her!' she suggested I throw the ring to the ground in disgust. At weekends I continued to work on these scenes at my home which, in those days, was on the banks of the Thames. I lost two of my mother's rings in this way. My mother was wonderfully understanding.

"The crunch came when I applied for RADA and the Central School of Speech and Drama. They both turned me down, kindly saying that I had talent but they could not foresee a professional career for someone whose leg had been affected by a childhood bout of polio. In my naivety I had simply not foreseen any problems. In this difficult time it was only the faith of my parents and Beatie and Jean, who shared the same disability, which kept me going. I will never forget that. LAMDA, however, came to the rescue. They were not only prepared to take a chance on me, but suggested I apply for a scholarship. Armed with Saint Joan and Viola and all of Beatie's wonderful advice, I auditioned for John Gielgud and Sybil Thorndike. I was apprehensive as I had heard Dame Sybil only two days previously saying how difficult she found listening to other actresses playing Joan as she had been coached in every intonation by Shaw himself. But all went well, and I won the Ellen Terry Award. Tears of joy all round, not least from Beatie and Jean.

"My thanks, then, to Beatie for putting my foot squarely on the first rung of the ladder, for her big heart, her warmth, her energy and love of life, her faith in me. She was a truly remarkable person."

"Summer Schools were nine days long," recalled David Owen-Bell who directed the course for several years. "We would meet them on a Friday and the following Saturday week we would do an hour's production with as many as thirty in the cast. We tried to devise it as an onward going learning process, doing exercises which would lead to the production rather than simply working on the text. The most successful one from my point of view was called *Yesterday's Dreams*. A company arriving at a theatre which was about to be demolished find props, costumes and the bric-a-brac of a former era. These remind them of scenes and characters which they perform. There were about thirty five in that, all getting a fair crack of the whip, all playing as a company. At the beginning of the week you would think, 'Are we ever going to get this on?' But then it was the end of the week and everyone was telling you how marvellous it had been."

John Wiles answered a summons to assist with a Summer School. "I can't imagine anyone saying no to Beatie. I daresay, in the course of her long and frenetic life, there were those who have refused her some small request, but I have never met them, and neither has anyone else I know. On the contrary, the merest hint of that breathless voice on the phone or simply a glimpse of those eager eyes peering up from under the scrap of lace she always wears on her hair, and one was lost. There was no saying no. Instead, 'Whatever you say, Beatie. Of course, Beatie. Two pounds fifty to do the whole production? Why not, Beatie?'

"When she phoned me up to say, 'That play of yours that was in the play competition, did quite well, didn't it? What was it called now, something to do with Madness wasn't it?' She was looking for somebody to direct her Summer School students. A mutual friend (James Roose-Evans, I believe) had told her I was doing a lot of work with young people at the time. In the end I did four, or was it five, Summer Schools for her - a Ugo Betti play, a Kafka, *Everyman* in the round - working at the Richmond College in a tiny hall on an improvised stage, sometimes perched high on boxes, sometimes flat on the floor. Jean joined us, doing speech and poetry classes. Oh, they were happy days, long summer hours filled with sunshine and hard work.

"Hand in hand with all this high drama, classes in movement and exercises in directorial tantrums ('You're awful, you're all awful. I don't know why I am wasting my time with you all!') there were also appearances on Brains Trusts, talks on being a writer, talks on being a director, talks on being a talker, and always Beatie and Jean in the front row, the former (God help us) with a notebook and pencil, peering up eagerly at the rostrum, scribbling notes. 'You don't mind, do you dear. I thought I'd try that with my own students. We all learn from one another, don't we?' and conducting unwhispered conversations with her daughter and anybody else while the talk progressed ..."

Apart from Anna Calder-Marshall, another actor of potential took his first steps at a De Leon Summer School. "In the early sixties," he recalled, "I was teaching in Staffordshire and involved with amateur theatre. My wife had been aware of my 'faraway look' for some time, when she pointed out an advertisement in one of the Sunday newspapers. That was how I came to meet Beatie de Leon and her lovely daughter. Beatie's enthusiasm was monumental and highly infectious. We, the students, from all kinds of occupations and backgrounds, threw ourselves into the activities with a will. I played Peer Gynt in a shortened version of the play - endlessly encouraged by Beatie and Jean. Beatie asked whether I had thought of becoming a professional actor. I told her I'd often dreamed of it.

"For all her encouragement I sensed her concern for my wife and children, but honestly feel that we both knew it was inevitable. I never regretted my decision, though I doubt I would have made it without Beatie's sympathetic understanding. The humorous wink and smile of approval have meant a great deal to me over the years."

Windsor Davies, the actor in question, would eventually team up with another actor who has reason to bless Beatie. With Donald Sinden he would form a long-lasting television partnership in the situation comedy, *Never The Twain*.

Until Margery Leslie took over at Richmond, Jean continued to divide her time between the City Lit., where she put in about fifteen hours a week, and Richmond where she still put in one whole day. Mrs Leslie suggested she might become a full time lecturer in charge of Music and Drama. Ultimately this seemed sensible as though she earned more on an hourly basis, a full-time post would mean she was paid in the holidays. As it transpired, by working two evenings a week at Richmond she qualified for one whole day off. On that day she would go to the City Lit. where she kept going her classes in The Art of Conversation and her lunch-time London Theatre course.

"Beatie always said that the advice given to Mrs Worthington was wrong," recalled Margery Leslie. "Any daughter, or son for that matter, who is passionately interested in theatre though not possessed of any significant acting talent, can train in stage-management and find a good career in a sphere that is suitable and enjoyable. Every single acting student was trained in stage-management. Several people have established themselves in the profession simply because of their stage-management skills."

Mrs Leslie was able to take a first-hand interest in the full-time drama school when she offered to integrate it into Richmond Adult College, such full integration being finally achieved in 1972, after several years of association with the college. "The general student involvement at the college," continued Mrs Leslie, "was very much on a part-time basis. This meant that Drama played a very great part in the life of the place. It was a focus. A production drew all the courses together - the art department, the dress-making classes - all contributed. It gave a heart and soul to the college.

"My collaboration with Beatie lasted more than twenty years. Her best qualities stemmed from her real understanding of people. She understood two completely different elements - she understood their potential and she understood their needs. As an educationalist I always felt she was able to marry the two main requirements of education, the need to satisfy society's requirements and the need to develop fully the individual. I have never known anyone with her resourcefulness. If there was a way to be found to overcome an obstacle Beatie would find it. If such and such a place were not available, she would somehow locate another. If she were short of helpers, she found them. I have known her to go out into the street and return with several puzzled looking but willing young men who proceeded to help move the scenery. She was an excellent judge of people, particularly the young and uncertain, and she knew how to get the best out of them, and, what is more, to do the best for them as she understood their real needs. Although she didn't think her geese were swans, she located and developed every talent.

"She assessed each situation, worked out what she was going to do and then went ahead and did it. I remember there was an annual row about advertising. All advertisements had to be placed with the Chief Executive and it would take up to six weeks for anything to be done. This was extremely irritating. Sometimes Beatie was short of just one student and needed to be able to place an advertisement quickly. On one such occasion she wrote to the Town Clerk for an interview. He was a bit taken aback but he invited her along, together with the Director of Education, the local Education Officer, myself and my Administrative Officer.

"He talked at length, giving reasoned arguments as to why his department operated in the way it did, claiming that he had been able to obtain advantageous rates and so on, that were to the benefit of each and every rate-payer. This went on for about half an hour, during which time Beatie said nothing. Finally she looked up at him and smiled and said, 'I suppose you get the Educational rate?' Well, of course, he hadn't heard of it. It transpired he was paying twice as much as he need do and let Beatie's advertisement go through!"

David Owen Bell worked for several years with Beatie's students. He directed end-of-term productions including *A Midsummer Night's Dream*, a punk *Macbeth* and a nineteen thirties/forties *A Winter's Tale*. "After an introduction by Greta Colson I first worked with the students in workshop. Beatie then invited me to direct the pantomime which was, I think, one of the highlights of the course. I wrote the scripts around the available students. One year she asked me to put on a pantomime in a day! About twenty five twelve to sixteen year olds arrived at nine in the morning and the show was performed at seven-thirty that evening. There was no script. I would just throw lines at them as we went along. The lyrics of the songs were pasted up on the back wall. The audience was warned that the show was got together in less than eleven hours. It was a great success, so much so that they begged me to do another one the following year.

"Beatie was a perfectionist. I'll never forget, there was a charming lady who often helped with various menial jobs on performance days. She had set up a table where she was going to sell tickets as the audience arrived. Beatie stormed in and said, 'That is *not* a box-office!' The table was moved, the tickets were arranged, a bowl of flowers was brought, the lady was asked to smarten up her hair, a chair was brought for her to sit down. 'That,' Beatie said, 'is a box-office.'

"Early on in my teaching at the school I suggested directing scenes from Shakespeare in which fights occurred, in cooperation with Ian Barber who taught stage-fighting. We would work on the scenes in the morning and then Ian would choreograph the fights in his class in the afternoon. Beatie would turn anything into a production at the drop of a hat and decided to present these scenes for the public. "Beatie had a habit of creeping into classes, standing at the back and making comments and suggestions at the end. I always found this useful. We were working on one of the fight scenes when she crept in one day. I pointed out to some of the students that in their stage-falls during the fights they weren't *feeling* the fall, just doing them accurately, but technically. At the end of the class Beatie said, 'He's right, you know.' Anyway we broke for lunch and Beatie, myself and all the students set out to cross the road to the pub. It was a really bleak mid-winter's day, the ground thick with snow. Suddenly, to everyone's alarm, Beatie collapsed in the snow. Everyone rushed to help her. She promptly sat up and said, 'There you are! That's feeling it!'"

"I frequently sat in on auditions with her," continued Margery Leslie, "and I sometimes thought she accepted people because she was sorry for them. 'I've seen worse,' she would say, 'and I think he'll be able to do something.' Generally, she was right. She helped people to realize themselves through a combination of her understanding and application of the practical skills. As well as her own practical skills Beatie also had long term goals which she achieved through an understanding of what was there. Ninety nine per cent of students responded to her."

During the latter years of the De Leon Drama School, a young school leaver of German and South American extraction, who had very little idea of what to do with his life, attended an audition. "Someone said, 'Buy The Stage newspaper,'" he recalled. "I saw an advert for the De Leon School and applied. I knew nothing about the theatre. Apart from the odd pantomime or musical I was taken to as a child, I had only seen one play. I knew nothing about drama schools. Of course I'd heard about RADA, but nothing more. I went along and Beatie and Jean auditioned me. I did the Prince of Morocco from *The Merchant of Venice*, that's how green I was. After the interview, Beatie took me to her office and launched into a lesson on performing in Shakespeare. I was already nervous, now I was completely tongue-tied. Anyway I was offered a place and I decided to go for it. If, on my last day at school, anyone had suggested that only three months hence I would be lying flat on my back on the floor, breathing deeply and making strange noises towards an invisible spot on the ceiling, I would have killed myself laughing. Within a week I was saying, 'Yes, this is it!' I was really enjoying myself, making a fool of myself, finding I had a voice, and so on. It had opened me up as a human being."

Three years after leaving the De Leon School, Gordon Warnecke won international recognition as one of the stars of the award winning film *My Beautiful Laundrette* for his sensitive portrayal of the laundrette manager in love with the punk played by Daniel Day Lewis.

At the school he had played Macduff and Banquo in *Macbeth*, Leontes in *A Winter's Tale* and, by contrast, Ugly Sister in *Cinderella*! "Beatie would slip into classes, thinking she was unnoticed at the back of the room," he continued. "The class was, say, doing an improvisation and you'd suddenly find everyone was performing to the back of the room! Everyone had a tremendous amount of respect for Beatie. Mind you having run the Q Theatre for so many years, she was still the great entrepreneur, determined to have a full house, if necessary at the expense of the actors' toil and sweat. Waiting for our first entrance for the matinee performance of one of our pantomimes, we heard the whole audience calling to one another in German. Our hearts sank to the floor. She had filled the entire house with German students, few of whom spoke a *word* of English!"

Michael Bennett, fledgling farceur and impresario, and a contemporary of Gordon's, sums up the feelings of most of the people who trained at the De Leon School. "It was like being in the *real theatre*. It prepared us for a professional career."

Beatie had been training students from the age of sixteen. It was nothing new for her. However, her background at Q had informed her with experience few drama teachers have. She could not help but pass some of this on to her students. In her late eighties she was *still* teaching students. She would still have been doing it at the De Leon Drama School had not some officious busybody pointed out that she was a mere twenty three years over the retirement age. What's a year or two when you're having fun? She scarcely missed a day. When London experienced its last great fog no-one thought it possible that Beatie would show up for her class in Mortlake but, according to Margery Leslie, she persuaded a taxi-driver to follow her as she went ahead with a torch. No other teacher had made the journey. There was only one major occasion when she couldn't make it. Normal illness would never detain her, but in 1967 she needed an operation on a polyp.

My time in hospital seemed a nightmare and a dream. I had been in the midst of organising a public performance by the full-time drama students of *Colombe*. Jean had to take over. It was the only drama school production that I missed. My health insurance provided me with a private room at University

College Hospital and private nurses, as they were very short-staffed. The operation was successful, but I then had a pulmonary embolism. Jean arrived, breathless and anxious from Richmond Adult College. She had hired a car and driven up and had been caught in heavy traffic. By the time she came in, the crisis was over.

"Her energy was amazing," added Margery Leslie. "Even after a major operation, she was sitting up in bed after only a matter of days, planning her next Summer School ..."

"Beatie is ageless," John Wiles wrote in 1989. "I've got old. I daresay Jean has got older, but Beatie is a rock and rocks don't crumble, and if old ladies live for all eternity, then Beatie is surely one of them. If one day she simply ceases to be, we will all be bereft, but eternally grateful that at no time did we say no, Beatie, no, it's out of the question. She is and was one of the great characters in the theatre, and because you didn't say no to Beatrice de Leon, even when you were asked to write a memory for a book about her you said, Yes, and were happy to do it."

CHAPTER TWO - THE HOUSE ON KEW GREEN

ALTHOUGH it would seem from the haphazard chronology of this book that Beatie and Jean have been living in Delia's small back bedroom all this time, work was not such a preoccupation that it excluded house-hunting and other such luxuries. In fact, after a long search, they put a deposit on a new house in Kensington soon to be available. But before the final contract was signed, providence, with its irresistible magnet, drew them back once more to Kew. When on its thirtieth anniversary the management of the Q Theatre decided to hold a national play competition, one of the chosen panel of judges was the Marchioness of Carisbrooke. Jean would occasionally visit King's Lodge, the pleasant house on Kew Green where Lady Carisbrooke lived, with piles of manuscripts for her perusal.

Lady Carisbrooke was a charming person and had been a patron of Q for many years. I remember her coming along and sharing smoked salmon sandwiches in the office. It seems she had, herself, once been an actress. A one time neighbour, Mrs Claiden, whose husband worked in Kew Gardens as a bird-keeper, helped in King's Cottage and remembers the dear Marchioness coming into the kitchen in full regalia after a ball, sitting on the table and saying, "You know, cookie, I could eat some bread and dripping."

In the winter of 1958 we heard that King's Lodge was up for sale. The house was Crown property and had been a grace and favour abode. It was a listed Georgian house overlooking the church of St Anne's on the Green and several magnificent chestnut trees.

Jean and I went along to view it. Although it was a cold winter's day and the house was nearly empty, we fell for it immediately. The only drawback was that, although there was a fine view of Kew Gardens from the side, it had no garden of its own. I felt desperate because, in the summer when Jean was teaching, I did want to be able to sit outside. Mrs Roundell, who had converted the adjoining King's Cottage for herself and was arranging the sale of the Lodge, lingered a moment and then led us along the side passage lined with leafless hydrangeas. She showed us a tiny space through an archway, bounded by lovely old walls, but littered with bricks and earth and rubbish. We considered for a while, and when she suggested that this space could be made available to us for use as a patio we agreed to purchase a lease.

In those days it was very difficult for a woman to get a mortgage. All my relations said that Jean and I, being two unemployed females, would never obtain the necessary mortgage unless we were guaranteed. I did not want to beg a guarantee from my brothers. It was my bank manager, Alan Garnham, who came to my aid. From his branch in Long Acre he had helped Jack through many a financial difficulty during his West End days and, when he

The de Leons abroad

Jean, Jack, Beatie and Q

Jack, back to camera, supervising a Q rehearsal

Jack in the London Clinic

Dr and Mrs James Mason

Student successes.
(Top right) Beatie awards the
Jack de Leon prize to Anna
Calder-Marshall.
(Top left) Windsor Davies as
Peer Gynt.
(Below) Gordon Warnecke
(right) with Daniel Day-Lewis
in *My Beautiful Laundrette*

Jim, Jean and Beatie outside the house on Kew Green

was ill in the London Clinic, had kindly sent him a huge box of peaches from Covent Garden. Alan took me to the Alliance Assurance Company and cleverly convinced them that Jean and I had earning potential and deserved their support. He got the mortgage for the house in our joint names. It matured after fifteen years and was paid off. Later we arranged for a longer lease. I was always an optimist. One of my tame bank managers, after a splendid meal and drinks, told Jean that I had a lucky aura.

But there were no longer only two inhabitants of the house on Kew Green. Jean's insatiable quest for the improvement of her mind took her one weekend in 1959 to Pendley Manor. This was an Adult Educational Centre at Tring in Hertfordshire run by Dorian Williams. The weekend course which had been suggested by her friend, the Hon. Philip Samuel, was on Clear Speaking and Jean found herself sitting next to a rather shy gentleman named Jim.

Although she can more than hold her own in philosophical and psychological debate, Jean had, and still has, a quality of gentle but flirtatious shyness of her own on first encounter. She sounds out each new person with simple, non-probing questions until she finds a level where both she and her new acquaintance are comfortable. Added to this she has a genuine fascination in everyone she meets. It is built into her character that there is a vast amount to learn from everyone she befriends. This is one of the greatest legacies she has from her parents.

This particular new acquaintance was born in Rhyl in North Wales on April 10th 1911, the only child of a baker and confectioner. After public school in Derbyshire he attended Liverpool University reading Medicine and graduated to jobs in many different hospitals. At the time of the weekend in Tring he was working in a small hospital in the East End of London taking care of the mentally sub normal. He would later claim this post which he held for fifteen years, to be the most satisfying of his career. "He rang me up several times after that weekend before we arranged to meet," recalled Jean. "I was still working for Dr Salmon and asked him if I could leave promptly at five-thirty. 'Is he nice?' he asked me. 'Yes, very,' I replied. We decided to eat at a Chinese restaurant, but Jim couldn't eat a thing. He felt ill. Probably nervous of me. Then he sent me postcards of dew-covered roses for several weeks. He told me he was going to a Buddhist summer school. Like Daddy, and, indeed, all my close friends, he was interested in things spiritual."

They were drawn together and over the next seven years saw as much as they could of one another. "I was always painfully shy," comments Jim. "Naturally I was alarmed by the size of Jean's family and I thought it would be an ordeal to meet them. However they were all warm and welcoming. I had no particular interest in the theatre. My parents didn't go to the theatre, though I remember being taken to pantomimes as a child; I enjoyed them and looked forward to them - George Robey, Dorothy Ward, Bill Mercer and so on. I would go to the cinema much more often. I prefer the larger canvas."

On July 12th 1966, almost thirty years after feeling herself infatuated with the eponymous actor, Jean became Mrs James Mason.

The Richmond Registry Office overflowed with family and friends. Jim was smiling and seemed to have shed his shyness. He seemed relaxed when he greeted us. When Margery Leslie wished him every happiness, he replied, "Guaranteed". Jean wore a cream silk dress and matching shoes given by my brother, Caesar. We had an afternoon reception in the Shaw Room at the Questors Theatre at Ealing where we had been present for the laying of the foundation stone. Our old friend Hero de Rance kindly played the piano for us, providing a delightful contribution to the happy atmosphere. The couple chose 'This Is My Lovely Day' for the cutting of the cake.

After a honeymoon near Nice the couple moved into a newly decorated ground floor flat at King's Lodge. Jean's cousin Peter Winton-Lewis, the architect, had made plans for the conversion. Elizabeth Agombar suggested the decor and Harry Pegg, Q's long time stage carpenter made a long wooden pelmet to form a 'fireplace' to sit round. The little office off the hall which had been used by Beatie's part-time secretary was converted into a kitchen which explains the higgledy-piggledy mess of her business papers when Anna Calder-Marshall took over the secretarial duties temporarily. As her wedding present Beatie had velvet curtains made for the sitting-room and bedroom and furniture from the old Q clubroom and Jack's office was moved in.

It soon became clear that there were advantages to having a doctor in the house. Beatie's local G.P. had seemed completely unconcerned at the occurrence of the small polyp. It was only because of Jim's insistence that it needed microscopic examination that Beatie had entered hospital in 1968.

In 1969 when the Open University was inaugurated Jean decided to enrol on the Arts Foundation Course, as it was announced that a Drama course would be offered. During the following five years, although still full-time at Richmond Adult College, she studied an average of ten hours per week in a tiny den upstairs at King's Lodge which had been converted from a larder. It faced west and overlooked Kew Gardens and she enjoyed being there. Jim and I joined her in the weekly television viewing. I especially loved the analyses of *Hamlet*, *King Lear*, *Macbeth* and *Twelfth Night* and the drama course which opened with Sophocles' *Oedipus* and ended with Genet's *The Balcony*, which was banned from television. We had long discussions over late night tea about the various programmes. All our lives became involved in the course.

One scorching summer's day we went to the Alexandra Palace with Jean. It was here amid the gardens filled with roses and the crowds of smiling faces that she received the certificate which conferred upon her a B.A. Honours Degree. A photograph of Jean in her navy and gold gown has pride of place in my sitting-room.

In all Jean took nine courses, the first on Modern Poetry, the second on European Drama and finally, after receiving her Honours Degree, Comparative Religions, which she took simply out of interest. "At one stage," recalled Jim, "the Open University put on an optional short course in Florence and Beatie and I accompanied Jean. The plumbing at the hotel which had been allocated to us was as bad as you hear in all the jokes and we quickly moved on to another place called Augusto near the Ponte Vecchio. I signed the register and we had scarcely been in our room for half an hour when a call came through from reception. It seemed that Peter Shaffer, the playwright, was calling me from London and wished to reverse the charges. I had never met the man and refused the call. I have often speculated on a later meeting between the playwright and James Mason the actor when one would inevitably call the other a liar!"

Beatie would often go on holiday with her friend Edie Lukyn, Alan Garnham's cousin. On other occasions Jean and Jim would accompany her. Often they stayed with Jim's cousin Annie Mason in Rhyl, North Wales. One year they visited Israel. **We were met at Tel Aviv by my great niece Josephine who was a professional guide and a very dear person. I shall never forget her smiling face as we touched down at the airport. She came with us up to Haifa where we spent our first week. The lovely harbour and the splendid town with its breathtaking views was glorious.**

In Haifa I was delighted to be reunited with Lily Tobias who, decades before, had collaborated with my mother on the dramatisation of *Daniel Deronda*, and was now a distinguished Israeli writer. We learned she was the aunt of the poet Dannie Abse who often read at Richmond Adult College with Jean. Our final week was spent in Jerusalem. We roamed the cobbled streets, bowed at the Wailing Wall, motored into the surrounding hills and stood in silent wonder in the Garden of Gethsemane, suffused with a sense of history of generations of human beings. The whole visit to Israel seemed like a lovely dream. Above all I remember the friendly atmosphere and the beauty of the whole country as well as the golden domed temples and the ancient churches.

The three of us went to Yugoslavia and spent a long weekend in Leningrad, organised by Richmond Adult College for students of Russian. After all the hateful propaganda and anti-Russian hysteria in those pre-*glasnost* days it was exciting to be able to see Russia ourselves. We visited Pushkin's Palace with the sun shining on the thawing snow and the Eastertide country golden and white in the spring light. We visited the opera, a lovely graceful building with elegant decor, a Bulgarian company was performing. The Hermitage was so huge you could not take in all the wonderful paintings. We saw round the small ship on the river near our hotel where the Russian revolution had begun.

One of our first trips abroad together was to Greece. Jack and I had always hoped to go there together and after Jack's death I had thought that there

would not be any opportunity to go abroad again. However, we flew to Athens and stayed in an idyllic place fifteen kilometres outside called Vouliagmeni. Above all I was impressed by Delphi. We arrived at Easter. The village was full of people roasting lambs in the piazzas. The trees covered in tender leaves and the grass bright with spring flowers up the slopes and between the ruins. In the great theatre I stood alone in the centre orchestra circle where Drama first flowered and spoke aloud, throwing my arms heavenwards. I felt myself to be in the centre of the world.

Because she missed the excitement and uncertainty of theatre, Beatie became an 'angel', investing through Herby de Leon in various West End shows. Many failed, but there were successes too. Though they are diminishing in size, cheques still arrive with Beatie's earnings from her investment in the West End musical *Oliver!* Beatie would have continued to be a regular theatre-goer, especially to see some acclaimed new artist, or a classic she adored. However, unless she could sit in the first few rows, she found it difficult to hear. She was, nevertheless, quick to point out her admiration of the younger generation of today's actors in that she found them less melodramatic than many actors in the past. The last great performance she saw was Vanessa Redgrave's portrayal of Ellida in *The Lady From the Sea* at the Roundhouse.

On November 22nd 1980 Beatie notched up eighty years. The day began with bouquets from the Attenboroughs and Judi Dench. Anthony Lewison threw a surprise luncheon party in her honour at his Hampstead home. He had the invitations printed as replicas of the old Q programmes. Roy Plomley was the Master of Ceremonies and many old friends attended.

The last production at the De Leon Drama School before Beatie's retirement was *Arms and The Man*, directed by Pierre Rouve. Over a hundred past students and staff gathered to pay tribute to her. Rouve presented her with a huge card with Q as its centrepiece, signed by all those present. Beatie found the whole occasion overwhelming. The previous day, March 30th 1984, had been a day of tributes too. "I noticed in our local Oxfordshire paper," recalled Margery Leslie, "that Blackwell's in Oxford were to hold a literary lunch where the speaker was to be Dirk Bogarde. I had met him once or twice at various functions which Beatie had commandeered him to fulfil. I immediately applied for tickets but was disappointed to learn that the lunch was fully subscribed. However, I persisted and mentioned Beatie's part in Dirk Bogarde's life and the fact that she had featured in the first volume of his autobiography. They came up with tickets for Jean, Beatie and myself."

"I returned to Q some five years after the days of my early apprenticeship," Dirk Bogarde recalled in 1980. "In my rather tatty Captain's uniform I lined up with a row of elderly ladies who were offering their services as 'chars'. Beatie was standing at the end of the queue taking their particulars down in a little book. I was feeling happy to be once again in such familiar surroundings. Nothing had changed much since I had been to France, Holland, Belgium, Germany, India, Africa, Malaya and finally Java. When I got up to Beatie with her little book she looked up at me mildly and said, 'Hello dear; been away then?' Needless to say I didn't get a job, because Beatie felt, quite rightly, that after more than five years off the boards I would be a 'little rusty'. However time went on and I once again played Q to my delight and it was all it had ever been and is to this day, irreplaceable."

One of my former students, Ken Oxman, kindly drove us up to Oxford. When we arrived, we were called to an upstairs room for drinks. Dirk saw us across the crowded room and came towards us. I was overwhelmed. He kissed me on both cheeks, then fell on his knees before me, and kissed my hand. He called me, "My queen". I was moved that he remembered me with affection after so long. After lunch he gave a speech in which he said, "There she is over there - she was responsible for launching me on my career." Even Margery was in tears on this unique occasion, as he blew me a kiss across the room.

If there was one thing which frustrated Beatie it was that her mind was still alert and capable, as one by one the other departments of her frame shut up shop. She remained determined to let anyone know that, had she not had a midnight fall down the stairs at the age of eighty seven, she would still be the woman she had always been. In this she was resolutely determined that age should not wither her more than was reasonably possible nor custom stale that infinite capacity to bounce back in any given circumstance. Let someone mention 'stage falls'. "I can still do one," she would pipe up. No-one would challenge her in case she had actually got up to demonstrate. She admitted she no longer had the voice to imitate Gracie Fields or the coloratura sopranos of old, but there was that steely conviction in her eye and that chuckle under her breath that said, "You would have been rolling in the aisles if I could!"

She set out to be a performer. However, when her production of *The Barretts of Wimpole Street* was performed by her evening students and the final curtain was accorded a standing ovation, she felt too embarrassed to go out and take the call. Yet, at the drop of a hat - even before it touched the ground - among family and friends late into her eighties she would be up and off with one of the dramatic recitations she learned at her mother's knee. She didn't need to be asked twice to enter the video-age when Jean suggested she record the scene from *Comedy and Tragedy* which her beloved brother and sister, Victor and Helena, had taught her in her teens. However, Beatie knew her place. She hated public appearances because long ago she realized she was best suited to being one of the boys in the backroom as organiser, as director, as administrator, as teacher.

However, it is too easy to look at Jack and Beatie as poet and pragmatist. With all his cerebral spirituality he was a practical West End impresario, balancing complex budgets. With all her single-minded devotion to duty, she was an intuitive and creative teacher and director who brought out the best from many other human beings. Their union was not one of opposites, but of complementary kindred spirits, something which was not always easily apparent to an outsider.

Look at Beatie during the days approaching her ninetieth birthday, in the house on Kew Green. The slight stoop, one of the results of that dreadful midnight fall, means that she sits slightly forward all the time. She appears to be waiting, waiting for a particular something to happen. Could it be she is hatching new plots? Maybe she is planning a major career move. A production she has just got to do. Or another Q theatre.

One lovely thing about this room is the bay window which looks over Kew Green. Another is the little window at the side which looks out over Kew Gardens where Jack used to love to sit. Because it faces west I often see glorious sunsets. Evening skies have provided me with some of the most vivid and lovely memories of my life. My husband and I always shared sunsets.

Would that it were possible to let time stand still, that our story might end here as, once upon a time, it did. But Beatie, the true professional to the end, saw to it that the last act had its definitive final curtain.

She had been looking forward to her ninetieth birthday on November 22nd 1990. Any excuse for company and champagne and smoked salmon, with liberal scoops of ice-cream to follow, was always welcome. In the event, the occasion was marred by an unforseen accident.

Taking a few days by the sea with Jean and Jim, she endured another bad fall and broke her left arm. It says something of the indomitability of our heroine that the fracture healed without recourse to a pin or major surgery. Determinedly she set about exercising the arm, flexing her fingers to regain its use. Nevertheless she came to depend more and more on Mollie Evoy, the former nurse who, in return for light housekeeping duties, had lived in a room at Kings Lodge for three years. The trauma of the accident proved a setback, however, from which Beatie never really recovered. Her birthday was spent quietly with close family only. Though she was quite chipper when friends called she tired more easily. Early in the new year she went into a decline.

Constant nursing became essential. Molly, quietly conscientious as ever, volunteered for extra duties. Among the other nurses who came in was Gillian Liverton. "Off-stage, at home, and over ninety years of age, qualities were revealed to me in such an array of colour," she recalled, "that I assumed they were ones which had been with her and deeply rooted throughout her life; so deeply rooted that they remained with her to the end.

"Beatie, as she finally asked one or two of us to call her, used to greet us with reproach whether we were punctual or not. Even if we had been one minute late, explaining our prior professional commitments of greater urgency, we were shown little mercy. The nurse who withstood her ordeal with trepidation never to return missed the opportunity to spend more time with Beatie and to discover a quality of kindness which I personally felt was deliberately hidden out of sheer pride and strength of character.

"Even in sickness she seemed to retain those qualities which made her successful in the past. It was quite clear that she possessed enormous natural organisational powers. This was demonstrated in the way she dressed and planned her day. The smallest detail seemed not to be overlooked. On February 14th she asked me to make a complete list (she emphasised the word 'complete') of all her current symptoms which she would personally present to her own doctor due to visit later in the day, explaining that this was in case he arrived at a time when she did not have the energy to talk to him. She placed all useful objects around her with great consistent exactitude every day and night in order to achieve maximum independence.

"Mollie was a pillar of strength to me and was very much valued by Beatie. Replacing Mollie would never have been possible. There was a strong will, on Beatie's part, to keep up appearances and to keep all possible engagements made for her, and a strong sense of loyalty to her daughter whom she constantly praised. If she did not have the physical strength she waited until it returned rather than disappoint anyone who had travelled far to see her."

On February 13th, two of Beatie's earliest full-time students came to tea. She received them in her armchair in a bedroom filled with spring flowers. Jean brought in an 'Oscar Wilde tea' of cucumber sandwiches and they all chatted happily. A small bottle of champagne was opened and Beatie managed a sip. Two days later, for the first time in her illness, she hadn't the strength to leave her bed. Nevertheless, she was pleased to welcome Delia during the afternoon. Delia sat by her bedside and spoke Minnie Louise Hoskins' lines, "I said to the man who stood at the gate of the year." The following day she fell into a deep, untroubled sleep and died with the sun late that afternoon, Saturday February 16th. Her timing was impeccable. That weekend marked the thirty-fifth anniversary of the last performance of the last play presented at her beloved Q.

Most of the national newspapers carried prominent obituaries. Dirk Bogarde wrote a charming tribute for The Independent. Many relatives, friends and colleagues gathered at Golders Green for the simple liberal Jewish ceremony. As the coffin slid gently away, Jean waved her mother a touching farewell.

A few days later, one crisp, early spring-like morning, accompanied by Jim, she carried Beatie's ashes to Kew Gardens, scattering them in that same quiet spot where her father had loved to sit and where, almost thirty five years previously, Beatie had scattered his ashes.

Whenever Beatie referred to her marriage, she always spoke of 'Jack and Beatie,' both in the third person. "Jack and Beatie had wonderful holidays together," she would say. "Jack and Beatie saw the first night of every West End play." "There was not one single day of our married life that Jack and Beatie didn't see each other."

It is impossible not to imagine they are Jack and Beatie once again, united forever in that lovely place, a part of Kew for all eternity.

Beatie had always treasured the many love-letters Jack had written to her, guarding their privacy lest modern eyes might ridicule his tender but sentimental expressions of love.

There was one, however, which she chose to share, giving her permission that it might be included here. It was dated September 24th 1919, and was written on the eve of their engagement.

My own sweetheart,

Tonight is the close of the year; with the dawn of tomorrow a new epoch in our lives will begin: a new year approaching causing us to reflect on the events of the past months - and to look forward with eager anticipation for the time to come, the events that will be marked with indelible ink on the clean sheet with which we start our lives.

In looking back we see four months of a rose-strewn garden, four months lit up with the brilliant light of love - months of divine happiness in which we two, having found love, wandered together through the garden of the world, entranced with the ecstasy of its raptures.

Then the curtain falls before the crystal of the past, and rising displays the one in which I see a future of light, a bright light suspended from the gates of heaven, penetrating into the most obscure and darkest of corners, so that with tomorrow dawns the year that brightens up the whole world.

With this light to guide our steps we shall tread the path of life together and never lose our way.

As the curtain falls on the crystal of our future, a feeling of uncontrollable happiness comes over me - my soul is flooded with gratitude.

I am coming to you sweetheart,
Your own love,
Jack

APPENDIX ONE

The Acting career of BEATRICE LEWISOHN

The Sign of David, (film) (GB 1919) (unreleased)
The Young Person in Pink, Q 26.12.24
A Message From Mars, (Polly) Q, 13.1.25
Lithuania, (The Daughter), Q, 27.1.25
Eliza Comes to Stay, (Eliza), Q, 27.1.25
The Land of Promise, Q, 23.3.25
Tilly of Bloomsbury, (Tilly), Q, 13.4.25
The Man From Toronto, Q, 11.5.25
A Pair of Silk Stockings, Q, 1.6.25
The Czarina, (Annie Jashikoff), Q, 22.6.25
The Czarina, (Annie Jashikoff), Lyric, 20.7.25
The Lifting, Q, 14.12.25
The Mother, Q, 15.2.26
Young Mrs Greenshaw, Q, 15.3.26
Bongola, Q, 19.4.26
A Dog's Chance, Q, 21.6.26
Kimono, Q, 26.7.26
The Curate of St Chad's, Q, 9.8.26
A Night in Montmartre, Q, 20.12.26
Daniel Deronda, Q, 14.2.27

The Acting Career of VICTOR LEWISOHN

Twelfth Night, (Second Officer), His Majesty's, April 1913
Joseph and His Brethren, (Second Slave), His Majesty's, 2.9.13
Old Vic Company, 1915
Touring in Shakespeare, 1921
The Cenci, (Marzio), New, 13.11.22
Cymbeline, (Caius Lucius), New, September 1923
Saint Joan, (de Poulegny, Executioner), New, 26.3.24
Heraclius, (Nicetas, Mahomet), Holborn Empire, November 1924
Saint Joan, (de Poulegny, Executioner), Regent, January 1925
The Man From Toronto, Q, 11.5.25
Common Clay, Q, 18.5.25
Idle Hands, (Mr Rogers), Q, 25.5.25
A Pair of Silk Stockings, (Sir John Gower), 1.6.25

The Czarina, (General Malakoff), Q, 22.6.25
The Truth About Blaydes, Q, 29.6.25
Comfort, (Sir Brooke Wickham), Q, 6.7.25
The Czarina, (General Malakoff), Lyric, 20.7.25
The Designers, Q, 25.10.25
Saint Joan, (de Poulegny, Executioner), Lyceum, March 1926
The Prince's Harem, (Al Saitan), Q, 17.5.26
For None Can Tell, Q, 7.6.26
Ask Beccles, (Inspector Daniel), Q, 12.7.26
A Night in Montmartre, Q, 20.12.26
The Way of the Cross, (Paul Bernese), Q, 24.1.27
Daniel Deronda, (Mordecai), Q, 14.2.27
The Anonymous Letter, Q, 7.3.27
The Lonely Road, Q, 5.9.27
Monna Vanna, (Prinzivalle), Q, 19.9.27
Bluff, Q, 10.10.27
The Lovely Liar, (Simon Rubinstein), Q, 7.11.27
Enchantment, (Bill), Q, 12.12.27
The Man At Six, (Wolmer), Q, 6.1.28
Judith of Israel, (Herald), Strand, 15.2.28
Pelleas and Melisande, Q, 18.3.28
O'Flaherty's Star, Q, 16.4.28
The Gates of Paradise, Q, 14.5.28
The Master Builder, (Solness), Q, 11.6.28
The Big Idea, (Michael Hudson), Q, 13.8.28
Earthbound, (Capt. Zachary Margrove), Q, 10.9.28
John Gabriel Borkman, (Borkman), Q, 15.10.28
These Fathers, Q, 29.10.28
The Man In The Dock, Q, 26.11.28
The Man At Six, (Wolmer), Queens, March 1929
Tunnel Trench, (German Private), Duchess, 25.11.29
The Silent Witness, (Arthur Dinton), Comedy, 30.4.30
White Cargo, (Weston), Q, 19.10.31
Playground, (Dr Evan Griffith), Q, 2.11.31
The Master Builder, (Solness), Duchess, 19.11.31
Robin Hood, (Hugo de Longespel), Q, 29.12.31
Julius Caesar, (Mark Anthony), Q, 25.1.32
Hamlet, (Hamlet), Q, 22.2.32
The School for Scandal, (Sir Peter Teazle), Q, 28.3.32
As You Like It, (Jaques), Q, 6.6.32
Prince for Pimlico, (Leonard Wraymond), Q, 4.7.32

Times Fool, (Sir John Orme), Q, 1.8.32
Cohen and Family, (Mr Moses), Regent, 3.10.32
The Merchant of Venice, (Shylock), Q, 30.10.32
Third Degree, (Henry Jones), Q, 14.11.32
The Scoop, (Danby), Q, 9.1.33
Trust Berkely, (General Baroda), Q, 16.1.33
The Silent Menace, (Sgt Williams), Q 23.1.33
Henry IV, Part One, (King Henry IV), Q, 27.3.33
The Fourth Wall, (Edward Carter), Q, 14.8.33
The Passing of the Third Floor Back, (Third Floor Back), Q, 28.8.33
It's a Wise Wife, (Dr Anthropoulos), Q, 18.9.33
The School for Scandal, (Sir Peter Teazle), Q, 19.2.34
The Purple Mask, Q, 21.5.34
The Flame, (Luigi Benedetti), Q, 4.6.34
House on Fire, (Simon), Q, 18.6.34
Triumph, (Valerius Caesar), Q, 25.6.34
And So To Bed, (Charles II), Q, 30.7.34
The Three Sisters, (Chebutykin), Q, 20.7.34

The Acting Career of DELIA DELVINA

The Barton Mystery, Q, 23.2.25
The Round Table, Q, 16.3.25
South of the Line, (Musk Drop), Q, 12.6.25
The Prince's Harem, Q, 17.5.26
Children of the Moon, Q, 2.10.26
Children of the Moon, Royalty, October 1926
The Master Builder, (Hilde), Q, 11.6.28
Uncle Vanya, (Sonya), Theatre Royal, Huddersfield, Summer 1928
The Rose Without a Thorn, (Mary Lassells), Q, 28.10.35

The Acting Career of AMINTA DE LEON

Lord Richard in the Pantry, Q, 13.4.31
Interference, Q, 27.4.31
The Silent Witness, Q, 1.6.31
A Message from Mars, (Minnie), Q, 18.12.33
The Barretts of Wimpole Street, (Henrietta), Q, 1.1.34
At the Villa Rose, (Adele), Q, 8.1.34
The Chinese Puzzle, (Naomi Melsham), Q, 5.2.34
London Wall, (Miss Hooper), Q, 12.2.34

Saint Joan, (Joan), Q, 5.3.34
Dance Macabre, (Sister Claudia), Q, 19.3.34
Parody for Living, (Jean Fletcher), Q, 17.6.35
Frosted Glass, (Elsie Field), Q, 8.7.35
The Rose Without a Thorn, (Katherine Tilney), Q, 28.10.35
Widower's Houses, (Blanche), Q, 18.11.35

Films from plays by JACK DE LEON and JACK CELESTIN

The Man at Six, (GB 1931) BIP. Directed by Harry Hughes.
With Anne Grey, Lester Matthews.
The Silent Witness, (US 1932) Fox. Directed by Marcel Varnel.
With Lionel Atwill, Helen Mack, Greta Nissen, Bramwell Fletcher, Alan Mowbray.
Crime on the Hill, (GB 1933) BIP. Directed by Bernard Vorhaus.
With Sally Blane, Phyllis Dare, Anthony Bushell, Lewis Casson, Nigel Playfair.
Jury's Evidence, (GB 1935) British Lion. Directed by Ralph Ince.
With Hartley Power, Margaret Lockwood.
Line Engaged, (GB 1935) British Lion. Directed by Bernard Mainwaring.
With Bramwall Fletcher, Jane Baxter, Coral Browne.
The Gables Mystery, (GB 1938) Welwyn-MGM. directed by Harry Hughes.
With Antoinette Cellier, Francis L. Sullivan. (Remake of *The Man at Six*.)

A complete list of the plays of Jack de Leon can be found in the Index under his name.

APPENDIX TWO

Here are listed all of the new plays presented at the Q Theatre between 1925 and 1956. Among these are plays which may have been presented previously in other countries, or in earlier provincial try-outs. The criterion observed is that all were new to the London area and had never previously been performed in the West End. The plays are listed in author order with the dates of the first performance. An asterisk (*) indicates that the play transferred to the West End.

ABBOT, Ada G.
Mother of Men, * 23.7.46

ABDULLA, Achmed
The Prince's Harem, 17.5.26
(with Robert Davis)

ADDYMAN, Elizabeth
The Secret Tent, 24.5.55.

ADKINS, Ella
It Might Happen To You, 8.4.35
The Case of Dr Ambrose, 5.10.54
(with Gordon Harbord)

AGAR, Herbert
Storm Over Europe, 9.11.36
(with Eleanor Chilton)

AGATE, James
I Accuse, 25.10.37,
(from a play by Wilhelm Herzog
and Hans Rehfisch)

AGNEW, Ewan
The Shingling of Jupiter, 2.11.25

ALLNOTT, Kenneth
The Prickly Pear, 27.1.36
(with Stephen Tate)

AMES, Delano
Uneasily to Bed, 14.7.39

ANDERSON, Clement
Angelina Pantaloon, 22.6.54

ANSTHRUTHER, Gerald
The Third Visitor, * 12.6.45

ANTHONY, Jonquil
The Years of the Locust, 7.11.44

ARCHER, William
The Joy Ride, 8.2.26

ARMITAGE, D.
Oflag 3, 26.6.45
(with Douglas Baber, Hugh Falkus)

ATKINSON, Alex
Nightmare, 4.2.47
Night Call, 23.10.51
Spring Model, 7.6.54

ATTIWILL, Ken
Who Killed My Sister, 18.8.42
(with Evadne Price)
Three Wives Called Roland, 2.11.43
(with Evadne Price)

BABER, Douglas
Oflag 3, 26.6.45
(with D. Armitage, Hugh Falkus)

BACON, Allon
Cry For the Moon, 2.10.51

BACON, Roger
Barren Gain, 7.12.29
(with Jane Wood)

BAGNOLD, Enid
Little Idiot, 10.11.53

BAILES, David
Cat's Cradle, * 28.9.25
(with Aimee Cavendish)

BAINES, John
Rovina, 20.2.39

BARLOW, Vernon
Youth Unarmed, 23.4.41
(with W.T. Maxwell)

BARRETT, Philip
The Wasted Years, 26.8.47

BARWELL, Peggy
Prison Without Bars, 24.4.39

BARZINA, L.
(see Athole Stewart)

BATES, Florence
Uncle Hiram's Here, 12.10.25
(with Edith Carter)

BAX, Clifford
A Day, A Night and a Morrow, 19.10.48

BEALE, Jack
Time On Our Hands, 6.7.54
(with Patrick Cargill)

BEAUMONT, William
This Woman, 21.3.27

BECKWITH, Reginald
Happy as Kings, 28.1.47

BEER, Georges
A Lady Reflects, 22.4.40
(with Louis Verneuil)
(and see Audry and Waveney Carten)

BELA, Nicholas
Fire-weed, 28.3.50

BELL, GORDON
Claudius the Bee, 23.12.43
(with John Leeming)

BELL, Robert
Poisoned Chalice, 27.1.48
Golden Leaves, 24.2.48

BENTLEY, Wilford
Yew Tree Farm, 4.7.38

BERINGER, Vera
Beltane Night, 20.4.25

BERNARD, Henry
Miss Smith, * 27.4.36
The Old Master, 29.8.38

BERRYMAN, Noel
Age of Indiscretion, 23.11.54

BIRCH, Frank
Mountebanks, 12.11.34

BIRO, Lajos
School for Slavery, 18.11.41

BIRO, Ludwig
The Czarina, * 22.6.25
(with Melchior Lengyel)

BLACK, Ian Stuart
We Must Kill Toni, 17.4.51

187

BLACKMAN, A.
Sparring Partners, 25.2.29
(with Brock Williams, George Carney)

BLACKMORE, Peter
Down Came a Blackbird, 1.9.53

BLACKWELL, Donald
The Annexe, 5.10.48
(with Theodore St John)

BLAKE, Grey
Too Late For Anger, 2.7.46

BOEHM, David
Courtship Dance, * 22.10.34

BOLTON, Guy
Adam and Eva, * 30.3.25
(With George Middleton)
Humoresque, 26.10.48

BORLAND, Barlow
(see George Douglas)

BOULTON, Guy Pelham
Mirabelle, * 14.6.37

BOULTON, Matthew
Silver Threads, 21.10.29

BOWER, Marion
The Quince Bush, 25.7.32

BOWMAN, Fanny
Priscilla the Rake, 7.2.27

BOX, Muriel
Love In These Days, 19.6.45

BRAMPTON, Joan
The Old One Smiles, 22.11.37

BRANDANE, John
The Lifting, 14.12.25

BRANDON-THOMAS, Jevan
The Glory of the Sun, 19.10.25

BRETT, Michael
Four in Hand, 13.10.53
Lucky Strike, 11.4.55

BROADWATER, Henry
Anniversary, 2.7.34

BROMFIELD, Louis
The House of Women, 3.9.28

BROOKER, Wolfe
The Flame, 4.6.34
(with Beatrice Erskine)

BROWN, Lionel
To Have and to Hold, * 25.1.37
The Constant Sinner, 5.4.37
Square Pegs, 4.10.37
This Land of Ours, 14.8.45
Not Proven, 5.2.52

BROWN, Thomas
The Man Who Has Nothing, 7.6.37
(with Maud Flannery)

BROWNE, Thomas
Grand Slam, 13.3.39

BROWNING, H.
The Tame Cat, 4.1.26

BRUCE, Kate Mary
The Rocking Horse, 24.9.46

BUCKLE, Richard
Gossip Column, 14.4.53

BURDEN, Hugh
The Young and Lovely, 2.3.43

BURFORD, Roger
A Poor, Weak Woman, 20.9.49

BURKE, A.L.
A Disturbed Night, 16.5.27

BURTON, Betty
Youth and Mrs Meredith, 23.5.38
(with Margerie Scott)

BUTLER, Ivan
Joking Apart, 7.10.52

CALDWELL, H.H.
Little Stranger, 6.6.37
(with Katherine Hilliker)

CALVADORE, Louis
The Way of the Cross, 24.1.27

CAMPBELL, J.L.
The Praying Mantis, 9.3.54

CAMPBELL, Keith
Flat Spin, 6.9.49

CAMPION, Cyril
Ask Beccles, * 12.7.26
(with Edward Dignon)
The Lash, * 18.10.26
Asleep, * 25.4.27
The Admiral's Secret, 20.8.28
(with Edward Dignon)
Watch Beverley, 17.2.30
Trust Berkely, * 16.1.33
This Money Business, * 6.12.37
Calling Bellamy, 13.6.38
Temporary Residence, * 1.4.40
The Lady Killer, 10.10.44
Madeleine, 14.12.48

CAPEK, Karel
The Mother, * 13.2.39
(adapted by Paul Selver, Miles Malleson)

CARGILL, Patrick
Time On Our Hands, 6.7.54
(with Jack Beale)

CARNEY, George
Sparring Partners, 25.2.29
(with A. Blackman, Brock Williams)

CAROLE, Joseph
Start from Scratch, 3.1.56

CARSON, Frances
The Unknown Woman, 27.6.27
(with Grace Edwin)

CARTEN, Audry and Waveney
Gay Love, * 20.2.33
Destination Unknown, * 5.7.37
My Crime, 20.6.38 (from a play by
Louis Verneuil, George Beers)

CARTER, Conrad
Bad Name, 11.7.27
Your Brother George, 6.8.45

CARTER, Edith
Uncle Hiram's Here, 12.10.25
(with Florence Bates)
Wanted A Wife, 13.9.26
The Lovely Liar, 7.11.27

CARTER, Gertrude
The Snow Storm, 12.4.26

CARTER, Winifred
The Two Mrs Camerons, 1.2.32
Marriage Harvest, 5.12.32

CARVIC, Heron
The Widow of Forty, * 21.11.44

CASPARY, Vera
Laura, * 30.1.45
(with George Sklar)

CASTON, Charles
Are You Married?, 31.10.27

CATTO, Max
They Walk Alone, * 21.11.38
Punch Without Judy, * 12.6.39
Wise Guys, 27.5.40
Black Racket, 5.5.42
Gather No Moss, 18.11.47

CAVENDISH, Aimee
Cat's Cradle, * 28.9.25
(with David Bailes)

CELESTIN, Jack
The Man at Six, * 16.1.28
(with Jack de Leon)
The Silent Witness, * 26.11.28
(a.k.a. *The Man In The Dock*)
(with Jack de Leon)
Crime On The Hill, * 3.10.32
(with Jack de Leon)
Line Engaged, 23.7.34
(with Jack de Leon)

CHARLTON, John
The (K)Night of the Garter, 13.5.29

188

CHILTON, Eleanor
Storm Over Europe, 8.11.36
(with Herbert Agar)

CHRISTIE, Dorothy and Campbell
The Town Bowl, 26.7.49

CLARK, Cumberland
Money Makes a Difference, 9.10.33

CLARK, Dudley
Bluff, 10.10.27

CLAY, Tomasine
Full Tide, 16.6.53

CLAYTON-GREENE, Alice
The Last Guest, 20.2.28

CLEWES, Howard
Quay South, 5.12.50

CLOSE, Ella
The Gates of Paradise, 14.5.28

COLEBY, Wilfred T.
The Top Drawer, 28.2.27
(with Witheridge Hill)

COLLINS, Sewell
Anne-One Hundred, * 28.3.27

COLTMAN, Joseph
A Dog For Delmont, 13.2.51

COMPTON-RICKETT, Arthur
Sovereignty, 31.1.27

CONSTANDUROS, Denis
A Pig In A Poke, 17.10.50
(with Mabel Constanduros)

CONSTANDUROS, Mabel
Reluctant Lady, 11.11.47
A Pig In A Poke, 17.10.50
(with Denis Constanduros)

COOPER, A. Burton
We Are The People, * 25.8.42

COOPER, William
High Life, 23.1.51

CORNELIUS, Lillian
Bongola, 19.4.26
(with C. Owen Payne)

COSENS, Monica
Miss Black's Son, 20.9.26
(with Brenda Girven)
Cautious Campbell, * 15.11.26
(with Brenda Girven)
The Red Umbrella, * 24.10.27
(with Brenda Girven)
An Average Man, 23.5.32
(with Brenda Girven)

COUSINS, E.G.
Gaily I Go, 20.7.48
Star Witness, 6.1.53

COX, Constance
Vanity Fair, * 14.5.46
The Picture of Dorian Gray, 30.10.47

CRADDOCK, Reginald
Night Returns In Africa, 8.2.55

CRAIGIE, Jill
The Judge, 26.9.38
(with Jeffrey Dell)

CRAMPTON, Ernest
So This Is Romance, 22.2.26

CRAUFORD, Lane
The House at Bury Hill, 25.11.52

CROFT, Neville
To Christabel, 2.12.52

CROMBIE, Oliver
(see George Douglas)

CRONIN, A.J.
Jupiter Laughs, * 7.10.41

CROSSE, David
Identity Unknown, 30.5.55

CURRIE, Clive
Tamaresque, 18.2.29

DACRE, John
Rumpus on the River, 16.12.52

DARLING, Grenville
The Haunted Legacy, 12.6.22

DARLINGTON, W.A.
(see Jan Fabricius)

DARNLEY, Herbert
By Whose Hand?, 12.8.29

DAVIS, C.A.C.
Song In Leap Year, 20.4.43

DAVIS, Rhys
The Captive Maid, * 14.12.36

DAVIS, Robert
The Prince's Harem, 17.5.26
(with Achmed Abdullah)

DAVISON, John
Search, 7.5.34

DAWES, John Stanley
Wind Across The Tide, 22.5.39

DEARDEN, Harold
To Kill A Cat, * 1.5.39
(with Roland Pertwee)

DEARSLEY, A.P.
Fly Away Peter..., 26.9.44

DELAMERE, Margaret
The Ship's Bell, 16.1.39
(with Sebastian Shaw)

DELDERFIELD, R.F.
Printers Devil, 10.7.39
Follow The Plough, 1.12.53

DE LEON, Jack
The Man At Six, * 16.1.28
(with Jack Celestin)
Contraband, * 12.3.28
(with Warren Fawcett - Marion
Fawcett)
The Other Mrs Baverstock, 17.9.28
(Play by Wilfred Thornley,
reconstructed by Jack de Leon and
Marion Fawcett
The Silent Witness, * 26.11.28
(a.k.a. *The Man In The Dock*)
(with Jack Celestin)
Crime On the Hill, * 3.10.32
(with Jack Celestin)
Francis Thompson, * 6.3.33
(with Jack Celestin)
Line Engaged, * 23.7.34
(with Jack Celestin)
*The House In the Wood, being the Adventures of Goldilocks, the Three Bears and
the Big Bad Wolf*, 22.12.54
(with Felicity Douglas)

DELL, Jeffrey
The Judge, 26.9.38

DE MARNEY, Derrick
Whispering Gallery, 5.3.28

DE MARNEY, Terence
Wanted for Murder, * 28.6.37
(with Percy Robinson)
The Crime of Margaret Foley, * 2.5.44
(with Percy Robinson)

DENHAM, Lilian
The Man With Expensive, Tastes, 6.4.53
(with Edward Percy)

DENHAM, Reginald
Green Holly, * 30.5.38
(with Edward Percy)
The Distant Hand, 8.5.39
(with Edward Percy)
Dog's Delight, 2.4.46
(with Edward Percy)
The Coral Snake, 2.9.47
(with Mary Orr)

DENNYS, Joyce
The Bells Ring, 17.9.46

DES VEOUX, Carmaine
The Book and the Binding, 3.2.36
(with Christopher Sandeman)

DICKENS, Stafford
One Way Street, 9.5.38

189

DIGNON, Edward
Ask Beccles, * 12.7.26
(with Cyril Campion)
The Admiral's Secret, 20.8.28
(with Cyril Campion)

DINNER, William
Front Page Girl, 11.7.50
(with William Morum)

DIXON, Ruth
The Long Walk to China, 5.4.55

DONISTHORPE, Sheila
Children - To Bless You!, * 10.2.36
Guests at Lancaster Gate, 3.5.37
Society Blues, 17.10.38
Prelude to Marriage, 30.10.45

DORNHORST, Paul
They Fly By Twilight, * 19.9.38

DOUGLAS, Felicity
It's Never Too Late, 18.11.52
The House In the Wood, being the Adventures of Goldilocks, the Three Bears and the Big Bad Wolf, 22.12.54
(with Jack de Leon)

DOUGLAS, George
The House with Green Shutters, 29.10.34
(adapted by Barlow Borland, Oliver Crombie)

DREW, D.L.
Post Mortem, 9.4.34

DUDLEY, Ernest
Dr Morelle, 4.7.50
(with Arthur Watkyn)

DUDLY, Ernest
Trouble At Number Thirteen, 20.10.53

DUGDALE, Giles
Owner Gone Abroad, 3.2.30

DUNSANY, Lord
Mr Faithful, 22.8.27

DYER, C. Raymond
Who On Earth, 24.7.51

EDWIN, Grace
The Unknown Woman, 27.6.27
(with Frances Carson)

ELLETT, Eileen
Temporary Ladies, 21.5.45
...and All Things Nice, 16.10.51

ELLIS, Walter
The Lovely Lady, 13.8.46

ELLIS, W.W.
The Big Idea, 13.8.28

ELSNA, Hebe
Seasons Greetings, 29.9.53

ENSOR, Aubrey C.
Long Lane, 25.1.26
Come Out of Your Shell, * 20.5.40
(with Leslie Julian Jones)

ERICKSON, Paul
Jail-Break, 8.2.49
The Shadow of a Man, 19.2.52

ERSKINE, Beatrice
The Flame, 4.6.34
(with Wolfe Brooker)

ERVINE, St. John
Boyd's Shop, 30.9.47

EVANS, Caradoc
Taffy, * 8.9.25

EVANS, David
Up The Garden, 15.9.30
Putting Back the Clock, 27.5.35
(with Mary Forrester)

FABRICIUS, Jan
Night of Masquerade, 29.4.52
(adapted by W.A. Darlington)

FALKUS, Hugh
Oflag 3, 26.6.45
(with D. Armitage, Douglas Baber)

FARJEON, J. Jefferson
Enchantment, 12.12.27
The Hours Between, 12.11.29

FAWCETT, Marion
Contraband, 12.3.28
(with Jack de Leon)
The Other Mrs Baverstock, 17.9.28
(Play by Wilfred Thornley, reconstructed by Jack de Leon and Marion Fawcett)

FENN, Charles
School for Scoundrels, 24.1.50
The Sea Breeze, 22.4.52

FISHER, Daisy
A Ship Comes Home, * 16.11.36

FLACK, Mary Frances
Blind Corners, 28.3.38

FLANNERY, Maud
The Man Who Has Nothing, 7.6.37
(with Thomas Brown)

FLAVIN, Martin
Children of the Moon, * 4.10.26
Call Me A Gondola, 6.12.55

FLEET, Ben
Before Men's Eyes, 30.8.26
(with Clifford Pember)

FLEMING, Brandon
None But the Brave, * 19.7.26
(with Bernard Merrivale)

FLOWER, Dorothea
Triumph, 25.6.34

FODOR, Ladislaus
Trifles Light as Air, 6.6.49
(adapted by Arnold Ridley, St. Vincent Troubridge)

FORBES, Hugh
The Thursday Habit, 3.5.55

FORD, Richard
Six To Ten, 17.3.53

FORESTER, C.S.
Nurse Cavell, * 26.2.34
(with C.E. Bechhofer Roberts)

FORRESTER, Mary
Putting Back The Clock, 27.5.35
(with David Evans)

FOSS, Kenelm
Second Fiddle, 21.2.27

FRACAROLI, A.
(see Athole Stewart)

FRANCES, Charlotte
Western Wind, * 21.6.49

FRANCIS, John Derek
Two In the Bush, 22.9.53

FREEMAN, Gordon
A Prince from Pimlico, 4.7.32

FURNISS, Paul
Between Five and Seven, 24.3.30

GALBRAITH, Dorothy
Minder Duel, 11.12.45

GATES, Bill
The Earth Remains, 15.11.49

GEORGE, Carroll
Motives, 30.6.30

GIBBS, Margaret
The Hawthorne Tree, 29.11.55

GIBSON, R.R.
Mandalay, 4.6.28

GICK, Judith
The Golden Thread, 13.1.53

GILTINAN, Donal
The Gentle Maiden, 15.9.53

GINSBURY, Norman
Walk in the Sun, 23.1.39

GIRVEN, Brenda
Miss Black's Son, 20.9.26
(with Monica Cosens)
Cautious Campbell, * 15.11.26
(with Monica Cosens)

190

The Red Umbrella, * 24.10.27
(with Monica Cosens)
An Average Man, 23.5.32
(with Monica Cosens)

GLAISTER, Gerrard
Music for Murder, 24.5.49
(with Gavin Holt)

GLENNON, Gordon
Dust Before the Wind, 10.11.42

GODLEY, Elizabeth
The Immortal Minute, 13.5.52

GODWIN, Harold
Nothing Venture, 29.4.35

GORDON, Dahlia
Married Bachelors, 13.2.28

GORE-BROWN, Margaret and Robert
Finishing School, 14.9.54

GOULDING, Iris
Between Friends, 19.7.49

GOW, Ronald
Ma's Bit of Brass, * 31.10.38
The Full Treatment, 3.2.53
(with Robert Morley)

GRAHAM, Bertha N.
Young Mrs Greenshaw, 15.3.26

GRANT, Neil
Thy Name is Woman, * 16.8.26

GRIEVE, Rachel
If This Be Error, * 13.12.49
Birds of Sadness, 12.1.54
The Visiting Moon, 18.1.55

HACKFORTH, Gilbert
Sweethearts and Wives, * 28.9.48
(with Margaret Jones)

HADLEY-CHASE, James
Last Page, 19.3.46

HALL, Allan
The Third Party, 20.9.29

HAMILTON, John R.C.
The Crimson Crescent, 24.9.29

HARBORD, Gordon
The Case of Dr Ambrose, 5.10.54
(with Ella Adkins)

HARDING, D.C.F.
Sweet Adversity, 13.9.37

HARPER, Barbara
Close To The Wind, 4.10.49

HASTINGS, Charlotte
Uncertain Joy, 8.9.53

HASTINGS, Hugh
Red Dragon, 12.12.50

HAY, Ian
We Are Seven, 20.3.45

HEIMANN, Philip
First Episode * 11.9.33
(with Terence Rattigan)

HEMING, Jack
The Scoop, 9.1.53

HENDERSON, Robert
... Burning Bright, 11.5.54

HERBERT, F. Hugh
For Love or Money, 30.9.52

HERZOG, Wilhelm
(see James Agate)

HESLOP, Charles
Cuckoo Cottage, 9.5.27

HEWITT, K.D.
African Shadows, 23.9.29

HILL, Witheridge
The Top Drawer, 28.2.27
(with Wilfred T. Coleby)

HILLIKER, Katherine
Little Stranger, 6.6.37
(with H.H. Caldwell)

HODGE, Morton
The Island, * 26.7.37
To Whom We Belong, 11.12.39
Once There Was Music, 10.3.41

HODSON, Mildred
The Square Peg, 27.5.29

HOLLAND, Harold
The Big Drum, 17.10.27

HOLLOWAY, Sydney
Hitch Your Wagon, 6.12.26

HOLT, Gavin
Music for Murder, 24.5.49
(with Gerrard Glaister)

HOME, William Douglas
Great Possessions, * 8.2.37
Passing By, * 29.4.40

HOPE, Bertha
The Jolly Family, 28.11.27
(with Reginald Owen)

HOPWOOD, Avery
High Temperature, * 8.7.40

HORLER, Sydney
The House of Secrets, 10.1.27

HORNE, Kenneth
Ann's Lapse, 19.1.37
A Lass and A Lackey, 27.12.40

HUNTER, John
No Joy For the Wicked, 24.4.45
(with William Lees)

HUTCHINSON, Ross
Navy at Sea, 19.6.51

HUTH, Jochen
The Four Partners, 12.10.36
(adapted by Sewell Stokes)

HUTTON, Michael Clayton
Sleep On My Shoulder, 31.5.49

HYAMS, Hilda
The Master, 15.2.26

JACKSON, Frederick
The King's Messenger, 7.7.30

JACKSON, Harry
Young Man's Fancy, 9.10.51

JAFFA, Minnie Z.
In Walked Jimmy, 21.9.25

JAMES, Stanford
Strangers In Paradise, 6.8.34

JARVIS, Nina
Where Is Bohemia?, 6.9.37

JEANS, Ronald
Grace and Favour, 27.7.54

JOHNSON, Pamela Hansford
Corinth House, 4.12.51

JONES, Leslie Julian
Come Out of Your Shell, * 20.5.40
(with Aubrey Ensor)
Rise Above It, * 8.1.41.

JONES, Margaret
Sweetheart and Wives, * 28.9.48.
(with Gilbert Hackforth)

JONES, Paul
Birthday Honours, 17.2.53

JONES, Peter
Sweet Madness, * 11.3.52

JOYCE, James
Exiles, 15.5.50

KENNINGTON, Alan
Spring Harvest, 6.10.42
Flying Visitor, 10.4.45
(with William McElwee)

KILMARNOCK, Lord
The Anonymous Letter, 7.3.27

191

KILPATRICK, Florence
Virginia's Husband, * 28.6.26
Getting George Married, * 28.1.29

KING, Philip
See How They Run, * 21.12.44
Post Haste, 17.7.51

KINKEAD, Clive
Common Clay, 18.5.25

KLEIN, John
Charlotte Corday, 26.10.36

KNIGHT, Walter
... In Heaven and Earth, 15.12.42

KNIPE, John
The Dark River, 14.11.27

KOHN, Rose Simon
Green Laughter, * 28.8.45

LANE, Gerald
Thus Far, 16.9.35

LANGLEY, Noel
Little Lambs Eat Ivy, * 9.9.47

LATIMER, Norman
The Watchman, 6.2.51

LAURENCE, C.E.
The Year, 22.8.27

LEE, Norman
In The Palm of Your Hand, 10.12.46
(with Barbara Toy)

LEEMING, John
Claudius the Bee, 23.12.43
(with Gordon Bell)

LEES, William
No Joy for the Wicked, 24.4.45
(with John Hunter)

LEHMAN, Leo
Who Cares?, 14.2.56

LEIGH, Kathleen
House On Fire, * 18.6.34

LENGYEL, Melchior
The Czarina, * 22.6.25
(with Ludwig Biro)

LEWES, Cedric
Courage, 8.11.26

LEWISOHN, Lydia
Daniel Deronda, 14.2.27
(with Lily Tobias)

LIGGATT, James
Divorce on Tuesday, 3.12.46

LINCOLN, Charles
Stolen Time, 6.2.39

LION, Leon M.
The Capital Crime, 2.11.36
(with Basil Mitchell)

LISTER, Laurier
Forsaking All Other, 2.5.50
(with Hilda Vaughan)

LOMAX, W.J.
Conscience In Pawn, 22.10.28

LUMSDEN, Mary
Clouded Vision, 9.3.48

MACAULAY, Tom
This Tender Age, 28.8.39

MACDOUGALL, Roger
MacAdam and Eve, * 7.2.50

MADDEN, Cecil
The Hero, 21.5.28

MAINWARING, Frances
Portrait of a Woman, 7.12.54

MAINWARING, Richard
Apple Sauce, 15.4.40
(with Stratton Taylor)

MALCOLM, Charles Horace
Bachelor's Brides, 6.5.29

MALIK, Elsa
Louise, 31.1.50

MALLESON, Miles
Conflict, * 30.11.25
A Night in Montmartre, 20.12.26
(with Walter Peacock)
(and see Karel Capek)

MALLOCH, G.R,
Harvest, 30.4.34

MALLOCK, W. Wyndham
Vantage Point, 16.5.38

MALTBY, H.F.
The Age of Youth, 2.1.33
(with Freddie Wynne)
Learning to Love, 15.5.33
(with Charles Windermere)

MARCH, Richard
The Sentinel, 29.5.51

MARKHAM, F. Ellinor
Thy Name Is Woman, 17.1.56

MARKS, Enid
Running Away Money, 14.5.34
(with Winifred Walton)

MARLOWE, Patricia
The Uneasy Head, 9.12.41

MARSH, Brian
The Man Responsible, * 13.6.27

MARSH, Edward O.
(see Georges Neveux)

MARSHALL, Ken
The Painted Devil, 3.11.53

MARSHALL-HOLE, Molly
Water, * 8.10.28

MARTIN, Desmond
The Merry Month, 17.11.53
The Evidence I Shall Give, 25.1.55

MASSEY, Wilfred
I Walk Unseen, 7.12.48
(with Robert Ward)

MAXWELL, W.T.
Youth Unarmed, 23.4.41
(with Vernon Barlow)

McCORMICH, Ian
The Beautiful World, 11.10.49

McELWEE, William
Flying Visitor, 10.4.45
(with Alan Kennington)

McFADDEN, Elizabeth
He Signed His Name, 24.8.43

McGARRY, Kevin
Money For Jam, 18.5.54

McLELLAN, Mary
Sauce For The Goose, 21.2.50

MERRICK, Leonard
The Fraud, 9.2.25
(with Michael Horton)

MERRIVALE, Bernard
None But The Brave, * 19.7.26
(with Brandon Fleming)

MERRYN, Anthony
The Dreamers, 12.11.28
The Way of a Wife, 2.8.37

MEYRICK, Gordon
The Green Phantom, 11.11.35
The Second Shot, * 19.4.37

MIDDLETON, George
Adam and Eva, * 30.3.25
(with Guy Bolton)

MILLAR, Ronald
Zero Hour, * 15.2.44

MILLER, Hugh
One Flight Up, 24.11.42
(with Ronald Simpson)

MILLER, Stanley
The Girl from Rouen, 10.6.52

MILLS, H.V.
Do Let's Be Serious, 3.12.28

192

MITCHELL, Basil
The Capital Crime, 2.11.36
(with Leon M. Lion)

MONRO, Robert
Pardon My Claws, 2.6.52

MONTGOMERY, Doreen
The Summer House, 24.11.53

MORGAN, Joan
Dark Potential, * 25.1.44
Deep As A Well, 6.5.47
Who Goes Home, 31.10.50
Shadow On The Sun, 12.5.53

MORLEY, Robert
The Full Treatment, 3.2.53
(with Ronald Gow)

MORLEY-SMITH, Ann
Bless You, 20.5.52

MORRELL, Charles
The Choker, 6.1.30

MORRIS, Colin
Reluctant Heroes, 7.4.47

MORTON, Michael
The Fraud, 9.2.25
(with Leonard Merrick)
Salvage, 22.11.26
(with Peter Traill)

MORUM, William
Front Page Girl, 11.7.50
(with William Dinner)

MURRAY, T.C.
Autumn Fire, * 22.3.26

NASH, Aiden
The Sainted Sinners, 4.5.53

NEGRA, Nella
Educating Anne,
27.2.28

NEVEUX, Georges
Indictment, 16.11.48
(adapted by Edward O. Marsh)

NICOLAS, John
Wait My Love, * 29.5.45

NORMAN, Dolph
A Witch In Time, 20.12.55

O'DONNELL, Frank J. Hugh
Anti-Christ, 21.11.27
O'Flaherty's Star, 16.4.28

O'HANLON, Peter
The Bee Fool, 29.11.37

OLIVER, Roland
The Night Hawk, * 13.8.34

OPENSHAW, Charles Elton
Scapegoat, 5.6.33
The Shadow Princess, 23.10.33

ORME, Michael
The Lonely Road, 5.9.27
The Eternal Snows, 6.2.28

ORR, Mary
The Coral Snake, 2.9.47
(with Reginald Denham)

OWEN, Reginald
The Jolly Family, 28.11.27
(with Bertha Hope)

PASTON, George
When Adam Delved, 18.7.27

PAXTON, Peter
Mountains In Sunrise, 10.8.43

PAYNE, C. Owen
Bongola, 19.4.26
(with Lillian Cornelius)

PEACEY, Howard
Magic Hours, 27.4.25

PEACH, L. du Garde
The Devil Within, 20.1.42

PEACOCK, Walter
A Night In Montmartre, 20.12.26
(with Miles Malleson)

PEISEY, Frederick
Dance Macabre, 19.3.34
(with Percy Robinson)

PEMBER, Clifford
Before Men's Eyes, 30.8.26
(with Ben Fleet)

PERCIVAL, Jean
The Restless Room, 2.9.35

PERCY, Edward
Green Holly, * 30.5.38
(with Reginald Denham)
The Distant Hand, 8.5.39
(with Reginald Denham)
The Shop at Sly Corner, * 20.6.44
Dog's Delight, 2.4.46
(with Reginald Denham)
The Man With Expensive Tastes, 6.4.53
(with Lilian Denham)

PERTWEE, Roland
To Kill A Cat, * 1.5.39
(with Harold Dearden)
House On The Sand, 12.4.49
Many Happy Returns, 1.4.52
(with Noel Streatfield)

PETERSON, Margaret
The Summons, 4.4.27

PHELPS, Barry
Cry Wolf, * 29.4.47
By Adoption, 13.9.49

PHILPOTTS, Adelaide
The Good Old Days, 18.2.35
(with Eden Philpotts)

PHILPOTTS, Eden
The Mother, 15.2.26
The Good Old Days, 18.2.35
(with Adelaide Philpotts)

PHIPPS, Nicholas
Bold Lover, 1.10.46

PLOMLEY, Roy
All Expenses Paid, 1.5.51
Half Seas Over, 5.5.53

POLE, Joseph
The Hungry God, 12.2.52

POLLEY, S.A.
Portrait of a Lady, 26.8.29
Bridle-way, 3.3.30

POLLOCK, John
Anna Karenina, 27.7.43

POLLOCK, William
Kimono, 26.7.26

POPHAM-YOUNG, Sir Frank
A Dog's Chance, 21.6.26

POPPLEWELL, Jack
Blind Alley, 20.1.53

POWELL-ANDERSON, Constance
The Curate of St Chad's, 9.8.26

PREEDY, George (Marjorie Bowen)
Rose Giralda, 24.4.43

PRESNALL, Robert R.
Ruse, 12.1.26

PRICE, Evadne
Who Killed My Sister?, 18.8.42
(with Ken Attiwill)
Three Wives Called Roland, 2.11.43
(with Ken Attiwill)
Through The Door, 10.6.46

PRIESTLEY, J.B.
Bright Shadow, 25.4.50

PROSPER, John
See A Fine Lady, 18.3.29

PRYCE, Ronald
By Kind Permission, 26.4.55

PULLEIN-THOMPSON, H.J.
Tomorrow to be Wise, 19.6.33

PULLING, Geoffrey (Wallace Geoffrey)
Third Degree, * 14.11.32

PUNSHON, E.R.
Learning Business, 28.5.28

QUINN, Shirland
Man and Woman, 28.8.51

RATTIGAN, Terence
First Episode, * 11.9.33
(with Philip Heimann)

RAWSON, Graham
The Family Tree, 26.3.28
It's A Wise Wife, 18.9.33

RAYMOND, Ernest
The Berg, * 4.3.29

REHFISCH, Hans
(see James Agate)

RICHARDSON, Anthony
Portrait of the Artist, 1.12.42

RIDGEWELL, George
Casting Stones, 3.6.29

RIDLEY, Arnold
Easy Money, * 23.3.48
You, My Guests, 31.1.56
(and see Ladislaus Fodor)

RIGBY, Ray and Jean
The End Begins, 7.2.56

ROBERTS, C.E. Bechhopfer
Nurse Cavell, * 26.2.34
(with C.S. Forester)

ROBERTS, Lena & Maxwell
Fear In The Night, 24.1.56

ROBINSON, Lennox
The Round Table, * 16.3.25

ROBINSON, Percy
For None Can Tell, * 7.6.26
Whispering Gallery, 5.3.28
(with Derrick de Marney)
Dance Macabre, 19.3.34
(with Frederick Peisley)
Wanted For Murder, * 28.6.37
(with Terence de Marney)
Jenny Frensham, 1.11.37
The Crime of Margaret Foley, * 2.5.44
(with Terence de Marney)

ROBINSON, Martha
A House of Their Own, 30.1.51

ROFFE, Jack
No Other Verdict, 15.12.53

ROHMER, Sax
Secret Egypt, 4.8.28

ROWE, Reginald
The Worst of Being William, 11.2.29

RUEGG, Judge
John Clutterbuck, 10.2.30

RUSSELL, E.
All She Wants, 26.9.32

SADLER, Joan
Local Colour, 23.2.54

ST. BARBE-WEST, H.
The Silent Menace, 23.1.33

ST. JOHN, Theodore
The Annexe, 5.10.48
(with Donald Blackwell)

SANDEMAN, Christopher
The Temptation of Eve, 30.1.28
(with Desiree Welby)
The Book and the Binding, 3.2.36
(with Carmaine des Veoux)

SANDS, Leslie
Intent to Murder, 11.12.51

SANGSTER, Alfred
The Brontës, 29.6.43

SAUNDERS J.A.
Moonshine, 10.10.55

SAUNDERS, Lionel P.
Gossip, 17.11.30

SCOTT, Margerie
Youth and Mrs Meredith, 23.5.38
(with Betty Burton)

SCOTT, Noel
Playground, * 2.11.31
Man From Heaven, 7.9.43

SCOTT, Peter Graham
The Breath of Fools, 19.4.55.

SCOTT-GILBERT, Clement
Whirligig, 29.3.55
(with Ernest Vajda)

SCOTT-ROGERS, Jean
One Fair Daughter, 27.10.53

SELVER, Paul
(See Karel Capek)

SHAW, Sebastian
The Ship's Bell, 16.1.39
(with Margaret Delamere)

SHELLEY, Frank
Summer Serenade, 25.10.55

SHEPPARD, John
A Case of Murder, 31.7.39

SHERRY, Gordon
Black Limelight, * 12.4.37

SHUTE, E.L.
The Price, 6.6.27

SHUTE, Nerina
The Prodigal Mother, 17.1.38

SIGNALLER
The Reluctant Bachelor, * 15.7.47

SIMPSON, Doreen
The Sparks Fly Upwards, 21.10.47

SIMPSON, HAROLD
The Crime of Cannon Ward, 1.2.55
(with Robert Sladen)

SIMPSON, Ronald
One Flight Up, 24.11.42
(with Hugh Miller)

SKLAR, George
Laura, * 30.1.45
(with Vera Caspary)

SLADEN, Robert
The Crime of Cannon Ward, 1.2.55
(with Harold Simpson)

SLOAN, Farquhar
Times Fool, 1.8.32

SNOWDEN, Lewis
The Fugitives, 22.1.34

SOMERVILLE, Peter F.
The Local Raq, 7.1.29

SPARROW, Robert
Life Story, 9.2.54

STANSBURY, Harold
The New Romans, 17.5.55

STAUGHTON, Simon
Passionate Prelude, 3.7.33

STAYTON, Frank
The Intriguing Ladies, 15.8.27
The Last Day, 27.6.38
(with John Walton)

STEPHENSON, Ann
Shall We Say Grace, 10.7.33
(with Gordon Whitehead)

STEWART, Athole
Life-Palpitating Life, 5.12.27
(adapted from A. Fracaroli, L Barzina)

STEWART, Hal D.
Lacking A Title, 26.6.51

STEWART, John
Where There's a Will, 10.9.34

STOCK, Ralph
South of the Line, 12.6.25
Habit, 25.10.26

WILKINSON, Ronald
Mountain Air, * 22.4.47

WILLIAMS, Brock
Sparring Partners, 25.2.29
(with A Blackmore, George Carney)

WILSON, Andrew P.
Sandy, 13.12.26

WILSON, John
The Pagans, 4.7.27

WINDERMERE, Charles
Square Rigged, 28.11.32
Learning to Love, 15.5.33
(with H.F. Maltby)

WITNEY, Frederick
Idle Hands, 25.5.25

WOLF, Edmund
Wisely Wanton, 14.6.49

WOOD, Jane
Barren Gain, 7.12.29
(with Roger Bacon)

WOOD, T.P.
The Green Sash, 25.2.35
(with Debonnaire Sylvester)

WYNNE, Freddie
The Age of Youth, 2.1.
(with H.F. Maltby)

WYNNE-BOWER, Betty
Hostility, 11.10.26

YOUNG, G.H.R.
Just As You Say Dear, 23.1.28

YOUNG, Howard Irving
Strange Night at Rockland, 16.3.43

ZORN, D.F.L.
The Designers, 5.10.25

INDEX

(Page numbers in italics denote direct quotations from the persons indicated)

Maduro, Evey (see Evey de Leon)
Malleson, Miles 33, 101, 105, 192
March, Elspeth ix, xii, *92*, 104
Mason, Brewster 139
Mason, James (actor) 119, 141, 174, 175
Mason, Dr James viii, xii, xiii, 173, *173*, 174, *175*, 178, 179
Massey, Raymond 34
Matthews, Jessie 123
Matthews, Lester 63, 69, 186
Maudling, Reginald 164
Mayne, Ferdy 139
McEwan, Geraldine 150
McGoohan, Patrick 150
McKenna, Siobhan 150
McLerie, Allyn (Ann) 144
Melville, Alan 115
Merrall, Mary 39, 85, 136
Michell, Keith 143
Miles, Lord (Bernard) ix, 92, *148*
Millar, Sir Ronald ix, *121-2*, 122, 192
Milton, Ernest 48, 72, 73, 73-4, 86
Minster, Jack 134
Mitchell, Yvonne 123
Molesworth, Ida 62
Montgomery, Bruce (Monty) ix, xii, 137, *138*, *144, 145*
Montgomery, Douglass 139
Moore, Mark ix, xii, *106-7*
Moore, Roger ix, xvi, *141*
Morahan, Christopher ix, 140
Morley, Robert 134, 193
Morse, Barry ix, *130, 130-1*, 137, *157-8*
Mortimer, John 147
Moseiwitch, Tanya 109-10
Moss, Keith 22-3, 23, 24
Murray, Barbara 144

Naismith, Laurence 134
Nash, Barbara ix, xii, 115-6, *156*
Neilson-Terry, Dennis 19, 62-3, 64, 65-6, 67, 71, 72, 78, 100
Neilson-Terry, Phyllis 8, 100
Nesbitt, Cathleen 124
Newley, Anthony 150
Newman, Nanette 150
Nicholls, Nick ix, xii, *45*
Nicholls, Peggy (see Peggy Lewisohn)
Northen, Michael ix, xii, *107-8, 109*, 113

O'Connor, Una 34, 36

O'Conor, Joseph ix, *130*
Odin-Pearse, Daphne ix, xii, *59*, 60, *84, 86*
Olivier, Lord (Laurence) 97, 134, 135
O'Neill, Maire 98-9
O'Neill, Rose Mellor 10
Owen-Bell, David ix, xii, *166, 168-9*
Oxman, Ken xii, 177

Page, Norman 10, 16, 39
Palmer, Geoffrey 150
Parry, Natasha 150
Pasco, Richard ix, xii, *122-3*
Paul, Betty 143
Percy, Edward 27, 124, 193
Petrie, Hay 36, 37
Phillips, Leslie 150
Philpotts, Ambrosine 92
Pilbeam, Nova 72
Playfair, Sir Nigel 51, 69, 71, 73, 186
Pleasance, Donald 150
Plomley, Roy 147, 176, 193
Pollock, Ellen ix, 134, *140-1*, 147
Portman, Eric 106, 122
Power, Hartley 122, 186
Preedy, George (see Marjorie Bowen)
Price, Nancy 48, 52, 53, 53-4, 57, 85, 96-7, 135, 163
Proudfoot, James 147
Purdom, C.B. 79, *79*

Quayle, Sir Anthony ix, xvi, 60, *60*, 77

Rains, Claude 23, 38
Ramsay, Margaret (Peggy) 149
Rattigan, Sir Terence 90, 106, 135, 146, 194
Rawlings, Margaret ix, xii, 97, *97-8*
Reading, Charles 88, 89
Redgrave, Corin 142
Redgrave, Vanessa 176
Redman, Joyce 100
Reed, Maxwell 141
Reeve, Ada 119, 124
Relph, George 27, 57, 112
Richardson, Tony 133
Rise Above It (Jones/Melville) 114-8, 123, 191
Roberts, Dennis ix, 94, *98*, 101
Roberts, Florence 95, 137
Roberts, Pringle 104, 112
Roberts, Rita 94, 98, 101
Robey, Sir George 6, 173
Robinson, Lennox 26, 194